DESTROYER BATTLES

NAVY YARD, N.Y. JULY 17 '42
U.S.S. FLETCHER

DESTROYER BATTLES

EPICS OF
NAVAL CLOSE COMBAT

ROBERT C STERN

Seaforth
PUBLISHING

Dedication

To Beth, my lovely, long-suffering wife – far better than I deserve.

FRONTISPIECE: The *raison d'être* of the destroyer – the torpedo, represented here by the after bank of quintuple tubes on USS *Fletcher* (DD 445) in this shipyard view, taken at New York Navy Yard, 15 July 1942, just before she headed to the Pacific and her participation in the Battle of Tassafaronga. The cylindrical housing on these torpedo tubes protected the two-man crew (trainer and gyro setter) from the blast of the 5in (127mm) mount just aft. (The forward bank of torpedo tubes did not have this blast shield.) The wavy patches of Ocean Grey (5-O) over a base of Haze Grey (5-H) are part of the Ms 12 Mod camouflage scheme she carried at the time. (NARA via destroyerhistory.org)

Copyright © Robert C Stern 2008

First published in Great Britain in 2008 by
Seaforth Publishing
An imprint of Pen & Sword Books Ltd
47 Church Street, Barnsley
S Yorkshire S70 2AS

www.seaforthpublishing.com
Email info@seaforthpublishing.com

British Library Cataloguing in Publication Data
A CIP data record for this book is available from the British Library

ISBN 978-1-84832-007-9

Designed and Typeset by MATS Typesetters, Leigh-on-Sea
Printed and bound in Great Britain by Biddles Ltd, King's Lynn

Contents

Author's Acknowledgements

As is always the case, this book could not have been written without the aid and co-operation of many people, going back over the more than 30 years during which I have been collecting the materials – both photographic and documentary – used here. I'm afraid I failed to record the names of many who helped me early in this process, as then my collecting was out of personal interest, with little thought that books might result in the future. To any whose names I don't recall, I offer my apologies. Those I do remember are listed below.

To Janis Jorgensen and the staff at the US Naval Institute, I am most grateful for supplying multiple oral histories, invaluable in writing chapter 8; to Tosun Saral of Ankara, Turkey, I am truly indebted for supplying the translation from Turkish of the account of Lieutenant Ali Haydar, and for several valuable photographs; to Peter J Green, I am indebted for his excellent personal account of the Falklands War and especially for his permission to use several of the photographs on his website; to Dan Withers for his excellent web site covering the *"Nasty"* boats of the Vietnam War and for his assistance with photographs; to Dave McComb for his in-depth research into US Navy destroyers and his generous help with chapters 7, 8 and 9. Also for introducing me to Rick E Davis, who helped describe the gun fit of US destroyers in the Solomons; to Captain Russell S Crenshaw, Jr, USN (Ret) for permission to quote from his writings.

To any others I may have neglected to list here, thanks again.

As always, if despite this great help, errors have crept into this narrative, they are solely my responsibility.

Notes on Units of Measurement
(and a Few Other Things)

It is difficult, when looking through historical documents and reference works from any period, to find a consistent set of units by which ships and everything related to them were measured. Further, being an American author writing in 2007, it is impossible to ignore the fact that every other developed country besides the United States has adopted the metric system, at least officially.

Given all this, I have been forced to make decisions about which units to use in this book and have tried my best to stay consistent with these decisions. There are two places where my best efforts have been most challenged. One is in the area of gun calibres. I have decided in this case to simply use the designation system(s) of the nation whose weapon is being described and have added an appendix to explain as best I can how the various systems correspond to each other. The other case is when I'm quoting a source that used a measurement system other than the one I adopted for this book. In those cases, I have retained the original measurement system used by the source's author. In all other cases, I have attempted to use the following units consistently:

Distance/length – In general, distances are given in nautical miles. A nautical mile is 2025 yards; in metric terms, it is 1852 metres. It is equivalent to 1.1508 statute miles. For many uses, the US Navy historically simplified the nautical mile to 2000 yards. The British have sometimes used a definition of 6080ft, also known as an 'admiralty mile'. However, since 1929, an international standard has been generally accepted, based on a nautical mile being exactly 1852 metres. The US Navy adopted this standard only in 1954. Whenever I use the word 'mile', even when not preceded by the word 'nautical', I mean a nautical mile. Shorter lengths, typically those less than one mile, I give in metres. The only exception to these rules is when I am giving a distance that is purely a measure of travel on land, such as the distance from Paris to Berlin. In these cases, I use kilometres.

Time – I use the nautical twenty-four-hour clock throughout. Keeping track of time zones is next to impossible, as it was almost always true that when one destroyer sighted another, their clocks would not have agreed, any more than their politics. In general, I have used the time zone of the first ship mentioned in the narrative and adjusted the other ships' to agree.

Displacement – In this matter, I have made no attempt to reconcile long tons, short tons and metric tonnes, since knowing the exact displacement of a ship never alters the outcome of the stories. In most cases, the sources do not specify which 'ton' they're using. (Displacement is normally, but not always, given in long or English tons.) I give standard displacement when it is distinguished from other displacements (eg, normal or full load). I make no attempt to reconcile the various interpretations of what standard displacement means in different navies. In general, I try to find a consensus between sources before giving a displacement. Merchant ship displacements are given as GRT (Gross Registered Tons), which is actually a unit of volume (1 GRT is 100 cubic feet or 2.83 cubic metres).

Speed – Always given in knots (nautical miles per hour).

Weight – I use kilograms and tonnes whenever possible.

Place names are also a problem, in that much of this history took place at a time when many of the locations of the action in these stories were under colonial administration. Colonial powers tended either to give new names to the places they 'administered', or give the local names new pronunciations and spellings that fitted the ears and tongues of the administrators. As a result, many of the place names used by the combatants in these wars would not be found on a map today. I have opted to use the names and spellings of the period and power in question and to give the contemporary name when useful in footnotes.

When writing Japanese names, I use the traditional form, which is surname first.

I had to decide whether to call destroyers 'boats' or 'ships'. There seems to be no consensus of opinion even today as to which term to use, though modern destroyers have become so big and important that they are most often called 'ships' in current writing. Nevertheless, in order to be consistent, I had to choose one term or the other and I opted to use the term 'ships', and that term is used throughout this book to refer to destroyers. The exception is when I quote a source. If that source used the term 'boats', I did not change it.

Introduction

AT THE BEGINNING, the story of the destroyer was the story of the torpedo. This curious word initially referred to any one of a number of different explosive devices used on land or in the water, but towards the end of the nineteenth century it came to refer specifically to a particular type of self-propelled, self-guided underwater missile, capable of sinking even the biggest ship without warning. Before it became part of the military vocabulary, it was the name of a genus of electric ray, also known as the crampfish or numbfish – well known for its ability to stun an unwary swimmer who steps on or even brushes against it. By the beginning of the nineteenth century, it was a common term for what now would be called a land-mine. In 1800, the American inventor Robert Fulton used the term to describe the explosive charge towed behind his experimental submarine *Nautilus*. By the time of the American Civil War, the term referred to any naval mine, floating or tethered. (Rear Admiral David Farragut's famous quote: 'Damn the torpedoes, full speed ahead', referred to the tethered mines in a field laid by the Confederate defenders of Mobile Bay.)

The Whitehead torpedo

A sub-type of torpedo, known as a 'spar torpedo', was used by small craft of the time, including the primitive Confederate semi-submersible *Hunley*. A spar torpedo consisted of an explosive charge mounted at the end of a spar attached to the attacking boat. The idea was that the attacker would approach close enough to the target to explode the charge, either by a contact fuse or when deliberately detonated by the attacking vessel. The hope was that the spar was long enough for the resulting explosion to sink the target, but not the attacker. (*Hunley*'s spar was 6.7m (22ft) long.) In the case of *Hunley*'s historic attack on the sloop-of-war USS *Housatonic* in 1864, it is not certain if the explosion of the torpedo – which sank *Housatonic* – also accounted for *Hunley*. It is known that *Hunley* remained afloat long enough after the attack to signal success to observers on the shore, but she disappeared soon after that, most likely a delayed victim of her own torpedo.

The obvious danger that a spar torpedo represented for the attacker spurred a number of clever men to think about ways of propelling the explosive to a safer distance. In the late 1850s, a captain in the Austro-Hungarian navy, Giovanni Luppis, approached his superiors with an idea for a self-propelled torpedo delivery system. His idea employed a small, unmanned motorboat mounting a spar torpedo; the boat would be controlled from some distance away by means of ropes connected to the motorboat's tiller. His idea was rejected, but Luppis still felt it had promise and approached an acquaintance, the English-born engineer Robert Whitehead, who was manager of a business building marine engines at the port of Fiume (now Rijeka, Croatia) on the Dalmatian coast, Stabilimento Technico Fiumano. Whitehead saw the kernel of a good idea in Luppis' proposal and proceeded to develop a compressed-air-driven, fin-stabilised, spindle-shaped apparatus, designed to run underwater. The range of this first device was approximately 275 metres (300 yards) at a speed of six to eight knots. In this form it was tested by the Austro-Hungarian navy in December 1866, which agreed to fund further development.[1] When they accepted an improved version for series production two years later, Whitehead offered them an exclusive contract, but this was turned down, leaving him free to market his device to any and all customers.

So it was that the Whitehead torpedo began to appear in the weapons inventory of multiple navies within just a few years, and each one of those navies began the process of developing the means of delivering this new weapon against enemy warships.[2] The obvious first step was mounting torpedoes on existing warships. By the late 1870s, most naval vessels carried at least a few torpedoes and the means to launch them. But, on capital ships, the torpedo was not a primary weapon. The breech-loading naval rifle – in calibres that increased rapidly during this period – extended the range of accurate gunfire from a few hundred metres to five miles or more. The torpedo was considered solely a defensive weapon, intended to discourage an enemy from approaching too close or pursuing too aggressively.

From torpedo boats to destroyers

To fully exploit the potential of this new weapon would require a new type of warship. Given the relatively short range and slow speed of early torpedoes, this new vessel would have to be able to close to within a mile or less of its target to have any chance of success. This argued strongly for a boat of high speed and small dimensions, both because a small, fast boat stood a better chance individually against the defensive gunfire of the day and because small boats could be built and deployed in greater numbers, increasing the chance that some at least could survive long enough to complete an attack. The first boat specifically designed to carry torpedoes was probably HMS *Vesuvius* of 1874 – 90ft (27.4m) long and armed with a single, fixed, submerged torpedo tube at her bow. She had a very low silhouette and was designed to approach targets more by stealth than by speed, which was only 9.7 knots. She was immediately overshadowed by the next 'torpedo boat' built for the Royal Navy, John Thornycroft's HMS *Lightning* of 1876. *Lightning* had the then-extraordinary speed of nineteen knots and a pair of 'cradles' at either beam for dropping torpedoes into the water. The cradles only worked at very low speed and were replaced in 1879 by a single, conventional above-water torpedo tube at the bow.

The number and types of torpedo boats soon proliferated in the Royal Navy and in the navies of every other naval power. At 32.5 tons, *Lightning* was considered to be a First Class Torpedo Boat, meaning she was sufficient for coast defence, but was really too small and lightly constructed for service in the open ocean. Both the French and Austrians actually ordered similar torpedo boats before Thornycroft got his order from the Admiralty, but *Lightning* was almost certainly the first fast torpedo boat in service. Such was the appeal of the type that, before the decade was out, Italy, Russia and Japan also had similar boats under construction or in commission.

However, there were other threads of development going on at the same time. The Italians and Germans both tried out larger vessels. The Italian *Pietro Micca* was twice the size of HMS *Vesuvius* and the German *Zieten* was bigger still; both were significantly faster, but as a type they could not compete with more conventional torpedo boats, which were being produced in increasing numbers during the 1880s. Driven by tradition and policy to see this pro-liferation as a threat to its control of the seas, in 1885 the Royal Navy ordered the first of a class of larger boats intended to protect its battle fleet from enemy torpedo boats. HMS *Rattlesnake* was really nothing more than an improved version of large torpedo 'cruisers', such as *Pietro Micca* or *Zieten*. She was supposed to be as fast as a torpedo boat but better armed. In fact, *Rattlesnake* and her successors, called Torpedo Gunboats (or 'torpedo-boat catchers'), were disappointing as a type, being significantly slower than the torpedo boats they were supposed to catch. The best of the type were the eleven boats of the

Alarm class of 1889, which displaced 810 tons, carried five torpedo tubes and two 4.7in (120mm) guns, but could manage a top speed of only 18.7 knots, at least three knots slower than contemporary torpedo boats.

There was nothing wrong with the idea behind the 'catchers', and the need they were intended to meet was not going away. If anything, it was getting worse. Forced to revisit the problem of defending the fleet against torpedo boats, given the failure of the 'catchers', the Royal Navy ordered four ships of yet another new type in 1892, two each from Yarrow and Thornycroft. Both firms had been proposing for several years designs that would address the failings of the 'catchers', and several foreign navies, most notably the Austro-Hungarian, were building ships that were bigger than torpedo boats, but smaller and faster than the 'catchers' and nearly as well armed. The four ships from Yarrow and Thornycroft, delivered in 1894–5 to two slightly differing designs, were 275–280 tons, armed with three torpedo tubes and one 12 pdr (75mm) and three 6 pdr (57mm) guns. The slowest of the four made her contract speed of twenty-six knots. The fastest, HMS *Daring*, was timed at 28.5 knots on her trial run.

It was immediately obvious to all observers, not just in the Royal Navy, that this new type was a success. In order to distinguish these ships from the 'catchers' they were intended to replace, they were dubbed 'torpedo-boat destroyers', a name that was very quickly shortened to just 'destroyer'. Not only would this new ship defend larger ships against torpedo boats, but they would also do everything torpedo boats were supposed to do, as well as or better than the smaller boats. By the end of the decade, most of the major navies had essentially stopped building small torpedo boats.[3]

The submarine

The story of the torpedo would not be complete without mentioning the other main type developed towards the end of the nineteenth century to deliver this new weapon – the submarine. Unlike the torpedo boat – which the destroyer was designed to counter and ended up replacing – the submarine thrived as a type. Hunting submarines would become, for much of the history of destroyers, a main preoccupation of the type.

The idea of the submarine had been around for centuries, maybe even millennia, if legends are to be believed, but the active quest for a practical submersible really got its start in the middle of the nineteenth century, and the pace of experimentation increased as the necessary technologies began to mature. John Holland is generally credited with building the first, truly practical submersible in 1897, but there were other attempts in numerous countries in the preceding few years. The mating of the torpedo and the submarine was natural, as they were both in their element underwater. The first primitive submersible to carry a primitive torpedo was probably the first of Nordenfelt's submarines, bought by the Greek government in 1886. This steam-powered boat, however, never became operational. The first known firing of a torpedo by a submarine was by the second Nordenfelt submarine, which he sold to the Turks in 1887.

The demise of the battleship

Most of the ship types that comprised the primary fighting power of a fleet for much of the history of destroyers have now disappeared from the world's oceans. There are no more battleships or cruisers in the fleets of the world. The capital ships of the twenty-first century are the aircraft carrier, the submarine and the destroyer, the oldest of which types is the destroyer. That this type should survive in an era of such profound change in technology and tactics is a testament to the innate versatility of the original concept. Never again will fleets of warships line up and hurl projectiles at each other. The enemy now will come in a myriad of forms and from any of many directions. The threat will appear with little or no warning from over the horizon or beneath the waves, as well as on the surface, and could be in the form of a missile, a torpedo or even an explosives-laden small boat. Against all these, destroyers will continue to defend for the foreseeable future.

Creatures of the night

This book tells the stories of some of these ships and the men who served on them. For much of their history, destroyers were creatures of the night. Most of the encounters described here took place in the dark. Even after the fitting of effective radars to destroyers took some of the mystery out of the night, these encounters were generally short, sharp, confused and bloody. It was often not possible to know who 'won' until dawn came and there was time to count hulls in the water. Another characteristic of these engagements was that they almost always involved multiple destroyers on one or both sides. Destroyers were small enough and were available in sufficient numbers that they were rarely deployed singly. As often as not, these battles involved multiple ships on both sides, blundering about in the dark, sometimes as dangerous to friend as foe.

The men who fought these battles were also a unique breed. Most men who served on destroyers, of course, did so not from choice, but whether willingly or not, they soon developed a distinctive pride to go along with their distinctive gait. Sailors from bigger ships often derided destroyer-men for the way they reputedly rolled with the waves even on dry land, but 'tin-can' sailors take a perverse pride in their ability to deal with whatever man or nature can throw at them. It is the stories of these men that I try to tell in these pages.

Notes

1 Giovanni Biagio Luppis von Rammer was born in Fiume into a family of Italian and Croatian ancestry. The idea for a remote-controlled explosive motorboat was apparently not his originally, but was passed along to him by an unnamed inventor. Luppis demonstrated his 'Salvacoste' (coast saver) in 1860 without attracting any interest and then, in 1864, entered into a contract with Robert Whitehead to fund further development of the idea. Although Whitehead changed virtually every detail of the device before he successfully demonstrated his version, he always gave credit to Luppis for the invention and paid him a royalty on sales. Some Croatians claim Luppis as a compatriot, but he considered himself Italian and moved to Italy after retiring from the navy.

2 Whitehead called his device a *Minenschiff* (mine ship), but it soon became known as an 'automotive torpedo' or 'locomotive torpedo', to distinguish it from spar or tethered torpedoes, but in just a few years the name became simply 'torpedo'. It took a few years for the weapon to attract attention, and the firm that Whitehead managed at Fiume went bankrupt in 1873 due to sluggish sales of the weapon. Whitehead believed strongly in the idea and raised the necessary capital to buy out the former owners and restarted the company as 'Torpedo-Fabrik von Robert Whitehead' in 1875. A few sources dispute Whitehead's claim of precedence in producing a modern torpedo. The Russian engineer/inventor Ivan F Alexandrovsky is reported as having designed a device with all the same basic features as Whitehead's a full year earlier, but the Russian Admiralty took three years coming up with the funds to build a prototype and, in the meantime, Whitehead's patents had been granted and recognised internationally. When Russia began buying torpedoes, they were Whitehead's and not Alexandrosky's.

3 The obvious exception to this was the various small motor torpedo boats built by some navies for work close into shore. The type includes the Royal Navy's CMBs, Italian MAS boats and German LM boats built during World War I and similar boats, such as British MTBs, American PT boats and German *Schnellboote*, built during World War II.

Chapter 1

Beginnings – Peru (1877), The Black Sea (1877), Chile (1891) and China (1904–5)

IT IS NOT ENTIRELY clear when the first ship fired a 'locomotive' torpedo in anger at another ship. By the late 1870s, most navies had mounted torpedoes on at least some of their existing warships and were building dedicated torpedo boats. The opportunities to try out this new device were not long in coming. While the major European powers were, for the most part, at peace with each other between the end of the Franco–Prussian War in May 1871 and the beginning of World War I in August 1914, there were plenty of conflicts between the European powers and other countries as they attempted to bring their version of civilisation to the rest of the world.

Firing the first torpedo

Most sources agree that the first recorded instance of a torpedo being fired with the intent to sink another ship took place during the Battle of Pacocha on 29 May 1877. On that date in the bay of that name on the southern coast of Peru, a pair of Royal Navy warships – the new unarmoured iron frigate HMS *Shah*

The first ship to be the target of a torpedo fired in anger was almost certainly the Peruvian turret ironclad *Huáscar*. The incident took place during the Battle of Pacocha on 29 May 1877. This contemporary lithograph shows the monitor's single turret forward of her bridge. To make *Huáscar* more seaworthy, she had a downward-folding bulkhead alongside her turret, which could be raised when the turret was not in use.

The torpedo in question was fired by HMS *Shah*, an unarmoured iron frigate completed
only the year before. She was armed with two torpedo cradles, each carrying one
of the new-fangled Whitehead torpedoes, along with a mixed broadside of 7in (178mm),
6in (152mm) and 64-pdr muzzle-loading rifles. When her guns proved incapable
of piercing *Huáscar's* armour, Admiral de Horsey resorted to trying to disable the enemy
with one of her untried torpedoes. It missed.

and the wooden corvette HMS *Amethyst* – cornered the British-built Peruvian
turret ironclad *Huáscar*. The dispute was over the detention of a pair of British
merchantmen by *Huáscar*, which had sided with the rebels in a revolt against the
Peruvian government. Protests by British businessmen caused the British
Chargé d'Affaires in Lima to pressure the Royal Navy's Commander-in-Chief,
Pacific Station, the flamboyantly named Rear Admiral Algernon F R de Horsey,
to teach the rebels a lesson. With his two ships, he set off in pursuit of the
Peruvian ironclad, catching up with her at Pacocha Bay and demanding her
surrender. *Huáscar* had on board the leader of the rebellion, who defiantly
rejected the British demands.

At 1500 hours, de Horsey ordered his two ships to open fire on *Huáscar* at a
range of 1700 metres. For the next two hours, the three ships circled each other.
Huáscar was hit more than fifty times (out of more than 400 rounds fired at
nearly point blank range), but only one of those shots penetrated her armour,
and that did little damage. The Peruvian ship, with only two large 10in (254mm)

guns in her turret – compared to forty 64 pdr (6.3in/160mm) or larger guns in the batteries of the British warships – was able to achieve only a few hits, and they too caused only minor damage. Of greater concern to de Horsey was *Huáscar's* ram bow; his radical manoeuvres to avoid several attempts by the Peruvians to ram his ships contributed to the poor shooting on both sides. Finally, frustrated by the inconclusive combat and with only an hour of sunlight remaining, de Horsey reluctantly turned to a new weapon carried by his flagship. When completed a year earlier at Portsmouth Dockyard, *Shah* was fitted with a pair of torpedo cradles and a total of four 14in (356mm) diameter Whitehead torpedoes. A story has lingered, almost certainly apocryphal, stating that the officer on *Shah* responsible for launching the torpedo was so shocked by the order, apparently feeling that the Peruvians had proved themselves a gallant foe and were thus undeserving of being sunk by such a weapon,

Almost alone among the warships described in this book, *Huáscar* is still afloat and in something like her original condition. This is nothing short of incredible, considering the fact that she fought in two more major battles after Pacocha, the second of which left her seriously damaged and in the hands of the enemy. She was captured and repaired by the Chileans and retained in various capacities until she was recommissioned as a museum ship in 1934, a status she retains to this day. The bulkheads designed to give her more freeboard for ocean crossings have been removed, giving her a somewhat different profile. (Juan del Campo)

demanded the order be repeated in writing. He need not have worried, as the torpedo missed *Huáscar*, and there was insufficient time to load and launch another before the light failed.

The two sides separated in the dark. Damage had been minimal on both sides. The casualties on *Huáscar* were one dead and a few others wounded; on the British side there were only a few minor wounds. *Huáscar* exited the bay in the dark and surrendered to government forces two days later. She fought with distinction against Chile in 1879. During the first six months of that war, *Huáscar* single-handedly prevented the invasion of Peru by the far larger Chilean army. On 21 May 1879, she was in action in the port of Iquique, where she was in close combat with the Chilean corvette *Esmerelda*. *Huáscar* sank *Esmerelda* by ramming, while the *Esmerelda's* sailors were attempting to board *Huáscar*. At the Battle of Angamos on 8 October, *Huáscar* was overwhelmed by six Chilean warships and captured in sinking condition. Remarkably, the Chileans were able to stop the flooding and towed *Huáscar* into port, where she was repaired and returned to service under her new flag in time to participate in the late stages of the war against her former country. She remained in Chilean service, being decommissioned in 1897, but was kept in service as a hulk and later as a submarine tender until 1934, when she was declared a heritage ship, recommissioned and a long process of restoration begun. Today, she remains a commissioned warship and is open to visitors at Talcahuano, Chile, where she is in immaculate condition and is considered a shrine to the sailors of two nations.

HMS *Shah* remained in commission barely three years. She was paid off at Portsmouth in October 1879. There was no future use for an unarmoured cruiser in the Royal Navy. Admiral de Horsey was very nearly reprimanded in Parliament for being insufficiently aggressive in his attack on *Huáscar*. He retired in 1885.

A dubious hit in the Black Sea

According to some sources, the first use of a locomotive torpedo to sink a ship in combat actually took place four months before the Battle of Pacocha, on the night of 16 January 1877, when Russian torpedo boats operating in the Black Sea under the command of Captain Stepan Osipovich Makarov sank the Turkish *Intibah*. These accounts give little more detail than that. They state that a pair of torpedo boats carrying Whitehead-type torpedoes, along with possibly two others mounting spar torpedoes, attacked and sank the Turkish vessel. There is only one problem with this account: it most likely never happened, at least, not at all as that bare outline would have us believe. To begin with, it is unlikely that the incident took place on 16 January 1877, as war was not declared between Russia and Turkey until 24 April of that year.[1] Secondly, it appears that whenever the attack took place, the Turkish ship that was the target almost certainly was not named *Intibah*, as that name appears in no contemporary lists of Turkish warships. Third and most seriously, whatever Turkish ship was attacked, it almost certainly did not sink.

Actually, a good deal is known for certain about what went on in the Black Sea at the time. As war appeared likely to break out in the south, a number of Russian naval officers expressed concern about the weakness of the Russian Black Sea fleet, compared to the relatively more substantial Turkish fleet. One of these was Captain Makarov. In 1876, though posted in the Baltic at the time,

A passenger steamer converted to a tender for torpedo boats, *Velikiy Knyaz Konstantin* was the flagship of then Captain Stepan Osipovich Makarov in the Black Sea in 1877. Several small torpedo boats of various designs operated from this tender for at least three separate attacks on Turkish warships. Their greatest success appears to have been the sinking of a small boat tied up alongside a Turkish ironclad.

he saw that the Turks had a decided advantage in ironclad ships in the Black Sea and he proposed to the Russian Admiralty that a large passenger steamer be converted into a tender, capable of hoisting onboard four small torpedo boats and carrying them to Turkish waters where they could make night attacks on the enemy ships. The idea was approved by the head of the navy, Grand Admiral Konstantin Nikolaevich, and Makarov was dispatched to the Crimea to take charge of the project. When the converted tender was commissioned, under the command of Captain Makarov, she was given the name *Velikiy Knyaz Konstantin*, after the admiral who had sponsored the project.

Makarov immediately began working up the flotilla of small torpedo boats his tender would carry. They were a scratch lot of small motorboats fitted with a variety of torpedo types – spar and towed torpedoes, as well a few of the new locomotive type. He not only trained the captains and crews, but he devised the tactics they would employ. He was renowned for his attention to detail, such as making sure *Velikiy Knyaz Konstantin* burned only Welsh coal because it created less smoke, and painting his torpedo boats a dark blue colour that would make them harder to see at night.

This was because he understood that night attacks gave a crucial advantage to the primitive torpedo boats of the day. Each of the three attempts his boats made ocurred at night. The first came on 12 May 1877 at the port of Batûm.[2] There, Makarov sent in four boats to attack a small squadron of Turkish ironclads. The boats were sighted as they approached the big targets and were driven off by Turkish small craft before they could mount an effective attack. The next attempt was across the Black Sea on 12 June at the port of Sulina at the mouth of the Danube.[3] This time *Velikiy Knyaz Konstantin* was accompanied by a second converted steamer, *Vladimir*, which carried two more torpedo boats. The force of six boats, under the command of Lieutenant I M Zatzarennii went after three Turkish ironclads anchored there – *Idjalieh*, *Fethi Bulend* and *Mukaddami Khair*. These were a mixed lot of relatively new, small ironclads representing a fair proportion of the striking power of the Turkish fleet. The targets were well defended, having both nets and guardships connected by rope cables. It appears that only one of the attackers cleared the ropes and that one's torpedo was stopped by *Idjalieh*'s nets. One of the attackers was sunk in the explosion of its spar torpedo.

The third attack was on the central battery ship *Assari Shevket*, anchored in the port of Sukhum Kalé on the night of 24 August 1877.[4] Again, four torpedo boats attacked, two of which were armed with Whitehead-type torpedoes. These were *Chesma*, which had a single torpedo tube under her keel (which allowed it to be loaded only when the boat had been hoisted out of the water on the tender) and *Sinop*, which had a raft secured alongside from which the torpedo was launched by pushing it overboard (an even more primitive version of the torpedo cradles favoured at the time by the Royal Navy).[5] One of the boats never sighted the target and returned to *Velikiy Knyaz Konstantin* after an uneventful evening. This was one of the two boats armed with a locomotive torpedo. The two boats armed with spar torpedoes pressed home their attacks. One was nearly swamped by the explosion of its torpedo, a frequent result of the use of spar torpedoes. The other was attempting to drive its explosive through the nets surrounding the target when a massive explosion rocked *Assari Shevket,* nearly dragging the small boat under in the process. The explosion was the result of the Whitehead torpedo fired by the remaining attacker striking a motor launch tied alongside the Turkish ironclad. The launch was demolished, but the ironclad *Assari Shevket* was unharmed. Nevertheless, the excited commander of the Russian torpedo boat reported the sinking of his intended target; this claim was never questioned and became a standard component of Russian naval history.

Makarov, who was acclaimed a national hero and awarded various medals, was never in any doubt that the claimed sinking actually occurred. He went on to a highly successful naval career, gaining fame as an oceanographer and inventor, eventually reaching the rank of Vice Admiral.

The first torpedo sinking

This leaves open the question of the first use of a Whitehead-type torpedo to sink an enemy warship, assuming that the demolished launch tied up next to *Assari Shevket* does not really count. It is known that on 5 February 1895, a Japanese torpedo boat damaged the Chinese battleship *Ting Yuen*, which had survived the Battle of the Yalu, to the extent that she sank the next day at Weihaiwei, but that was certainly not the first time torpedoes had destroyed an enemy warship.[6] The Brazilian battleship *Aquidaban* had been sunk by the torpedo gunboat *Gustavo Sampaio* on 16 April 1894, during a rebellion by parts of the Brazilian fleet, but that was also probably not the first such occurrence. It is most likely that event occurred during yet another of the seemingly interminable internecine conflicts in South America in the second half of the nineteenth century.

Chile was typical of the nations that emerged from Spanish colonial rule in the 1860s in that its borders were drawn more by the timing and circumstance of the wars of independence than by any political or economic logic. The next few decades seemed to be dominated by regional conflicts between the new states to redraw borders and internal conflicts, as economic and political groups attempted to establish dominance. Chile fought a war against Spain in 1865 allied with Peru and then the war against Peru in 1879, during which the ironclad *Huáscar* was captured. But perhaps the bloodiest of Chile's conflicts was a long civil war that broke out in January 1891, when the Congressional party came out in rebellion against the dictatorial President Balmaceda. Each side had the support of a different branch of the military – the government controlled the army while the Congressional party controlled most, but not quite all, of the Chilean navy. Among the critical naval assets not controlled by the Congress were two just-delivered torpedo gunboats, *Almirante Lynch* and *Almirante Condell*. Similar to the torpedo-boat 'catchers' built for the Royal Navy in the late 1880s, they had the same strengths and weaknesses. They were armed with three 14 pdr (approx 75mm) guns, some smaller weapons and five 14in (356mm) torpedo tubes, one fixed at the bow, the other four single trainable broadside mounts. Compared to most contemporary torpedo boats, they were bigger, better armed and somewhat slower. They were delivered to Chile in March from England where they had been built by Laird's of Birkenhead. This was only two months after the rebellion began, and thus they were manned by crews which had been in England since before the rebellion and were, thus, loyal to the government. On the west coast of South America in 1891, they were the most dangerous adversaries for the Congressional navy.

In the early morning of 23 April, the two *torpederas* caught the Congressional fleet anchored in Caldera Bay, and *Almirante Lynch* put a torpedo into the side of the rebel flagship, the ironclad *Blanco Encalada*. The victim was renowned in Chile for the capture of *Huáscar* and for being, with her sister, *Almirante Cochrane*, the most powerful ship in the region. She had put in at the port of Caldera the day before to coal and to support the cruiser *Esmeralda*, which had landed troops in an attempt to capture the town. At anchor that evening, *Blanco Encalada* was obviously not expecting to be attacked, as she had minimal watch set, her fires were banked and no guns were manned. She did have torpedo nets deployed to seaward.

At 0330, the officer of the deck on *Blanco Encalada* noticed lights moving to seaward, but at first thought it was just *Huáscar* and another Congressional ironclad, which were expected to join the squadron at Caldera the next day. Instead it was the two *torpederas* manoeuvering into attack position. They had completed their post-transit overhauls at Valparaiso just a few days before and had set out for Caldera the previous morning. By 0400, the two *torpederas* had organised their attack and began a high-speed approach in line ahead with *Almirante Condell* leading. Lookouts on *Blanco Encalada* finally realised their peril and alarms were raised. Before this could have any effect, the attackers each fired one torpedo, probably from the fixed bow tube, and then bore away.[7] Both of those torpedoes missed.

At that point any semblance of order vanished, as erratic gunfire erupted from *Blanco Encalada* and the *torpederas* began manoeuvering independently, trying to avoid the defensive fire and launch their remaining torpedoes. In the ensuing chaos, *Almirante Condell* launched two more torpedoes and *Almirante Lynch* fired three. These all missed as well. In the meanwhile, *Blanco Encalada* had raised sufficient steam to start moving and began to turn towards her attackers, perhaps to present a smaller target to their torpedoes. This had the effect of exposing her unprotected starboard side to *Almirante Lynch*, which had separated from the other *torpedera*. She aimed well this time and put her last torpedo on *Blanco Encalada*'s starboard side abaft her foremast from a range of 200 metres.

The explosion was tremendous and the result fatal. The ship quickly heeled over and sank, taking with her 182 out of a crew of 288. Survivors accused the *torpederas* of firing on them as they were abandoning ship. The two torpedo boats realised they were now down to a pair of torpedoes and stood little chance against the aroused Congressional squadron when day broke, so they exited the scene heading south. At dawn they ran into the rebel steamer *Aconcagua* heading towards Caldera with a deck full of troops and were about to attack when a cruiser was seen approaching from the north. Believing it was the rebel *Esmeralda*, the loyalist *torpederas* chose discretion and resumed their run to the south. The ship turned out to be HMS *Warspite* on her way to Caldera to check out rumours of an impending battle. Her captain wrote up an extensive report on the torpedo attack, which was the first word to Europe of the success of this new weapon.

Torpedo tactics and the Russo-Japanese War

Until the sinking of *Blanco Encalada*, the danger represented by the Whitehead torpedo and the boats that carried them was more theoretical than real, and even after that the threat was hard to quantify. The events in Chile, Brazil and China at the end of the nineteenth century showed that torpedoes could sink warships under the right circumstances. In each of those incidents the target was stationary or very nearly so and, as often as not, caught unawares by the attack and, even then, the results were far from impressive. For torpedo boats to live up to the great fear that they aroused in the world's navies, they would have to show they could be effective in battle against alert and mobile opponents.

Typical of first-generation destroyers, this ship of the Japanese *Ikazuchi* class has a 'turtleback' forecastle designed to help it survive broaching waves at high speed or in bad weather. Six ships of this class were built for the Japanese at Yarrows between 1898 and 1900. They displaced 305 tons, measured sixty-seven metres on the waterline and carried one 12 pdr, five 6 pdrs and two 18in (457mm) torpedo tubes. At least one ship from this class, *Oboro*, participated in the attack on Port Arthur, 8–9 February 1904.

In order to demonstrate that kind of effectiveness, things would have to change. For one thing, torpedoes would have to improve, and they did. The invention of the gyroscope in 1898 was rapidly applied to torpedoes and resolved one of the weapon's fundamental problems – erratic course and depth keeping after launch. This would clearly increase the odds that any one torpedo would find its target. Added to this were increases in speed, range and warhead size, so that by the turn of the century, torpedoes typically would have a range of more than 1000 metres at a speed of twenty-five or more knots with a warhead of fifty kilograms of guncotton.[8] Despite these improvements to the weapon itself, it remained a relatively inaccurate weapon due to its slow speed and the still primitive state of the aiming and firing systems.

It became obvious that the only way to increase the chances of success in a torpedo attack was to increase the number of torpedoes being fired at a target. Since torpedo boats of the 1890s rarely carried more than four torpedo tubes and the first of the larger, more powerful destroyers generally carried no more than two, having sacrificed torpedo armament to carry more and bigger guns, the only way to launch a significant number of torpedoes was to dramatically increase the number of boats involved in an attack. A further impetus towards increasing the number of attackers was the improved defence against torpedo attacks. Not only were destroyers being introduced specifically to repel torpedo attacks, but the number of smaller calibre, quick-firing guns on warships rapidly increased, specifically to defend against torpedo attacks.

The net effect of these trends was that the number of torpedo boats in the world's navies increased dramatically up to the mid-1890s. It is estimated that in 1890, there were approximately 1000 torpedo boats in service, 90 per cent of them in the world's five largest navies.[9] Even as torpedo boats were largely replaced by bigger, more expensive destroyers, these numbers did not decrease significantly. For example, in the 1896–7 budget year, a typical year for the time period, the Royal Navy ordered sixteen destroyers and three somewhat larger and faster 'specials'. This meant that there were enough destroyers available of roughly similar characteristics that they could be organised in flotillas of generally between five and ten ships, which deployed together and trained together in co-ordinated simultaneous attacks against single targets.

The first opportunity to try out these evolving tactics came with the outbreak of the Russo-Japanese War in February 1904. In fact, it came right at the beginning of that war. The dispute was a typical colonial squabble between two of the powers intent on extending their influence in the crumbling Chinese empire. Russia and Japan both lusted after mineral-rich North Korea, wherein lay the seeds of the conflict. After exchanges of increasingly hostile diplomatic notes, the Japanese decided on a strategy with a long and honorable tradition in the history of their island culture – a surprise attack. Throughout Japanese history were instances of one opponent in a struggle taking the initiative and attacking the other side before it was ready. There were strict rules governing when such a move was allowed. Only the weaker of the two sides was allowed to use this option and only in cases where the formalities leading up to war had all been observed.[10] In this case, every necessary step was followed. A Japanese ultimatum to Russia expired on 4 February 1904 and the Japanese ambassador left St Petersburg the next day. The formal breaking of relations between the two countries came on the 6th, the same day that Russian troops crossed the Yalu River and began occupying the disputed region. The Japanese waited two more days before making their 'surprise' attack.

Even then, the attack on Port Arthur was not the first act of hostilities by the Japanese.[11] The telegraph line to Port Arthur was cut by the Japanese on 7 February and, the next day, Japanese ships entered the harbour at Chemulpo, on the western coast of Korea, at 1415 local time, and troops began landing near the port four hours later. But in those last days before the widespread introduction of wireless communications and with the telegraph line cut, there was no way for the Russians at Chemulpo to alert the base at Port Arthur of the outbreak of war.

Nevertheless, it is hard to understand why the Russian squadron at Port Arthur, comprising seven battleships and five cruisers, was not at some state of alert when the sun went down on 8 February 1904. In fact, the mood at the port was one of relaxation, almost festivity. Despite being aware of the break in diplomatic relations, the last word received from St Petersburg the day before had predicted that a diplomatic solution was probable and that war would be avoided. Regardless, orders stated that if war were to begin, it should be the Japanese who fired the first shot. As the sun set, the wife of the fleet commander, Rear Admiral Oskar Stark, was holding a reception for her name day, but far more of the fleet's officers were in town, where a circus was performing. The defensive batteries on the heights above the port were only lightly manned, and no exceptional alert had been ordered. As usual, the fleet was anchored in two lines in the outer harbour, six ships in the outer line and five in the inner, with the cruisers at the northern end of the lines.[12] A short distance to the east, two more cruisers were anchored. The lamps were lit on all buoys, ships had anchor lights lit and no torpedo nets were rigged. Several Russian destroyers were on patrol further out in the bay. The remainder of the Russian destroyers were anchored in the inner harbour. The night was clear and moonless, and the sea calm as midnight neared.[13]

The Japanese were approaching from the south. The original plan of Vice Admiral Togo Heihachiro had been to attack with his heavy squadrons – six battleships and five cruisers – but he had been given false intelligence that the Russian shore batteries were on alert, and therefore decided to keep his big ships out of range and sent in only the fifteen destroyers accompanying the fleet. These were split into two divisions; five destroyers were to attack the larger commercial port at Dalny further up the peninsula, while the remaining ten were to attack the fleet at Port Arthur.[14] The decision to split his attack, despite knowing that there were probably no major targets at Dalny, was perhaps a necessary precaution, but it guaranteed that the attack at Port Arthur would be less effective. The ten destroyers in the main attack were from three flotillas – the 1st with four ships, the newest ships in the fleet, and the other two with three each. At first the approach went well. The Japanese destroyers were moving at slow speed in order to reduce noise and prevent sparks coming from their funnels. Out of the darkness loomed a pair of patrolling Russian destroyers. The lead Japanese ships swerved sharply to avoid the Russian pickets, throwing the following flotillas into such confusion that two destroyers of the 3rd flotilla collided. Neither was seriously damaged, but it took some time to work those ships back up to speed. The 1st flotilla proceeded, unaware of the chaos behind them; the other two fell behind and lost any semblance of organisation. The Japanese believed they had not been sighted by the Russian ships, because the pickets had not reacted to their presence and quickly disappeared in the darkness. In fact the Japanese had been sighted, but the Russians were under strict orders not to fire first and thus had no recourse but to turn away and head back towards port at best speed.[15] It is interesting to speculate what might have happened had any of the Russian captains opted to disobey orders. Even a little bit of warning might have made a difference. From the point of view of the Russian officers in town, all was peaceful until the cruiser *Pallada* opened fire.

> At about midnight everybody was surprised by the squadron opening fire. It appeared that this was night target practice, and it soon ceased. But after half an hour the firing was resumed and this time it was irregular and ragged. But all the same we thought that it was target practice still continuing. Soon afterwards all the troops were summoned by the alarm signal to the line of fortifications . . .[16]

The first sign the Russians had that an attack was imminent came at 2337, just before midnight.[17] The cruiser *Pallada* had lookout responsibility that evening and was making periodic sweeps of the water to seaward with her searchlight, giving the commander of the 1st flotilla of Japanese destroyers a precise target to steer towards. (Another cruiser, *Novik*, the last in the outer line just aft of *Pallada*, had steam up in case the patrolling destroyers needed heavier support.) As the four destroyers of the 1st flotilla approached from the south, the line of Russian ships was dark and could barely be discerned against the dark mass of the shoreline in the background. The flotilla commander, Commander Fujimoto, saw he was aiming towards the middle of the line of targets, so he turned slightly towards the left, planning on then making a sweeping turn to starboard to bring his ships parallel to the Russians, whose line of anchored ships ran roughly northeast to southwest. Visibility was better for the Russians looking out to sea. Thus it was at 2337 that a lookout on *Pallada* sighted lights moving to the west of due south and ordered searchlights aimed in that direction. The lights revealed a line of four destroyers, almost head on, moving relatively slowly and just starting to swing to starboard on a course that would take them along the line of Russian ships. It took a few moments to ascertain that the ships they were tracking were not friendly. After all, the lookouts knew that there were Russian destroyers to the south patrolling in the bay. Complicating the issue was the fact that Russian and Japanese destroyers of the time looked much alike. They all had four funnels with the middle two closer together. The Russian ships differed mainly in having a built-up superstructure between the second and third funnels, which Japanese destroyers lacked. That was a give away, plus the puffs of light and smoke as the destroyers launched torpedoes at their targets. Only after they were sure that the destroyers were hostile did the Russians begin to fire at the attackers.

The Japanese had no similar problem. They knew the ships they saw off to port were enemy and they fired their torpedoes as soon as they came into range and lined up a shot. This was made all the easier on the first four ships as the Russians, incredibly, remained silent, even after they had straightened on to the parallel course at a range at which they must have been visible. Each ship in turn aimed and fired its pair of torpedoes. Firing at short range against no opposition, the success rate of the 1st flotilla was impressive. Three out of eight torpedoes found a target.

The first of three warships torpedoed by Japanese destroyers was the protected cruiser *Pallada*, which was anchored near the northern end of the outer line of Russian ships. She was hit by a single torpedo abreast her third funnel on the portside, in way of a nearly full coal bunker. Taking on water and fighting a fire in the bunker, her captain opted to beach her near the Tiger's Tail lighthouse rather than risk her sinking. She was repaired and returned to duty, only to be trapped in the harbour and sunk by Japanese siege guns. She was later raised again and served in the Japanese navy until 1923.

A more serious blow was the torpedoing of the battleship *Retvisan*. Completed in 1901, she was, along with *Tsessarevich*, the newest and best of the Russian battleships at Port Arthur at the beginning of the Russo-Japanese War. More by luck than planning, the Japanese were able to damage both battleships. This photograph shows *Retvizan* beached outside the entrance to the narrow channel leading to Port Arthur's inner harbour. She had taken a torpedo abreast her forward turret and was beached to prevent her sinking in the channel.

The exact order in which these events occurred is hard to determine, but it appears that the lead destroyer, *Shirakumo,* was the first to obtain a hit. The cruiser *Pallada* was the first to be hit. This torpedo struck her exposed portside abreast the third funnel, between frames 68 and 78. The result was:

> . . . a column of flame and water shooting high in the air, some of the water coming on board and drenching the officers and crew on the upper deck in the vicinity.
>
> The shock to the ship was not violent, she first lifted easily a little, then settled back as if on springs, and listing about five degrees to port.[18]

Pallada was hit alongside a coal bunker, which was nearly full. This absorbed much of the force of the explosion, but some of the gases broke through the inner bulkhead of the bunker and ignited some rounds in a magazine storing

12pdr cartridges, and water leakage through this bulkhead flooded one engine room. Fortunately, the explosion in the magazine space did not set off the remaining rounds stored there, but it was sufficient to blow out the vents into an adjoining space where crewmen were sleeping. The subsequent fire killed five of the crewmen.

Within seconds of the first hit, another torpedo struck the next ship forward of *Pallada*, the battleship *Retvizan*. This one was almost certainly fired by the second destroyer in line, *Asashio*. *Retvizan* was hit abreast the forward turret, a hole of twenty square metres blown in her side plating. Only moments later a third explosion was heard. The victim this time was the newer battleship *Tsessarevich*.[19] This ship, built in France starting in 1899, had an important innovation: a torpedo bulkhead inside the outer shell plating under the narrow waterline armour belt. This was an inner watertight barrier of 1½in (3.8cm) steel, 6ft 8in (2m) inboard of the outer hull. The idea was that the intervening compartments, either filled with coal or empty, would absorb the explosion of a torpedo and the inner bulkhead would prevent flooding. This ran for approximately 80 per cent of the length of the hull between the main turrets. Unfortunately, the torpedo hit *Tsessarevich* just aft of the after turret, causing extensive flooding, so much so that her fantail was nearly awash, and disabling her steering gear. It is not known which of the two remaining 1st flotilla destroyers, *Asagiri* or *Harusame*, fired that torpedo.

The four destroyers turned and headed south, pursued shortly by *Novik*, which was able to get off a few shots before losing them in the dark. The rest of the Russian fleet, now fully alert, rigged torpedo nets, manned all guns and raised steam, so as to be ready to move at first light. It was this enemy that was attacked by the six ships of the remaining two Japanese flotillas. Starting about half an hour after the 1st flotilla made its exit, individual ships attempted to approach close enough to attack and were each driven off by Russian defensive fire. Between the six ships, a total of eight more torpedoes were fired, but none of these hit. The last attacker, the destroyer *Oboro*, one of the ships that had collided earlier, made her run at just after 0200 and then cleared the area.

The moon rose just after 0300 and first light came not long after, revealing a scene of apparent devastation. None of the three damaged ships had sunk, but all three had been beached to prevent that possibility, the two battleships on either side of the harbour entrance and *Pallada* further up the shore near the Tiger's Tail light. Port Arthur's repair capabilities were minimal, with no dry dock large enough to take the battleships. All three ships would be repaired, but would be out of action for months.[20] The formal declaration of war by the Japanese was delivered to St Petersburg the next day.

Whatever opinion the world may have formed of the Japanese decision to attack Port Arthur before war was declared, the tactic was effective, robbing the Russians of any initiative they may have contemplated exercising. Rear Admiral Stark was soon replaced by a new commander sent out from St Petersburg, none other than Vice Admiral Stepan Osipovich Makarov, the same officer who, twenty-seven years earlier had commanded the torpedo attacks in the Black Sea. His task was to stiffen resolve and infuse the fleet at Port Arthur with a more aggressive spirit. Even before Makarov's arrival, the Russians made periodic sweeps of the surrounding waters with destroyers.[21] After his arrival on 8 March, the frequency and aggression of these patrols increased.

A little after midnight on 10 March, a flotilla of Japanese destroyers was spotted and fired on by shore batteries around the harbour entrance at Port Arthur, but soon disappeared down the coast to the southwest. A squadron of four Russian destroyers was alerted and left the harbor at 0240 and headed in the same direction in which the enemy had disappeared more than two hours earlier.[22] This squadron blundered into a flotilla of Japanese destroyers some fifteen nautical miles southwest of the harbour entrance at approximately 0400. There ensued a confused melée as the two sides fired their small guns at each other while trying their level best to line up a torpedo shot. It is not known how many torpedoes were actually fired, but it appears that no hits were obtained. The commander of the Russian destroyer *Vlastni* claimed the sinking of one of the enemy, but what he took to be the explosion of a torpedo was more likely the sudden venting of steam on the Japanese destroyer *Akatsuki* after some feed pipes were severed by a shell hit. The commander of the Russian squadron was wounded and, believing his squadron was getting the worse of the engagement, ordered his ships back into the harbour.

Shortly after the first group of Russian destroyers had left the harbour at 0240, a second squadron of four followed to sweep to the south and east.[23] The squadron split at some point into two groups of two ships. One group returned to harbour without incident, but the other, comprising the destroyers *Steregushchi* and *Ryeshitelni*, was on a return course at 0700 when it was intercepted by another flotilla of Japanese ships. *Ryeshitelni* took some damage but was able to make a high-speed escape into the harbour. *Steregushchi* was not so fortunate. One shell from the Japanese severed her steam pipes and, losing way, she was surrounded by enemy ships, which proceeded to bombard her from short range. Admiral Makarov, watching the plight of *Steregushchi* from the bridge of the cruiser *Novik*, decided to attempt a rescue. Along with another cruiser, *Novik* came out of the harbor at 0830 heading in the direction of *Steregushchi*. However, besides the destroyers he had seen earlier, Makarov found

Steregushchi was now being shelled by five Japanese cruisers and he quickly called off the gallant, but potentially suicidal, rescue attempt. When all four of the destroyer's officers and most of her crew were dead, the remaining crew surrendered. The Japanese attempted to take *Steregushchi* under tow, but she was damaged to the extent that she sank before a tow line could be rigged. Only four of her crew survived.

These may well be the first instances of destroyers fighting destroyers. It is noteworthy that once again torpedoes proved to be a difficult weapon to employ in this kind of confused engagement. The one sinking that did occur came as a result of gunfire.

Twelve days later, the Japanese again sent destroyers in towards Port Arthur, backed up by heavier units in an attempt to draw the Russians out of the harbour. The ploy failed on this occasion, but it set a pattern for future engagements. One side or the other would send destroyers into the waters around the harbour and see if the other side reacted. On the night of 12/13 April, the Russians sent out two divisions of four destroyers each, looking for the Japanese fleet. Makarov, who wanted to be ready for any action, was spending the night on board the cruiser *Diana*, which had guardship duty that evening. Lookouts on board *Diana* saw shapes moving outside the harbour entrance and correctly concluded that these were Japanese ships laying a new minefield. When informed of this activity, Makarov ordered that the area should be swept in the morning and retired for the night. The cruiser *Bayan* was ordered out at first light to support the returning destroyers. She had just cleared the harbour when word arrived that a single Russian destroyer was in sight, under attack by numerous Japanese ships. *Bayan* immediately increased speed and headed for the fray.

The destroyer in this plight was *Strashni*. She had been the fourth ship in one of the two Russian squadrons that had put out the night before. Apparently, around 2300, she had become separated from the rest of her squadron and, after blundering about on her own for nearly three hours, stumbled on to a line of four destroyers at 0200 and, assuming it was the other Russian squadron, fell in line behind it.[24] Equally as bizarre, a pair of Japanese destroyers, also separated from their flotilla, fell in behind the Russian squadron to which *Strashni* had originally belonged. Officers on the other Russian ships, who had failed to notice *Strashni*'s absence, did notice that their line had now grown to five and spent several hours pondering what, if anything, they should do about it. It appears that around 0300 the Japanese captains realised their mistake and slipped off the end of the Russian line. The Russians did not fire on them, fearing that one of them might be *Strashni*.[25]

Strashni remained at the end of her line of destroyers until, at first light, they approached a squadron of six Japanese cruisers. Only when, rather than attacking the cruisers, the destroyers fell in line with them, did it finally dawn on *Strashni's* captain that something was amiss. Whatever he may have lacked in experience (and perhaps common sense), he certainly did not lack in courage. Faced with overwhelming odds, he raised his colours and tried to mount a torpedo attack on the cruisers, but before he could get into range, the Japanese reacted and one of the many enemy shots detonated the warhead of *Strashni's* forward torpedo and brought her to a halt. *Bayan* came up at this point and put herself between *Strashni* and the Japanese ships. Nothing could be done to save the destroyer, which was clearly sinking, but *Bayan* managed to put a boat down in the water and was able to rescue five of *Strashni's* crew.

Makarov had been watching all this with great frustration from Port Arthur. The cruiser *Diana* was ordered out and the rest of the Russian ships were told to raise steam and head for the Japanese cruisers as soon as they could move. The first Russian battleship to be ready was *Petropavlovsk* and Makarov moved his flag to that ship and ordered her out at her best speed. It looked for a few moments as if a full-scale fleet engagement might ensue, as four Japanese battleships appeared from the south to support the cruisers and Russian ships came pouring out of the harbour in somewhat random sequence. Seeing no chance for an easy victory and not wishing to risk the fleet on which so much depended, the Japanese withdrew to the south. Makarov formed his fleet into two columns and made a sweep of the area, but no attempt was made to pursue the faster Japanese squadrons. Satisfied that the immediate threat was averted, he turned his fleet back towards the harbour. At 0943, *Petropavlovsk*, leading a column of four battleships, ran on to a mine, one of those laid the night before by Japanese torpedo boats. His order to sweep the area got lost in the haste to rescue *Strashni*; *Petropavlovsk* and Makarov paid the price of this oversight. The relatively small detonation of the mine was followed by the much bigger explosion as the battleship's magazines erupted, tearing out the ship's bottom forward. In less than two minutes, *Petropavlovsk* disappeared bow first, her screws still turning. Seven officers and seventy-three men were rescued. Makarov was not among them.

The way forward

By the time of the Russo-Japanese War, the torpedo and the ships designed to carry torpedoes had evolved to the extent that something recognisable as a destroyer faced off against other destroyers in the first of many such

Prints of military subjects, particularly ones showing great feats, especially in victory, were as popular in Japan as in Western countries. The Japanese brought their own style to the depiction of the tumultuous night action that followed the Battle of Tsushima, 27–28 May 1905. Destroyers and torpedo boats battled high seas as much as they did the remnants of the Russian fleet. They succeeded in sinking four Russian warships for the loss of three torpedo boats.

engagements. The weapon and the type continued to evolve to the point that in World War II, destroyer torpedoes could reach fifty knots at a range of 20,000 metres carrying nearly 500 kilograms of explosive, and destroyers grew to the size of small cruisers and carried five or more guns of generally 5in (127mm) calibre and eight or ten torpedoes.[26] This evolution, while dramatic, was only to be expected, as destroyers proved themselves to be workhorses, capable of taking on tasks as diverse as convoy escort, shore bombardment, search and rescue, high-speed transport and anti-aircraft picket, as well as the surface attack role for which they were originally designed. The numbers in which they were built, particularly by the United States during World War II, is ample testimony to the type's utility – more than 400 destroyers joined the US Navy during the war years, not counting an even larger number of somewhat smaller destroyer escorts.

What did not evolve in anything like the same straight path of development was the tactics with which these ships would be employed. In 1904, destroyer engagements generally evolved into chaotic melées in which ships were often as much a danger to their compatriots as their enemies. No incident in that war exemplifies this better than the aftermath of the Battle of Tsushima. Having successfully met and defeated the Russian Baltic fleet after the latter's epic voyage halfway around the world, the Japanese fleet remained between the Russians and Vladivostok, their intended destination. As night fell, the damaged remnants of the Russian fleet reorganised and tried to grope their way north through the Japanese fleet.

The Japanese responded by sending in their torpedo craft – a total of twenty-one destroyers and approximately forty torpedo boats. The former had been accompanying the Japanese fleet, the latter had been sheltering in the lee of Tsushima Island due to high seas. The number of torpedoes fired by the Japanese flotillas before morning is not known, but seven hits were claimed and that number appears to be correct. Two battleships and two cruisers were on the receiving end of those seven torpedoes. Four found their mark on *Navarin* – two on each side – and sent her to the bottom. Single hits stopped *Sissoi Veliki* and the cruisers *Vladimir Monomakh* and *Admiral Nakhimov*. All three of those sank the next day. The Japanese forces were roughly handled by the Russians and their own forces. Two torpedo boats were sunk by enemy gunfire and a third sank after colliding with the destroyer *Akatsuki*. There were five other collisions, which damaged three other destroyers and three more torpedo boats to the point that they had to pull out of the action.

The Japanese, in particular, learned the lessons of this war and developed excellent night-fighting doctrine that gave them a distinct advantage in their first encounters with their American counterparts in the South Pacific. They worked decades to perfect their torpedoes, night optics and fire discipline to allow them to sight the enemy first and strike more swiftly and accurately. The Americans responded not by emulating the enemy, but rather with new and innovative technology. By deploying radars that effectively lit up the night, they eventually were able to nullify the Japanese advantages and ushered in the modern era of electronic warfare that is still evolving today.

Notes

1   All dates in this account are given 'new style', meaning that they are twelve days later than the dates the Russians would have recorded at the time. The Russians did not switch from the Julian to the Gregorian calendar until after the 1917 Revolution. In 1877, 24 April would have been 12 April on Russian calendars.

2   Now the port of Batúmi in the Republic of Georgia.

3   Sulina is now part of Romania.

4   Now the Georgian port city of Sokhumi.

5   The tender *Velikiy Knyaz Konstantin* carried four torpedo boats that night. Besides *Chesma* and *Sinop*, these were named *Navarin* and *Miner*. It is believed that the latter two did not carry Whitehead-type torpedoes, instead employing spar torpedoes. One source gives the fourth boat's name as *Sukhum Kalé*, but that is almost certainly a mistake, as that was the Turkish name for the port where the attack took place, an unlikely name for a Russian torpedo boat. It is also possible that the tender carried different boats on different occasions.

6   Weihaiwei is now known as Weihai, a major port city in Shandong province, PRC.

7   Even with the earliest torpedoes, which, if they functioned correctly, could only run a straight course, aiming accurately was not easy. Even if the target was stationary, the firing boat was moving, and that introduced an element of offset into the aiming of the torpedo. The fixed bow tube would be the easiest to aim because, as long as the boat's course was straight, no account need be taken of the boat's motion.

8   Guncotton, also known as nitrocellulose, is made by treating cotton with nitric acid. It is far more powerful than black powder, but is very unstable during production and was most often mixed with nitroglycerin to make cordite for use as a propellant or was replaced by TNT (trinitrotoluene), which is less powerful but far more stable.

9   *McSh*, p. 1.

10   In the case of the most famous Japanese surprise attack – the attack on Pearl Harbor – they had intended to follow all formal diplomatic procedures, including the breaking of diplomatic relations, prior to the attack, but through poor planning and a series of mis-steps, the delivery of the note breaking relations came hours after the attack had started. This allowed American propaganda to picture the Japanese as a treacherous adversary from the beginning of the war. In any case, the Japanese did not consider a formal declaration of war necessary; in their mind, the breaking of diplomatic relations was considered sufficient warning that acts of war were imminent.

11   Known as Port Arthur to the Russians and most of the west, and as Ryojun to the Japanese, this natural harbour is today Lüshun, a commercial and fishing port at the southern tip of the Liaodong peninsula, PRC. In 1904, it was the main Russian naval base in the region, along with Vladivostok (on the Sea of Japan) and Chemulpo (now Inch'on, ROK).

12   The inner harbour at Port Arthur was well protected but rather small and the entrance was very narrow, making the movement of larger ships in or out of the inner harbour a slow process. Thus it was standard Russian practice to moor their capital ships in the unprotected outer harbour.

13   The following account comes primarily from *McCul*, pp. 49–51 and 53, and from www.russojapanesewar.com and www.navy.ru. These accounts differ in many details and I have tried to form the most cohesive narrative possible from the various available pieces.

14   Dalny, rendered Dairen by the Japanese, is now known as Dalian.

15   It would appear that the Russians had no system of flares or signal lamps that would have

allowed the patrolling destroyers to warn the fleet of the approaching Japanese from a distance. Either that or the destroyer captains opted not to make use of them. At no time during the next several hours do these Russian ships reappear.

16 www.russojapanesewar.com/torp-attk-pa.html, p. 1. The quotation is anonymous, but from context it is likely that the author was an officer in the army garrison at Port Arthur.

17 Japanese accounts use a different time zone and report the action beginning shortly after 0020 on the 9th.

18 *McCul*, p. 50.

19 The name of this ship is rendered in English in many forms. Besides *Tsessarevich*, it is sometimes spelled *Tsarevich* or *Tsessarevitch*.

20 *Pallada* was able to use the dry dock at Port Arthur and was repaired within a month of the attack. The repairs to the battleships took longer, but both were with the Russian fleet for the attempted breakout in August.

21 The Russian navy had twenty-five destroyers at Port Arthur when the war began in 1904. Twelve of these were relatively small (220–240 ton) ships of the *Puilki* class which had been completed in sections at several different Baltic yards and sent to Port Arthur by rail where they were assembled. The rest were larger ships, built at a number of different Russian, French, British and German yards. Of these, only fifteen were operational at the beginning of the war.

22 The names of three of these ships are listed in *McCul* p. 71 as *Vlastni*, *Vuinoslivi* and *Bezstrashni* and the squadron commander as Captain Nikolai A. Matusevich.

23 Ibid. These were *Silni*, *Razyashchi*, *Ryeshitelni* and *Steregushchi*.

24 This incredible behaviour can be at least in part explained by the fact that *Strashni* was commanded by a young and very inexperienced captain, Commander Yurasovski, just arrived from St Petersburg, and that *Strashni* had only recently been made serviceable, so that her crew and remaining officers could offer Yurasovski little assistance.

25 In the days before radio, this kind of confusion recurs, though it is hard to understand why signal lamps or flare pistols would not have allowed the identity of the extra ships to be established, unless doctrine forbade the use of such methods.

26 The torpedo specifications relate to the Japanese Type 93 Model 1 torpedo, often – though inaccurately – called the 'Long Lance', used by that nation's destroyers for most of World War II. It is generally conceded to have been the best surface-ship torpedo of the era.

Chapter 2

David and Goliath – The Dardanelles (May 1915)

IF THERE WAS such a thing as a 'typical' battleship of the pre-dreadnought era, then HMS *Goliath* was that ship. Sir William White had become the Royal Navy's Director of Naval Construction in 1886, in an era when capital-ship design was evolving rapidly along many parallel courses of development. White

About as typical an example of a Royal Navy pre-dreadnought battleship as can be found, HMS *Goliath* was obsolete by the time World War War began, but use was found for her and her sisters in distant waters. She was serving as fire support for the ill-conceived Gallipoli campaign, when she crossed paths with an unexpected adversary on the night of 12–13 May 1915. This photograph shows *Goliath*'s sister, HMS *Canopus* in pre-war Victorian livery – black hull, white superstructure and buff funnels and masts. (NHC)

insisted that certain features were necessary in a British battleship, including sufficient freeboard to make them seaworthy, a small number of large breech-loading rifles for hitting power and extensive armour protection to allow them to take on any ship an enemy might possess. The result of this was almost twenty years of stable development ending only with the design of the revolutionary HMS *Dreadnought* in 1905.[1]

HMS *Goliath* was as typical as a White-era battleship could get. She was laid down in 1897, the fifth of six sisters of the *Canopus* class. Taking advantage of advances in metallurgy, this class substituted 6in (152mm) of Krupp steel for 9in (229mm) of Harvey nickel steel in the main armour belt, compared to the preceding *Majestic* class, and in the process saved almost 2000 tons of displacement on similar dimensions.[2] Nevertheless, the substitution was not quite one-for-one and left the *Canopus* class with less effective overall armour protection than their predecessors and prompted some in the Royal Navy to insist that these ships be classed as 'Second Class' rather than 'First Class' battleships. The savings in weight from the reduced armour thickness and improved performance due to the introduction of Belleville water-tube boilers gave them higher speed and greater range than the *Majestics*. Both classes were useful, as the *Canopus* class was intended from the beginning for service on the China station, where it was felt necessary to counter the threat of Japanese armament and to keep an eye on the various European powers interested in carving up the decaying Chinese empire. All six sisters served in the Far East until the alliance with Japan reduced the need for such a major force in Chinese waters and the development of dreadnoughts made *Goliath* and all the other White-era battleships effectively obsolete.

By 1909, *Goliath* was back in home waters and part of the reserve fleet. In 1913 she was decommissioned and in all likelihood would have been stricken in a few more years had war not broken out in August 1914. Placed back in service immediately and manned by a reserve crew, there was no lack of work for the old ship. Initially employed as part of a standing patrol of the Western Approaches out of Devonport, she was soon transferred to Loch Ewe to defend the Grand Fleet anchorage there and, before the war was two months old, she was again on her way to the Far East because she was still a good steamer and no newer capital ships could be spared for such distant duty.

The threat of German cruisers

The presence of major fleet units was needed away from home waters because the start of the war found many units of the German High Seas Fleet scattered across the world's oceans. Most of the German units in the Pacific joined Admiral Graf Spee's squadron, which briefly threw a scare into the British before he rounded Cape Horn and ran into a far superior Royal Navy force off the Falklands on 8 December 1914. But that still left a handful of small German cruisers operating singly in the most inconvenient locations – SMS *Emden* in the eastern Indian Ocean, *Dresden* off the west coast of South America, *Karlsruhe* in the Caribbean and *Königsberg* on the east coast of Africa.[3] While each of these ships had the potential to disrupt the seaborne commerce on which Britain's survival depended, they had a number of serious problems that limited the actual threat. Germany lacked the world-wide network of naval bases and friendly ports on which the Royal Navy depended to support its distant operations. This meant that these solitary German cruisers would have to depend on their own resources finding coal and other provisions and there would be few, if any, friendly ports where maintenance or repairs could be performed.

Nevertheless, the threat of these cruisers was real and was taken very seriously by the Admiralty. *Emden* appeared to be the most dangerous and became the object of a massive search, eventually ending with her destruction by HMS *Sydney* off Cocos Island on 9 November 1914. *Karlsruhe* was by far the newest and most capable of the four raiders and, being in the Caribbean at the outbreak of war, had considerable early success there and off the coast of Brazil. Then, with no warning, she simply disappeared and was never heard from again.[4] Her disappearance must have indeed seemed utterly mysterious to the British because she sank out of sight of land. While headed for Barbados for a raid, she suffered an internal explosion forward, which blew off her bow and caused her to sink in half an hour. Most of the crew survived, picked up by an accompanying collier. The exact cause of the mishap has never been determined, but clearly something set off the forward magazine.

Dresden, which had been part of von Spee's squadron, survived the Falklands battle and re-rounded Cape Horn. Finding pickings slim among the sparse traffic along the Chilean coast, she was soon running low on coal and provisions and allowed herself to be interned by the local authorities at Cumberland Bay on Isla Más a Tierra on 10 March 1915.[5] The crew remained on board *Dresden* as the island had no facilities to accommodate the 360 men. The Royal Navy was unhappy with this situation, fearing that the Germans might change their mind once the crew had some rest. Clearly the Chileans lacked the means to prevent *Dresden* from leaving. Ignoring Chilean sovereignty and neutrality, a Royal Navy squadron, including the cruisers HMSs *Kent* and *Glasgow*, appeared off Cumberland Bay the morning of 14 March and began shelling the German

Three Royal Navy officers in pith helmets approach the wreck of SMS *Königsberg* in the Rufiji delta, July 1915. *Goliath* had spent time between November 1914 and early April 1915 as the flagship of Rear Admiral King-Hall, in charge of the blockading squadron. (NHC)

cruiser. *Dresden* ran up a white flag and sent a young English-speaking *Leutnant zur See* out in a longboat to protest the firing on *Dresden* in neutral waters.[6] The British responded that they would resume the bombardment unless *Dresden* surrendered unconditionally to them. Unwilling to allow his ship to be captured and seeing no other option, her captain ordered the ship scuttled.

The fourth of the scattered German cruisers was *Königsberg*. Assigned to the base at Dar es Salaam, the capital of German East Africa in June 1914, she represented a serious threat to the merchant traffic between the Suez Canal and all points east. The Royal Navy's presence off the east African coast was a squadron of three older, slower cruisers, HMSs *Astraea*, *Hyacinth* and *Pegasus*.[7] *Königsberg* was at sea in the Gulf of Aden at the outbreak of war and immediately began searching for British shipping. Two days later, she captured the SS *City of Winchester*, the first merchant casualty of the war. Two days after that, *Astraea* bombarded Dar es Salaam, leaving the port unusable to *Königsberg*. With no home port at which to re-provision and perform basic maintenance, *Königsberg* rapidly declined into a state of low fuel and poor mechanical condition. She took refuge in the delta of the Rufiji river, emerging thereafter only once.

On 19 September, she made a quick sortie across to Zanzibar, having been informed that *Pegasus* was laid up there performing boiler maintenance. Unable to move, the British cruiser was a stationary target for *Königsberg* the next morning, which steamed slowly offshore and soon left the smaller British ship on fire.[8] Satisfied that *Pegasus* was no longer a threat, *Königsberg* headed south, hoping to make her way back to Germany, but a serious engine failure forced her back into the Rufiji, from which she never again emerged.

By 30 September, the first of three newer and larger light cruisers had arrived, effectively bottling up *Königsberg* in the delta. Gunfire from the three cruisers sank *Königsberg*'s collier and forced the German cruiser further upstream. In November, *Goliath*, en route to the China station was ordered to join the Rufiji blockade and attempt, with her longer-ranging 12in (305mm) rifles, to reach the elusive *Königsberg*, which had effectively disappeared in the multiple twisting channels of the delta. The effort proved futile, as *Königsberg*, lightened by removal of all top hamper and excess stores, was moved still further up the Rufiji, while the British ships were obliged by their deep draft to remain outside. Nevertheless, *Goliath* stayed on as flagship of Rear Admiral Herbert King-Hall, in command of the growing Royal Navy squadron.

The wreck of *Königsberg* seen from the air after she was sunk by gunfire from a pair of shallow draft monitors, July 1915. The use of aircraft for spotting fall of shot was critical in the eventual destruction of the raider. (NHC)

The British brought in a pair of seaplanes in hopes of finding and possibly bombing the elusive German cruiser, but one crashed soon after arrival and the other proved too underpowered to carry a bomb in the heat. Three more aircraft were dispatched and this rag-tag force was able to keep tabs on *Königsberg*, though they were unable to damage her in any way. Finally, in June 1915, two river monitors, HMSs *Severn* and *Mersey*, arrived and made their way upstream until they were in range of *Königsberg*. It took two attempts, but finally, on 11 July, they were able to disable the cruiser and force her to be abandoned and scuttled. *Goliath* was not there to witness *Königsberg*'s demise. She had been sent north again in early April to support the disastrous Gallipoli landings. Having tried unsuccessfully to force the Dardanelles with a purely naval force in March, the British incredibly decided to land troops at Cape Helles and fight their way up the narrow Gallipoli peninsula.[9] To guard the flanks of the troops and provide fire support, the Royal Navy brought in additional old battleships, including *Goliath*.

Engagements with the Turks

To oppose this naval force, the Turks relied mainly on mine fields and shore-based artillery. The Turkish navy was a hodge-podge of antique hulks with only a few modern units of significant military value. Earlier in the ironclad era, the Turks had attempted to build a modern navy capable of challenging Russia in the Black Sea, but internal politics had caused this effort to be abandoned and the powerful fleet of the 1870s was now less than useless. The best, and best-known units in the fleet were a pair of modern German ships that had been caught in the Mediterranean by the outbreak of war. Rather than risk attempting to steam out into the Atlantic, around the British Isles and across the North Sea – an almost certainly doomed effort – the battlecruiser SMS *Goeben* and light cruiser *Breslau* were directed towards the Dardanelles and ultimately Constantinople.[10] In the first weeks of the war, the Ottoman Empire was still officially neutral, but German influence was strong, and the Turks were long time enemies of the Russians and resented British and French inroads into Ottoman territory. The arrival of the German warships without invitation and the subsequent offer by the Germans to transfer the ships and their crews were critical factors in the decision by the Turks to enter the war on the side of the Central Powers.[11] Nevertheless, these ships were far too valuable to be risked against the Allied fleet in the narrow waters of the Dardanelles. For that, the Turks had destroyers.

The best of the Turkish destroyers were also of German make.[12] The four destroyers of the *S.165* class, laid down at the Schichau yard at Elbing in 1909,

TCG *Muavenet-i Milliye* was a German–built destroyer of the *S.165* class, acquired
by Turkey in 1909 while still under construction. This photograph shows the destroyer
in port with other ships behind her. The leftmost mast, the funnel to the left
of the destroyer's bridge and the mast visible between the destroyer's funnels belong
to one or more ships in the background. (Tosun Saral)

The officers and crew of *Muavenet-i Milliye* pose by one of the three single 17.7in (450mm)
torpedo tubes she carried, seen some time after the sinking of *Goliath*. The two officers
to the right, in front of the torpedo tube, are (left) KL Rudolf Firle of the German navy
and now-Lieutenant Commander Ahmet Saffet Bey. Firle wears the Iron Cross 1st Class
that he was awarded for his role in the sinking; Saffet already has the extra half-stripe that
indicates his promotion from Senior Lieutenant. (Tosun Saral)

were purchased by the Turkish navy before they were completed and transferred by sea from the Baltic to Constantinople.[13] They were typical destroyers of the time, displacing 665 tons, each armed with a pair of 75mm and 37mm guns and three single 17.7in (450mm) torpedo tubes and capable of a maximum speed of thirty-two knots. The lead ship of the class, *S.165*, was renamed *Muavenet-i Milliye*.[14] As with the others of her class, she retained a significant German complement, though the commanding officer was Turkish, *Birindji Yuzbachi* (Senior Lieutenant) Ahmet Saffet Efendi.[15]

The paths of *Goliath* and *Muavenet-i Milliye* converged on the night of 12–13 May 1915. Turkish destroyers had been reported in the Narrows, upstream of the Allied positions, for the last few nights, but this seemed to elicit little concern. The pace of operations in support of the troops was rather leisurely. The Allied ships would awaken soon after first light from their anchorage in Morto Bay, just inside the straits, move up to near the front lines, barely two miles further into the Dardanelles, fire a few shells at the enemy forts, weather permitting, and then retire back to the anchorage again before dusk. (The Turks nicknamed the two battleships *Kocakari*, which means 'old lady' or 'crone' in Turkish slang, referring to their nasty habit of talking too much.) Disdainful of the Turkish threat, the only precaution taken against torpedo attack was the posting of a nightly patrol of four destroyers just up the straits.[16]

Returning to Morto Bay at 1900 on 12 May, *Goliath* anchored in the out-board position. (The other occupant of the bay that night was the somewhat newer HMS *Cornwallis*, anchored closer in towards shore.) The moon was a mere sliver, just a day shy of new. A fog began drifting across the straits from the Asian shore soon after midnight. Following standing orders, *Goliath* periodically switched on her searchlights and swept the surrounding waters.[17] If anything, this reduced the effectiveness of her lookouts to near zero and made her easy to find in the gloom. What she did not do was deploy her torpedo nets. The rigging and taking in of torpedo nets was a slow and difficult procedure, taking at least an hour, especially difficult when done in the dark. Given that *Goliath* expected to be on the move again at first light on the 13th, it is small wonder that Captain T L Shelford chose not to deploy these nets when dropping anchor on the 12th. It was to be a fatal error.

The sinking of Goliath

As the sun set on 12 May, *Muavenet-i Milliye* was at anchor in Kephez Bay on the Asiatic side, just south of the Narrows, waiting for full dark. She had been forward based at Pasalimani, an island in the western part of the Sea of

Marmara, starting in late April, as part of an effort to combat British submarines operating in those waters. There was no road link between Constantinople and the Gallipoli front, so all supplies for the Turkish troops had to be sent by ship through the Sea of Marmara. After only three days on station at Pasalimani, *Muavenet-i Milliye* received orders putting Saffet under the command of the commander of the naval base at Canakkale (Chanak) with specific instructions to attack the British battleships that were inflicting serious casualties on the Turkish troops defending the line of the Kerevizdere, a stream that defined the eastern part of the Gallipoli front. Departing Pasalmani in the morning of 10 May, *Muavenet-i Milliye* headed for Gelibolu (Gallipoli), on the western shore at the head of the Dardanelles and then continued on to Canakkale on the Asian shore at the Narrows, which was reached at 1330. The next day, Saffet, accompanied by the German executive officer KL Firle, crossed the Narrows and travelled down as far as the front lines to get a good view of the British battleships.

Preparing *Muavenet-i Milliye* for the sortie, extra funnel cowls were fitted to reduce the chance of visible sparks, plus all four of her guns and most of her stores had been landed to reduce draft, in case she encountered any uncharted minefields.[18] She carried only one reload besides the three torpedoes for her single tubes. The crew prepared mentally as best they could. According to the ship's Torpedo Officer, Lieutenant Ali Haydar:

> Nobody in the boat considered it likely that we would return safely, even if our attack was successful. We all assumed we'd be able to swim to shore after our boat was sunk. Our crew, most of them unmarried, were mainly concerned about finding dry clothing and new uniforms once ashore. This was a concern because we'd all seen crewmen from sunken ships walking the gardens and corridors of the Naval Ministry in their night clothes. Such was the heedlessness of the ruling government at the time. . . . Our First Lieutenant and some of the men packed up their personal belongings and clothing and handed them over to the captain of ss *Kütahya*, which was sailing for Istanbul, for delivery to their families.[19]

Muavenet-i Milliye left Kephez Bay at 1900 on 12 May and headed across the Narrows. She then started creeping slowly south along the western shore, before anchoring to await full dark. The hope was that she would be able to slip past the British destroyer patrol because the steeper cliffs on that side of the straits would make for a darker backdrop. Even that short journey had its moments of excitement:

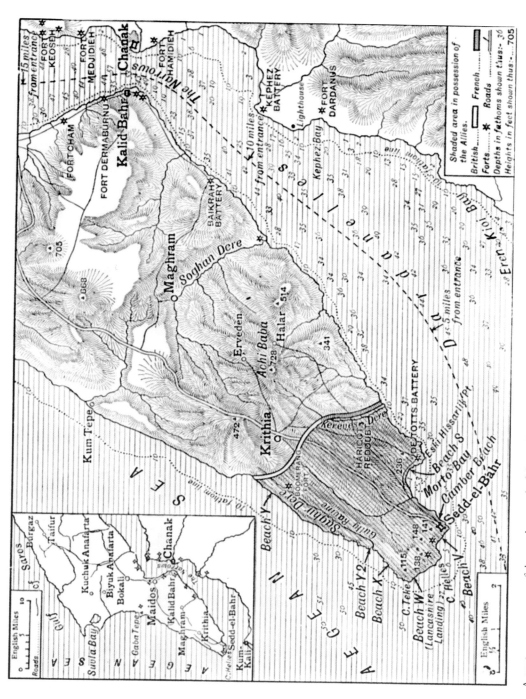

A contemporary map of the southern end of the Gallipoli peninsula, which shows Morto Bay towards the bottom left where *Goliath* was sunk. The route taken by *Muavenet-i Milliye* included a stop at Canakkale (Chanak) at the Narrows, at Kephez Bay just to the south and then continued south along the western shore of the Dardanelles.

To hide our vessel from the enemy and avoid any mine fields, we sailed close in to the opposite shore . . .

Suddenly something happened that startled us: The starboard propeller hit a submerged rock. 'Alas!' However, by Allah's grace the damage wasn't great. Only a small nick had been taken out of one propeller blade.

At 1950 we anchored in nine fathoms of water near the mouth of the Soganlidere.[20] Determining that this was not a safe place to wait, we moved our vessel closer in to shore. At that time we sent our pilot ashore.[21]

She weighed anchor again at 0045 on the 13th and started slowly south. The tactic of hugging the western shore worked, because *Muavenet-i Milliye* was able to slip past the destroyer screen unobserved, even though she was able to see and identify two of the British destroyers silhouetted against the incoming fog at a range of a few hundred metres.[22]

Safely past the defensive screen, Saffet let the strong current carry *Muavenet-i Milliye* along, using his engines only to maintain a steady course towards the strong illumination in the southwest. At 0110, *Muavenet-i Milliye* emerged from the fog in full view of the two British battleships anchored in Morto Bay. By then it was too late for anything but the most rudimentary defensive measures.

As we were approaching *Goliath*, they noticed us. They began sending us a series of signals. They were asking us for countersigns. I know English, so I went immediately to the bridge and began sending back a meaningless series of countersigns. My purpose was to make the enemy hesitant, to gain time so we could approach as close as possible to *Goliath*. Every second was precious. We'd approached to within 400–500 metres. We wanted to get within 300 metres to have the greatest chance of success.[23]

The oncoming destroyer was challenged by signal lamp and hailed by megaphone, which, according to one account, was answered in good English.[24] Even if the ship had gone to battle stations when the destroyer was sighted, there would not have been time to man guns before *Muavenet-i Milliye*, increasing speed, turned on a course parallel to *Goliath* and, at a range of less than 500 metres, launched all three loaded torpedoes at the stationary target.

We fired our first torpedo. We waited impatiently a short interval, then we fired our second torpedo. The first torpedo hit *Goliath*. In my opinion, it was not necessary to fire the third, but in the excitement of the attack, the crew of the aft torpedo tube had fired theirs without waiting for orders. We watched as the second and then the third torpedo hit *Goliath*. She began to roll on to her starboard side. The giant was burning! Dense smoke covered her

A dramatic rendition of the sinking of *Goliath* that was created for a German tabloid naturally
made the scene appear considerably more dramatic that it in fact was. *Muavenet-i Milliye*
did not stay around while *Goliath*'s crew abandoned ship and, in the event, the battleship
capsized too rapidly for any boats to be launched.

entire length, a column of flame rising around her mainmast. *Goliath* sank in
almost no time.[25]

Torpedoes had improved significantly in the ten years since the Port Arthur
attack. The addition of better propulsion, which made them faster and
gyroscopic guidance, which made them run straighter, improved the chances of
a hit if the aim was good. Moving at relatively slow speed and firing at short
range, *Muavenet–i Milliye* could hardly miss. All three torpedoes hit *Goliath*. The
first hit below her bridge, the second in way of her boiler room and the third
hit right aft. *Goliath*'s fate was sealed. Her side blown open, she took only
minutes to capsize. The explosions were not loud. In fact it was not until she
rolled over that lookouts on *Cornwallis* were even aware she had been
torpedoed. Many of the crew were trapped in the hull and went down with the
ship. Others jumped overboard but had no chance in the swift, cold current and
were swept out into the Aegean. In the end, only about 180 of her crew were
saved; more than 500 were lost, including Captain Shelford.

Obviously, this aroused the other Allied ships in the bay. Saffet had the option to load his one spare torpedo and make a run at *Cornwallis*, but he wisely decided that his chances would be slim and the risks high, and he opted to exit the scene heading back up the straits.

> We had achieved our task without a casualty, not even a nosebleed. All the men embraced me with great joy. My men kissed my hands. I kissed their cheeks and foreheads.[26] All our crew was happily cheering: '*Yasa!*'[27] But this was no time for cheering. I ordered my men to load the fourth torpedo in case we came under enemy attack.[28]

Now fighting the current, which was running at a steady five knots, *Muavenet-i Milliye*'s progress was slow and, with her engines running at full power, there was the constant risk that engine noise or sparks would give away her position to the now-alerted destroyer patrol. But luck and meteorology were with Saffet and the fog hid *Muavenet-i Milliye* as she made her way up the straits.

> We made our way back at full speed. We anchored at Soganlidere at 0200. We could move no further without a pilot guiding us through the minefields. After twenty minutes we saw two enemy patrol boats approaching. Our batteries at Soganlidere and Dardanos turned on their searchlights and began to fire on the enemy boats.[29] We were still in danger. We started north again, accepting the risks, entering into the minefields. We passed through safely and anchored at Ciftehavuzlar on the western side, where we waited until dawn. At 0445, we crossed the straits and came to Canakkale. All the men in the fortifications at Canakkale cheered us until daybreak, singing patriotic songs, playing drums and trumpets.[30]

The next day she made a triumphal entrance into Constantinople. The officers and crew of *Muavenet-i Milliye* were grandly feted, as this was a major triumph for the small Turkish navy. Firle and the Engineering Officer Lieutenant Engineer Andrea were awarded the Iron Cross 1st Class – then still a very rare honour. Ahmed Saffet was promoted to the rank of *Corvette Capitani* (Lieutenant Commander) and awarded the right to be addressed as 'Bey', a considerable increase in prestige.[31] Firle returned to Germany and served on the Admiralty staff. He survived the war, wrote a popular book on operations in the Baltic, and went on to a successful career in the merchant marine. Saffet also survived the war, remaining in the navy after the Turkish surrender and the dismemberment of the Ottoman Empire. Though he never rose above the rank of *Galion Capitani* (Captain), he sided with the forces of Turkish independence under Atatürk and served briefly as War Minister in the nascent Turkish government. He later stood for Parliament and served eight years as MP for Elazig. He retired in 1935 and died in 1938.

Notes

1 Of course, the design of HMS *Dreadnought* had its antecedents. The idea of an 'all-big-gun' battleship had its origin in several navies at the end of the nineteenth century. Some of the early sketch designs for the last classes of RN pre-dreadnoughts had called for an increased main battery, but it was the writings of the Italian General Cuniberti in 1903 and knowledge that the US Navy had began the design of an 'all-big-gun' battleship in 1904 that pushed the First Sea Lord Jackie Fisher to rush *Dreadnought* to completion in 1906.

2 The difference between Harvey nickel steel and Krupp cemented steel was so pronounced that the latter rapidly replaced the former as the standard naval armour plating from the date of its introduction in 1893. They both were face-hardened steels, but the Krupp version added chromium to the iron as well as nickel, which increased the resistance of the entire plate, and improved 'cementing' (a specific type of face-hardening, not the adhesion of two different plates) processes increased the hardness of the facing surface.

3 *Dresden* had been part of von Spee's squadron; the only unit to escape the slaughter off the Falklands. The other three cruisers had been operating independently before the war started.

4 The British did not learn anything of the fate of *Karlsruhe* until March 1915, when wreckage washed ashore in the Grenadines.

5 Isla Más a Tierra (literally 'island closer to land') is 674 kilometres west of the Chilean mainland at the same latitude as Valparaiso. It was renamed Isla Robinsón Crusoe by the government in 1966 in an attempt to boost tourism. It is, in fact, the island on which the Scottish sailor Alexander Selkirk was stranded for more than four years between 1704 and 1709. The novelist Daniel Defoe heard Selkirk's story and fictionalised it as *Robinson Crusoe*, published in 1719.

6 This was Wilhelm Canaris, who later became the head of the *Abwehr*, Germany's military intelligence service and conspirator in several plots to eliminate Hitler.

7 Of these, *Hyacinth* was the newest, biggest and best armed, but she was eight years older than *Königsberg* and nominally two knots slower.

8 *Pegasus* burned out and sank that same day.

9 On 18 March 1915, while attempting to knock out the forts at the Narrows, the Allied fleet encountered a single line of mines laid near the Asian shore. Five Allied ships were mined, three of them sinking, effectively ending the naval assault of the straits. All three losses were old battleships, which the British and French had to spare. (One of the lost battleships was HMS *Ocean*, a sister of *Goliath*.) It was at that time estimated that the Dardanelles could have been forced for the loss of perhaps ten old battleships and 10,000 men. While those estimated losses seemed excessive at the time and led to the decision to land troops, they would have been tiny in comparison to the 120,000 casualties actually suffered in the subsequent land campaign.

10 Although Constantinople had been in Turkish hands for more than 350 years at the time, its name was not officially changed to Istanbul until 1930.

11 The ships were renamed TCG *Yavuz Sultan Selim* and *Medili* respectively. They served primarily in the Black Sea against the Russians, where they had little success. Nevertheless, they remained a powerful presence in the eastern Mediterranean throughout the war that the Allies could not ignore. A constant blockade was maintained off the entrance of the

Dardanelles. On 20 January 1918, the long-awaited sortie by the transplanted Germans occurred. Catching the Allied blockade by surprise with their major units absent, the monitors HMS *Raglan* and *M28* were sunk off the island of Imbros, but the Germans ran into a minefield, sinking *Medili* and damaging *Yavuz* to the point where she could only limp back into the Dardanelles to be beached in the Narrows.

12 Fourteen new and much more powerful destroyers were ordered from French, British and Italian yards in 1914, but none were completed before war broke out and none were subsequently delivered.

13 Elbing is now Elblag in Poland. Originally a maker of railroad locomotives founded at Elbing in 1837 by Ferdinand Schichau, the company grew to become a major shipyard with main facilities at Danzig (Gdansk) until 1945. The company re-emerged after the war at Bremerhaven and survives today as Schichau Seebeckwerft.

14 *Muavenet-i Milliye* translates into English as 'National Support'. She received this name because she was purchased with donations to the national naval league.

15 The executive officer and the lead engineer were both German, as were one other officer and several senior NCOs. This was of particular importance with these ships, as they were the first turbine-powered ships in the Turkish navy. Whether Senior Lieutenant Saffet or his German XO, KL Rudolf Firle, was making the command decisions during the attack on *Goliath* is a matter of some disagreement. Saffet's rank was technically the same as Firle's. The addition of 'Efendi' at the end of his name was an honorific title, roughly equivalent to 'Sir' in courteous English usage, with no connotation of nobility.

16 Some accounts say this patrol line was five destroyers.

17 The captain of the ship *Goliath* relieved on bombardment duty, HMS *Majestic,* had complained that this practice only made his ship easier for the enemy to find without offering much benefit. Events were to prove him correct.

18 The *S.165*-class destroyers had mixed oil and coal-fired boilers. One problem with coal-fired boilers was the chance that a highly visible burning ember would escape out of the funnel with the smoke. The chances of this increased when coal was poured on to increase speed.

19 *Ali.*

20 Soganlidere (rendered Soghan Dere or Soghan River on contemporary British maps) was a small stream that entered the Dardanelles about five miles northeast of Morto Bay.

21 Ibid.

22 These were HMSs *Beagle* and *Bulldog,* both larger and more heavily armed than *Muavenet-i Milliye.*

23 Ibid.

24 *Gol2.*

25 Op. cit.

26 A Turkish custom with feudal roots. At times of great emotion, sailors kiss the hands of their superior officers; the officers respond by kissing the men on their foreheads.

27 '*Yasa*' is Turkish for 'Hurrah' or 'Long Life'.

28 Ibid.

29 At this point the Dardanelles is about three nautical miles across. On the western shore, there was a fortification on the north bank of the Soganlidere; on the opposite shore, there was another fort at Dardanos above Kephez Bay, marked as Fort Dardanus on contemporary British maps.

30 Ibid.

31 Like 'Efendi', 'Bey' was an honorific title without implying noble rank.

Chapter 3

The Agony of the 4th Flotilla
(31 May–1 June 1916)

GERMANY AND GREAT BRITAIN had spent all those marks and pounds on two massive fleets of dreadnought battleships for a reason. The sheer cost in time, labour and materials it took to build and man those fleets was staggering. The purpose of all this effort was, of course, the prospect of a grand encounter, much in the style of an almighty Nelsonic clash, in which the naval power of two nations lines up against each other and attempts to pound the other side into submission. On rare occasions it worked out that way, such as when the British line faced and defeated the combined French and Spanish fleets at Trafalgar and effectively doomed Napoleon's hopes for a stable Europe under French control. Had Nelson lost that battle, there can be little doubt that Russian and Prussian resistance, largely financed by Britain's dominance of world trade, would never have been sustained.

The situation in 1916 had many similarities to that of 1805. Once again, Britain stood against a dominant continental enemy. Once again, that enemy knew that Britain was effectively unbeatable, as long as her command of the sea was unchallenged. By early 1916, submarines were just beginning to emerge as a potential threat to this dominance, but the on-again-off-again nature of the U-boat offensive made it unclear if, or when, that potential would be realised. The only proven threat to Britain's position was the German fleet.

The Anglo-German arms race

Kaiser Wilhelm II had put tremendous energy and a disproportionate share of his nation's resources into creating a fleet capable of challenging the Royal Navy. There were many within his own country who questioned the wisdom of this effort. After all, the German army was unquestionably the finest in Europe, especially after it had so rapidly and decisively humiliated the French in the Franco-Prussian War of 1870. Why, many asked, was it necessary to also

53

have a world-class fleet? After all, were not the British quite content to dominate the water and let others contend for who had the best army? But Wilhelm understood that Britain's dominance at sea gave it the freedom to intervene in continental affairs at the time and place of its choosing, while preventing any continental power from returning the favour. The British army had faced Napoleon only in Spain, which had never kept his interest for long, and at Waterloo, when he was far past his prime and his army was a mob of raw recruits and over-age veterans, yet they had hounded the Emperor of France mercilessly, forcing him to make increasingly bad decisions. Wilhelm knew that as long as a hostile Britain remained inviolate across the North Sea, domination of the continent would be to little avail.

With this in mind, he appointed Alfred Tirpitz his Navy Secretary in 1897 and began an aggressive programme of naval construction, with the avowed intent of providing Germany with a navy of nearly forty battleships by 1920. This naturally caught the attention of the British, who famously had a policy of maintaining a navy as strong as its two nearest rivals' combined fleets, and led directly to the First Sea Lord Jackie Fisher's decision to build the revolutionary HMS *Dreadnought* in 1906. The launching of *Dreadnought* effectively rendered obsolete all battleships built before her, including twenty-nine German ships of varying age and quality. Wilhelm didn't flinch for a moment. He ordered the immediate design of German equivalents, but it would be 1910 before SMS *Nassau* joined the fleet, by which time the Royal Navy had seven dreadnoughts in service and three battlecruisers, a hybrid type with cruiser speed and armour and battleship guns. Rather than accept second-class status, Wilhelm saw to it that battleships and battlecruisers continued to be built as fast as his shipyards and economy would allow, forcing the British to continue building at an accelerated rate just to keep ahead.

There are many who argue that this frantic naval arms 'race' was the true cause of World War I. Regardless, the war on the naval front soon settled into a familiar pattern. The British, safe in their islands, instituted a tight blockade on all imports into Germany. The Germans, with a navy too small to openly challenge the Royal Navy's dominance, used the classic strategy of the weaker nation, tying down massive enemy resources through the mere existence of their fleet and occasionally raiding the enemy's coast or fishing fleets.[1] This strategy had led the Germans to send their battlecruisers across the North Sea several times in 1914 and early 1915, ending with the Dogger Bank action.

Undeterred, the Germans kept looking for an opportunity that might allow them to bring their entire High Seas Fleet against a portion of the British Grand Fleet and thus change the status quo in the North Sea. The Germans returned to the idea of a battlecruiser raid, this time on Sunderland, but different from the early raids in that the full might of the High Seas Fleet would be following fifty nautical miles behind. The hope was that the Grand Fleet would respond as before, with a detachment of battlecruisers, and that this detachment could be annihilated by the superior German forces, before the full might of the Grand Fleet could intervene. The Germans knew that the British had detached a force of six battlecruisers and four of their newest, fastest battleships to Rosyth, where they would be better able to respond to German raids. If this force could be lured back towards the High Seas Fleet's sixteen battleships by Hipper's five battlecruisers, the results should be just what the Germans wanted. What the Germans did not know was that the British suspected a trap and sent the full Grand Fleet out of Scapa Flow hard on the heels of Beatty's battlecruisers.

The stage was set for exactly the battle the British both most wanted and most feared, a full-on confrontation between the two fleets. With a 28:16 advantage in dreadnoughts and similar margins in all other types, the British

In this pre-war photograph, the dreadnoughts of the High Seas Fleet are in the order they approached the 4th Flotilla on the night of 1 June 1916. Because of the various evolutions that had occurred during the late afternoon, the German line was actually in reverse of normal order, with SMS *Westfalen*, on the left in this view, leading the line, followed by *Nassau* and *Rheinland*. These three were instrumental in the destruction of the 4th Flotilla. (NHC)

should have been able to prevail easily, barring unforeseen events. But this was not 1805, and Nelson was not in command of the British fleet. The British commander, Admiral John Jellicoe, faced an array of threats that Nelson never had to worry about, most particularly the torpedo and the swarms of torpedo-carrying destroyers that accompanied the fleets. (The British had seventy-eight destroyers between their two main detachments; the Germans had sixty-one.) Jellicoe was acutely aware, given the losses at the Dardanelles, that his advantage in battleships could be nullified in minutes by a well-executed torpedo attack or a newly laid minefield.[2] To his critics, he was no Nelson, but he had good reason to be cautious. He was famously described by Winston Churchill as 'the only man on either side who could lose the war in an afternoon'.

The first destroyer encounter

The battle that followed on the last day of May 1916 was indecisive. The main action was joined only after 1800 and died down at dusk around 2100.[3] There were some spectacular events, mainly involving the inadequate armour of British battlecruisers, but when the two sides settled on nearly parallel courses heading south as darkness fell, the main fleets were intact. A southerly course would bring the Germans closer to the safety of their base at Wilhelmshaven and, perhaps more importantly, the extensive minefields in the Helgoland Bight, so Jellicoe had reason to proceed cautiously, but there were also strong reasons to maintain this course. Dusk had left the Grand Fleet east of the Germans, blocking their path to safety. If he could hold this relative position, dawn would bring a renewal of battle with the Grand Fleet in a very advantageous position. Thus, at 2117, Jellicoe disposed his fleet in a compact, flexible formation on a course of 167 degrees, just east of south-by-east.[4] His battleships were supposed to be in three parallel columns with a mile between columns, though in reality, it was not quite so orderly. (The 5th Battle Squadron of now three new fast battleships and the 6th Division – half of the 1st Battle Squadron – lagged some distance behind and somewhat east of Grand Fleet's track.) His destroyers were arranged by flotilla, in five parallel columns, five miles behind the battleships, where Jellicoe hoped there would be no accidental encounters with friendly forces.[5] Also, Jellicoe hoped the destroyers might alert him if the Germans made an attempt to cut behind his main fleet and head for the northernmost swept channel in their coastal minefields at Horns Reef.[6] This latter course was, for some reason, considered unlikely.

Yet that was exactly the course chosen by the German admiral, Reinhold Scheer. Horns Reef was the closest of the three main entrances through the

HMS *Spitfire* was a typical 'K'-class destroyer of the type that comprised most of the Grand Fleet's 4th Flotilla. At Jutland, she was second in line, behind only the leader, HMS *Tipperary*. At that battle, *Spitfire* had the misfortune to get too close to SMS *Nassau* and suffered accordingly.

minefields and thus offered the best hope of bringing his smaller and slower fleet to safety before the British could renew the battle at dawn.[7] Therefore, Scheer issued the following order to his fleet at 2110:

SSE-¼E to Horns Reef Light – Speed 16 kt – Maintain this course![8]

He knew this course would most likely cause his leading ships to encounter British units in the dark. He also knew that training and natural inclination would cause these ships to turn away from night engagements. His admonition was to hold this course, regardless of the risks. Nevertheless, it took another hour-and-a-half for the Germans to correctly organise their line with dreadnoughts in front and the intact battlecruisers bringing up the rear, and Scheer ordered a further turn to port on to a southeasterly course to keep his fleet headed towards Horns Reef.[9]

The first encounter in the dark was at 2150 and lasted just a few minutes. It resulted in nothing more than confusion on both sides. The Royal Navy's 4th Flotilla was still trying to gain its assigned position five miles aft of the battleships and was therefore steering north, but was about to turn back towards the south. This flotilla comprised the destroyer leaders HMS *Tipperary* and *Broke* and ten 'K'-class destroyers.[10] The 'K'-class destroyers were the penultimate pre-war design, large at 1072 tons, fast at twenty-nine knots and well armed. As was British practice, they favoured guns over torpedoes, carrying three 4in (102mm) guns and only two 21in (533mm) torpedo tubes in single mounts, though a reload was carried for each tube. The two leaders were of a type new to the Royal Navy. It was normal in navies of the time that a destroyer flotilla would be led by a larger ship. This would have facilities for the flotilla commander and his staff and all the required communications gear, which at the time took up considerable space and required a large staff of technicians. However, the Royal Navy had been so focused since 1905 on gaining a lead in the race to build dreadnoughts that much of the needed supporting cast of scouting forces had been neglected. To address this need, the British designed and built with typical speed a class of fast, small light cruisers, the *Arethusa* class, specifically intended for the flotilla-leader role, but as these very useful ships joined the fleet in the first months of the war, the need for fast scouts was so great that they were rarely used in their intended role. Anticipating that something just like this might happen, in 1907 Fisher pushed through the construction of a large, very fast destroyer specifically intended as a flotilla leader. The resulting ship, HMS *Swift*, was not without its problems. In 1912, she was assigned to lead the newly formed 4th Flotilla, with its brand-new 'K'-class destroyers, but when they followed the Grand Fleet north to Scapa Flow in August 1914, *Swift* proved a poor sea boat and was reassigned to the calmer waters of the Dover Patrol.

A fortuitous chance allowed the Royal Navy to replace *Swift* at the head of the 4th Flotilla. The Chilean navy had ordered six large destroyers from the J S White yard in Cowes in 1912, and, as war broke out, two had recently been launched and two more were not far behind. These four were immediately purchased from Chile and rushed to completion with minimal alteration, only the substitution of standard British guns and torpedo tubes for the planned armament. They were big (1610 tons), fast (thirty-one knots), armed with six 4in (102mm) guns and four torpedo tubes in two double mounts and much better sea boats than *Swift*. Accordingly, two ships of the class, *Broke* and *Tipperary,* were assigned to lead 4th Flotilla as soon as they were commissioned. So, as the flotilla slowed in preparation for the turn to the south, their long line was led by *Tipperary*, flagship of Captain (D) Charles J Wintour, followed by four destroyers (*Spitfire, Sparrowhawk, Garland* and *Contest),* then by *Broke* and the remaining six destroyers of the flotilla (*Achates, Ambuscade, Ardent, Fortune, Porpoise* and *Unity).* This complicated manoeuvre, tricky enough in daylight, was even more dangerous in a pitch-dark night, with crews already exhausted from a day of active combat. Therefore, the flotilla's lookouts can be excused for not seeing another line of destroyers approaching out of the gloom to the northwest.

with these smaller guns specifically to defend against attack by enemy destroyers, and this was one of the rare instances when these guns were used for their intended purpose.

After the German searchlights were doused and the sea again became pitch dark, it became hard to sort out the inevitable confusion. At least five of the British destroyers fired torpedoes at the German battle line and then swung away to port, followed by the rest of the flotilla. All except *Spitfire*, which had been forced to swerve to avoid *Tipperary*, and, coming back on to her base course, found herself alone. She had suffered a number of hits in the brief firefight, including one which punched a large hole through the base of her middle funnel, but she still could steam and was basically intact, and her captain, Lieutenant Commander Clarence Trelawney, turned the ship to starboard intending to head back towards *Tipperary* to see if she could render any assistance to the flagship.

In the meanwhile, the three leading German battleships had turned to starboard to avoid the British torpedoes and were now swinging back to resume their original course. *Spitfire's* wide turn took her directly into the path of *Nassau*, the second in the German line:

> We closed the *Tipperary*, now a mass of burning wreckage and looking a very sad sight indeed. At a distance her bridge, wheel-house and chart-house appeared to be one sheet of flame . . . and so bright was the light from this part that it seemed to obliterate one's vision of the remainder of the ship and of the sea round about, except that part close to her which was all lit up, reflecting the flames. As we neared the *Tipperary*, we saw a German cruiser hovering near. Suddenly the Captain realised that she had seen us, and was trying to ram us.[18]

Nassau's captain saw *Spitfire* approaching his port bow at a range of about 450 metres. Realising that a collision was probably inevitable, he chose to continue his turn to port so as to reduce the angle at which the two ships hit. Perhaps, with luck, the two might slip past each other without hitting. Had *Spitfire* straightened her course, they might have indeed passed starboard-to-starboard, but her captain attempted to out-turn the oncoming behemoth, which only guaranteed that they would collide.

> She was coming at us full speed across our port bow. The Captain ordered: 'Hard-a-starboard: full speed ahead both,' and, leaning over the bridge screen, shouted, 'Clear the foc'sle.' It wasn't a minute too soon, as with an awful crash the two ships met end on, port bow to port bow, we steaming at almost 27

knots, she steaming not less than 10 knots (perhaps 20 or more). You can imagine how the ⅜-inch plates of a destroyer would feel such a blow. I can recollect a fearful crash, then being hurled across the deck, and feeling the *Spitfire* rolling over to starboard as no sea ever made her roll. As we bumped, the enemy opened fire with their foc'sle guns, though luckily they could not depress them to hit us, but the blast of the guns literally cleared everything before it. Our foremast came tumbling down, our for'ard searchlight found its way from its platform above the fore-bridge down to the deck, and the foremost funnel was blown back till it rested neatly between the two foremost ventilation cowls, like the hinging funnel of a penny river steamboat. The enemy . . . surged down our port side, clearing everything before her; the boats came crashing down and even the davits were torn out of their sockets, and all the time she was firing her guns just over our heads. But none of her shells hit us, except two fired from her foc'sle guns just before the ramming, which passed through the canvas screens round the bridge. The Captain was standing on the bridge, but bent down, whether or not with an object I don't know, and the shell passed across the top of his head taking his cap with it, and left only a skin-deep though nasty wound. With the exception of the Captain, the coxswain and one seaman, who later on were all extracted with much difficulty from the wreckage, everybody on the bridge was killed by these two shells. Eventually the cruiser passed down the length of us, cleared us astern and disappeared, leaving us still afloat, but drifting and in a somewhat pitiful condition.[19]

Nassau may have had more than fifteen times the mass of the little destroyer, but she felt the collision. She lurched and heeled ten degrees to starboard as the two ships scraped past each other. *Spitfire* took with her some seven metres of *Nassau*'s shell plating and some of her anchor tackle as a souvenir. All of *Nassau*'s damage was above the waterline, so that her speed was reduced only slightly. *Spitfire* was out of the battle, but not yet out of this narrative.

While *Spitfire* was jousting with *Nassau*, the rest of the 4th Flotilla was trying to organise itself. Commander W L Allen, the half-flotilla leader in HMS *Broke* attempted to gather the rest of the ships of 4th Flotilla and get them heading south again. By approximately 0030, he had been largely successful and was leading a line of eight destroyers at seventeen knots. In order, the flotilla now comprised *Broke*, *Sparrowhawk*, *Contest*, *Achates*, *Ambuscade*, *Ardent*, *Fortune* and *Porpoise*. Only *Garland* and *Unity* were unaccounted for. (*Unity*, after wandering about for some time, ended up falling in with the 9th Flotilla and plays no more part in this story; *Garland* was trailing some distance behind *Porpoise* and does get heard from again.)

HMS *Broke* is seen in the configuration she retained until after the Battle of Jutland. She was armed with six 4in (102mm) guns – two side-by-side on the forecastle, one on each side of the bridge and another sided pair right aft. When she was repaired after that battle, the two forecastle mounts were replaced by a single 6in (152mm) gun.

Broke *and* Sparrowhawk *collide*

This stable state of affairs lasted no more than ten minutes, because at 0040, the action started again. It began when *Broke's* lookouts sighted a gray mass to the west:

Almost as soon as the ship was steadied on her course south, the hull of a large ship was sighted on the starboard bow on a more or less parallel course, but this time well before the beam and not more than half a mile away.[20] The Captain immediately gave the order to challenge, but almost as he spoke the stranger switched on a vertical string of coloured lights, some green and some red, an unknown signal in our service.

'Starboard 20; full speed ahead both; starboard foremost tube fire when your sights come on; all guns–Green 40–a battleship,' and various other orders were simultaneously shouted down the various voice pipes on the bridge, but the German had evidently been watching our movements and we were too late.

Within a few seconds of our seeing his recognition signal, he switched on a blaze of searchlights straight into our eyes, and so great was the dazzling effect that it made us feel quite helpless. Then after another interval of about a second, shells could be heard screaming over our heads, and I vaguely remember seeing splashes in the water short of us and also hearing the sound of our 4-inch guns returning the fire of this German battleship, which we afterwards had strong reason to believe was *Westfalen*. I then remember feeling the ship give a lurch to one side as a salvo hit us, and the sound of broken glass and debris flying around, after which the searchlights went out, and we were once more in the darkness.[21]

The shells that hit *Broke* could have come from any or all of three German ships. The two leading battleships, *Westfalen* and *Rheinland*, which was second in line now that *Nassau* had dropped out, and the light cruiser *Rostock*, which was between the lines and was trying to push through the gap between the leading battleships, all illuminated *Broke* and fired at her during the brief engagement. It took all of forty-five seconds to wreck *Broke*'s bridge, and leave her in an uncontrolled turn hard to port. The best estimate is that during these few seconds, *Broke* was hit by at least seven 4.1in (105mm) shells from *Rostock* and one or two 5.9in (150mm) shells from *Westfalen* or *Rheinland*.

Broke's navigator continues:

At this moment I became conscious of the fact that I could get no answer from the quartermaster at the wheel, so shouting to the Captain that I was going below, I jumped down on to the lower bridge. There, in the darkness, I found complete chaos. The quartermaster and telegraph man were both killed, and the wheel and telegraphs were shattered and apparently useless. I found our midshipman had followed me down to assist, and we were both just starting to strike matches to make certain that communication with the engine-room was gone, when I heard the Captain's voice down the pipe shouting: 'Full speed astern both.'

I looked up for an instant and saw a green bow light of some other ship just ahead of us, and then with a terrific crash the ship brought up all standing, and we were hurled against the bridge screens by the force of the collision.[22]

Sparrowhawk, the ship in line just behind *Broke*, had just started a turn away to port to fire her torpedoes when *Broke*, still in an uncontrolled turn hard to port, caught her forward on the starboard side and penetrated to *Sparrowhawk*'s centreline. The force of the collision was such that a number of *Sparrowhawk*'s crewmen, some reports say as many as three, were thrown on to *Broke*'s deck. *Broke*'s navigator again:

On picking myself up I at once saw the we had one of our own destroyers bumping alongside, and an ugly-looking rent in her side abreast the bridge showed where we had hit her. Steam was roaring out of our foremost boiler rooms, and it was extremely difficult to see or hear anything. Our ship appeared to be settling by the bow . . . I went down on the forecastle to try and find out the extent of our damage, and to see what had happened, and to my surprise found a strange officer standing there, who turned out to be the sub-lieutenant of the *Sparrowhawk* . . . He informed me he had been pitched on board by the force of the collision . . . I remember vaguely telling him that I thought our ship was not much use, and that he had better go and find out if *Sparrowhawk* could steam, as he said he did not think she had been hit by gunfire.[23]

This is one of those interesting cases when we have an account of the same story from the other side. *Sparrowhawk*'s sub-lieutenant relates:

We were only half a cable (100 yards) apart, and I saw that a collision was absolutely inevitable; there was no time to avoid it. So, in addition to the enemy's gunfire which was straddling with every salvo, we saw *Broke* coming straight for our bridge, absolutely end on, at 28 knots. I remember shouting a warning to everybody in hearing to hold on, and cried out to the foc'sle gun's crew to clear off the foc'sle. Then I leant over the bridge and watched *Broke*'s bow coming absolutely dead straight for us. I really don't know why, but it was a fascinating sight; I clean forgot all about the Germans and their gunfire. Just as she hit us I remember shouting out 'Now!' and then nothing more till I found myself lying on the foc'sle, not of our ship, but of the *Broke*, illuminated in a bright light, but in a sort of fog which must have been due to the clouds of steam escaping from burst pipes. I sort of felt myself to see if arms and legs were all there, and then tried to stand up. My right leg hurt abominably, and I couldn't get any sort of movement into my right arm, but otherwise I was all right, and eventually I got up, though only to fall again owing to the deck being extraordinarily slippery . . .

The whole of *Broke*'s foc'sle was an absolute shambles, but I crawled along until I came to a place where I could stand up. There was a perishing noise going on all the time, as the Germans were still endeavouring to sink the ship, and I could not see the *Sparrowhawk* owing to the clouds of escaping steam. As I was getting to my feet, I met a fellow, who said: 'Who the hell are you?' I told him that I was the sub-lieutenant of the *Sparrowhawk*, and added that *Sparrowhawk* had sunk, and that I was going to report to the Captain of the *Broke* to ask for a job. He told me that the Captain was on the remains of the bridge, and disappeared.

I eventually found a ladder up to the bridge and went up, picking my way over the wreckage of the lower bridge, and found the Captain, whom I knew slightly, and reported myself to him. . . . He told me to go back to my Captain and tell him he had given orders for the crew of *Broke* to be transferred to *Sparrowhawk*, because *Broke* was sinking, and I was also to ask for *Sparrowhawk*'s engines to be worked so as to endeavour to get the two ships apart, as they were now locked together and straining badly. I informed him that I was unable to see any sign of the *Sparrowhawk*, but he pointed her out to me, and I went to carry out my orders.

I had to jump across a gap of about six feet from one ship to the other, and owing to my leg I didn't succeed in clearing it, but luckily caught the lower rail of *Sparrowhawk* with my left arm, and hung there with my body between the two ships. I halloaed out and somebody heard me and hauled me on board.

SMS *Rheinland* takes target practice before the war. Of more interest than the main battery in the large turrets on the upper deck are the secondary battery of (5.9in) 150mm guns in casemates below this deck. These were the guns that did such damage to *Broke* and *Fortune*, among others. (NARA)

I found my Captain and gave him the message from the Captain of the *Broke*. His remarks were: 'But that's a pity, Sub., because I've sent across precisely the same message to him. This ship is also sinking fast!' The orders for the men to cross had actually been given, and about 20 of our ship's company went into *Broke* and about 15 men from *Broke* came across to us.

By this time the escaping steam had been got under control and the appalling noise stopped, and by means of megaphones the two Captains were able to communicate, the engines were worked, and the two ships drew apart with a sickening rending and crunching of steel plates. . . . *Broke* then disappeared stern first into the darkness, and we were left alone – not in a very healthy condition.[24]

While the sub-lieutenant was on *Broke*, conditions on *Sparrowhawk* were going from bad to worse. The momentum of the collision had swung *Sparrowhawk* to port, right into the path of the next ship astern, *Contest*. A second collision was unavoidable. *Contest* rammed *Sparrowhawk's* port quarter, neatly taking off ten metres of her stern before she too came to a stop alongside the other two ships. This trio of damaged destroyers might have presented a very tempting target to the gunners on the leading German battleships, but they were having troubles of their own, and switched off their searchlights and ceased firing. *Rostock* had been hit by several shells and one of the torpedoes fired by remaining ships of the 4th Flotilla. She barely avoided a collision with *Rheinland*, but managed to get through the German line before drifting to a stop off to the west. Unhappy with the intensity of action enveloping the head of his line, Scheer ordered a simultaneous turn to port. This course was maintained for almost ten minutes before he again ordered the fleet back on the necessary southeasterly heading.

Westfalen *sinks* Fortune *and* Ardent

Meanwhile, Commander Reginald Hutchinson on *Achates* took command of what was left of 4th Flotilla, which now comprised six or seven ships (*Garland* had again caught up with the line; some accounts mention that *Contest* rejoined the line as well aft of *Garland*) and resumed a course to the south. Yet again, the German battle line and 4th Flotilla were converging. At around 0100, *Westfalen*, still leading the German line, was executing yet another turn away to south, this time to let two friendly light cruisers pass ahead safely, when she again sighted shapes to the east. She turned on her searchlights and opened fire. The target this time was the third ship in line behind *Achates*, HMS *Fortune*. *Westfalen's* fire was devastatingly accurate. The first salvo destroyed *Fortune's* bridge and brought down her foremast. In just twenty-eight seconds, and having fired only fifteen rounds from her secondary battery, *Fortune* was a blazing wreck and *Westfalen* switched targets to the two leading destroyers, *Achates* and *Ambuscade*. *Porpoise*, the ship next aft of *Fortune*, was engaged by other German battleships.

Most of the remnants of 4th Flotilla fired off their remaining torpedoes, took a few shots at the German line and swung east and finally north, eventually joining up with one of the flotillas off to the east. *Porpoise* took one serious hit, a shell that tore through her main steam trunk and disabled her steering gear, but the rest escaped undamaged. One of them put a shell into *Oldenburg*'s forward searchlight platform, causing damage and casualties. The Germans, seeing torpedoes in the water, again briefly turned away before resuming a southeast course. Forgotten between the lines, *Fortune* appears to have slipped beneath the waves as the two sides separated, the first of 4th Flotilla's destroyers to sink.

The next wasn't far behind. Having become separated from the rest of the flotilla during the previous engagement, HMS *Ardent*, turned south when the rest turned north. In yet another spectacularly brief encounter around 0115, *Ardent* was sighted from *Westfalen* at a range of 900 metres, illuminated and engaged. *Westfalen* fired off approximately forty rounds from her 5.9in (150mm) and 3.5in (88mm) guns and then switched off her searchlights and again turned away, fearing *Ardent*'s torpedoes. They need not have worried. *Ardent* was reduced to wreckage in that brief fusillade, taking only a few minutes to sink in the darkness. Only her captain and one other crewman survived to be picked up by HMS *Marksman* at dawn.

Incredibly, this was not the end of 4th Flotilla's brushes with the enemy that night. The last ships in the German line, the light cruiser *Regensburg* with several destroyers, sighted a burning wreck off to the east. Three destroyers were sent to investigate. One got diverted to help another German cruiser, but the other two, *S.53* and *G.88*, found *Tipperary* on fire along her entire length and apparently abandoned. A raft with nine of *Tipperary*'s crew was found by *S.53* and the men taken aboard. Satisfied there was nothing more to be done, the two ships turned back towards *Regensburg* and almost immediately encountered the badly damaged cruiser *Elbing*, which requested assistance. As they turned to *Elbing*'s aid, however, they sighted another darkened ship to the north and went to investigate. Switching on their searchlights, they discovered yet another battered British destroyer.

From *Broke*'s point of view, finding herself facing a pair of German destroyers was far from good news.

Day was now slowly breaking, and our hopes of getting away safely were fast rising, but at 1.15 they sank almost to zero when we sighted two German destroyers on our starboard quarter, steaming towards us at full speed.[25]

We had only two serviceable guns left, and both of these were aft, so we turned our stern towards the enemy at once and increased our speed to our utmost safe limit – about 10 knots. As they closed, I remember a feeling of extreme disgust and disappointment at being thus caught after having been so lucky in making our escape from the other ships.

The Germans, however, appeared to be feeling even more scared than we were, which was saying a good deal. On approaching to within 500 or 600 yards they turned up together abreast of us, and the leader opened fire with his bow gun. We replied with our starboard after gun, which was the only one remaining that would bear, and to our astonishment and joy both ships put over their helms and disappeared into the early morning mist, leaving us alone, still above water. They had scored two hits amidships, but these fortunately did little or no damage.[26]

Despite appearances, the German destroyers turned away not out of fear but because they had received another signal from *Elbing* of greater urgency and turned to speed to the disabled cruiser's aid.

The 4th Flotilla's encounters with the enemy were now over, but the ordeal was not. Of the two leaders and ten 'K'-class destroyers that had made up 4th Flotilla the day before, two, *Fortune* and *Ardent*, had been sunk and six more had been damaged to greater or lesser extent. That left only four in relatively undamaged state. These were *Unity*, which had detached early in the night, and the rump of the flotilla, which now comprised *Achates*, *Ambuscade* and *Garland*, situated somewhere north and east of the two fleets.

The Germans continued in their plan to cross behind the Grand Fleet and reach the safety of Horns Reef. Around 0145, the German van encountered a mixed squadron of fourteen destroyers from four different flotillas that had formed from stragglers during the night's confusion. (*Unity* was part of this squadron.) The last ship in line, HMS *Turbulent*, was detected by *Westfalen* after the rest of the squadron had safely passed in front of the German battleships. *Turbulent* was demolished by gunfire from the leading battleships, while the rest of the squadron continued, apparently oblivious to her fate. At 0310, yet another British flotilla encountered the German line, this time not the van but the aft end, where the six obsolete pre-dreadnoughts had been positioned to keep them out of danger. Delivering a classic torpedo attack, they managed to put one or two torpedoes into *Pommern*, which exploded catastrophically and sank in minutes. Even that was not the last of the encounters, but *Pommern* was the last ship to be sunk by enemy action that night. By 0400, as dawn was fully breaking, the German fleet was clear, now to the east of the Grand Fleet and only twenty-five nautical miles from Horns Reef. They had made good their escape. Jellicoe, on encountering an empty sea around him at dawn, had no choice but to order the Grand Fleet back to port.

Astonishingly, during the nearly two hours and five separate engagements between 4th Flotilla and the German fleet, not to mention the several other dramatic encounters, not one message was sent to Jellicoe informing him of the events transpiring behind his fleet. Nevertheless, it is impossible to conceive that the bulk of the British fleet did not notice the various eruptions of searchlights, gunfire and explosions going on not many miles behind them. These were always explained away as chance encounters between small units or cases of 'friendly' fire due to mistaken identity in the dark. It appears that Jellicoe was genuinely surprised when he did not find the German fleet still to the west at dawn. In later years he was sharply criticised for allowing Scheer to escape, but it is hard to imagine what he could have done, even had he been well informed of events that night. He might have altered the Grand Fleet's course more to the east, but the last thing he wanted was a night encounter between his battleships and the enemy's, and a change of course towards the east would have brought him perilously close to the minefields he so correctly feared.

The survivors straggle home

This leaves the fate of the six damaged 4th Flotilla destroyers to be resolved. The least damaged, *Contest* and *Porpoise*, returned to port without incident. The most damaged, *Tipperary* and *Sparrowhawk*, both sank in the early hours of 1 June. *Tipperary* began to settle noticeably around 0200 and the first lieutenant, now the senior officer, ordered everyone into a pair of Carley floats that had survived the devastation. Shortly thereafter the battered *Tipperary* slipped beneath the waves. At about 0610, the crew of *Sparrowhawk* sighted what was at first taken to be a submarine but turned out to be the larger of the two Carley rafts from *Tipperary*. Some number of men – accounts differ as to whether it was twenty-three or twenty-six – were pulled alive on board *Sparrowhawk,* but some of them, perhaps as many as five, died from wounds and exposure soon after being pulled from the water.

Sparrowhawk was a poor haven for *Tipperary*'s survivors. Soon after *Tipperary*'s survivors were brought on board, her bow broke off just in front of the bridge, leaving just *Sparrowhawk*'s centre section afloat. At about 0715, the destroyer

HMS *Spitfire*, now much worse for the wear, is seen as she pulled into Rosyth on 2 June. Her bow shows the effects of scraping *Nassau's* side. Her bridge is nearly flattened, her foremast snapped off and her forward funnel toppled, yet she was repaired and served out the rest of war with distinction. Her markings are of interest – the '41' on the side of the hull is part of her 'pendant number' (or 'pennant number'), which was officially 'H41', but the 'H' is missing. The letter 'K' painted on her after funnel is more curious. It may be a class designator.

leader HMS *Marksman* found the wreck and took off all the survivors. She attempted to tow *Sparrowhawk*, stern first, but the seas were rising and the tow parted. Rather than leave the wreck adrift, *Marksman* sank what was left of *Sparrowhawk* and returned to Scapa Flow. Besides the approximately twenty survivors of *Tipperary* taken off *Sparrowhawk* and the nine rescued from the smaller raft by *S.53*, there was one more survivor from *Tipperary*. The ship's surgeon was pulled from the water by *Elbing's* cutter after that cruiser sank. After drifting for five hours, the cutter was found by a Dutch trawler and the men in the cutter, all German except for *Tipperary's* surgeon, were interned for the duration of the war.

That left only *Spitfire* and *Broke* unaccounted for. The former, her bow torn open and still carrying a length of *Nassau's* shell plating, survived a day and night of increasingly rough weather on 1 June, while steaming without charts or navigation aids generally westward. Fortunately the storm abated after midnight on 2 June and she made landfall near the Tyne soon after dawn and docked at Rosyth about noon. *Broke* took longer to get home. Moving more slowly westward, she was battered more severely by the storm. Her foremast was

Pendant numbers were changed periodically in order to confuse the enemy.
When HMS *Spitfire* returned from repairs, she was assigned a new designator: 'H1A'.
The paint scheme is definitely the lighter mid-grey.

carried away soon after midnight on 2 June and, shortly after that, it became obvious she could no longer fight the storm and she turned southeast, away from England, to protect her battered bow. Only late on the 2nd did the storm abate to the extent that *Broke* could turn westward again. By now she was perilously close to the German coastal minefields near Helgoland. As the seas calmed, she crept westward and then northwesterly all that night and the next day. She tied up at Rosyth at 2000 on 3 June, the last ship of the Grand Fleet to return from the Battle of Jutland.

With a casualty rate of 67 per cent, the record of the 4th Flotilla at Jutland is almost unmatched in naval history. Rarely has a unit been called upon to make sacrifices of this order with so little to show for it. There was little point in trying to draw direct lessons from this experience, as Jutland was in reality the last battle of an older era, rather than an early battle of the new one. Although Jutland was fought in the twentieth century, it had the tactics and strategy of a battle fought 100 years earlier. It really was far more of the era of Nelson than of Nimitz. Nevertheless, it must have been abundantly clear that much still needed to be learned about how to employ destroyers, particularly at night and in proximity to major enemy units. These would be lessons that needed to be periodically relearned.

One obvious lesson was that the two larger destroyer leaders in 4th Flotilla proved their worth in battle, being able to carry more and bigger weapons and absorb more punishment. *Broke* was able to return to base, having taken a beating that would have overwhelmed any of the smaller standard destroyers of the time. Future destroyers would grow in size until they were often half again as big as *Broke* or even bigger. Despite the damage, *Broke* was taken in hand for repairs after Jutland and returned to the war, though not as part of the Grand Fleet. Her story continues in the next chapter.

Notes

1 This strategy, known as the 'fleet in being', ties down the enemy's larger fleet, while allowing the smaller fleet to make selective nuisance attacks. The hope is that this strategy will force the enemy to divide his forces in a way that enables the weaker force to gain local superiority over isolated enemy detachments and thus change the balance of power.

2 The North Sea literally teemed with mines as both sides laid extensive mine barrages across choke points, such as the Dover Straits and Skagerrak and the wider gap between Norway and Scotland, and long minefields on the southern and western sides of the sea to protect coastal traffic.

3 As was frequently the case in naval encounters, the two sides were keeping time to different time zones. The British were using GMT (Greenwich Mean Time) while the Germans were using CET (Central European Time), which was one hour ahead. In this chapter all times are GMT.

4 South-by-east is one point east of due south. A point equals eleven degrees.

5 The five British flotillas were, from west to east, the 11th, 4th, 13th, 9th and 12th.

6 Horns Reef is a well-known area of shallow water off Blåvands Huk, the westernmost point on the Danish coast. A deep channel passes just west of the reef and south along the coast all the way to the Elbe estuary at Cuxhaven.

7 The other entrances were west of Helgoland leading to Wilhelmshaven and at the island of Borkum leading to Emden or the safe channel between the East Frisian Islands and the German coast.

8 *Hist,* p. 378. The word Scheer used for the last part of this order was *durchhalten,* which in military usage implies holding out against impossible odds. 'SSE-¼E' is approximately 155 degrees, one quarter-point east of south-southeast.

9 The following is not intended as a complete description of the night action on 31 May–1 June 1916, nor even a complete account of the action involving Royal Navy destroyers that night. It concentrates on the fate of 4th Flotilla.

10 In 1913, the Royal Navy decided to help distinguish destroyer classes by designating each class with a letter and then naming all ships in the class with names starting with the chosen letter. The intent had been to start with this class and names were chosen for the ships all starting with 'K', but this tidy plan was overtaken by events. By the time the idea was approved and 'K' names chosen, every one of the twenty ships in the class had already been launched, meaning they had already been given names, not one of which started with 'K'. The long-standing sailors' superstition against renaming a ship once it had been christened prevented the Royal Navy from imposing the uniform naming scheme on these ships, but did not keep them from being called the 'K'-class.

11 Royal Navy destroyer flotillas are always designated with Arabic numbers – eg, 4th Flotilla – while German flotillas are often, but not always, given Roman numeral designations – eg, VII

Flotilla. To help distinguish the units of the two sides in these chapters, I will stick to this convention.

12 The Germans gave their destroyers names composed of a manufacturer signifier and a one-up number. When they started the new series of somewhat smaller destroyers in 1911, they reset the counter. Thus the first of the new series was *V.1*. Six different manufacturers built destroyers for the German navy, but almost all of them were by just four – Blohm und Voss (B), Germaniawerft (G), F Schichau (S) and AG Vulkan (V). The Germans rarely called these ships destroyers, persisting in calling them *T-Boote*, even though they reached the size and capabilities of contemporary destroyers. For the sake of consistency, I will refer to them as destroyers throughout.

13 *V.189* had a sister in VII Flotilla, but *V.186* had developed engine trouble and had turned back early the previous morning.

14 Cf., *Rules*. This book is essentially an examination of why so many Grand Fleet officers lacked initiative, believing that following orders to the letter was all that was required of an officer. Wintour was not the only officer this night to exhibit an astonishing lack of curiosity and feel no obligation to report events to Jellicoe.

15 11th Flotilla should have been the westernmost flotilla, but it had encountered some German light cruisers soon after dark and had turned away to the east. It never attempted to regain its assigned position, leaving 4th Flotilla exposed.

16 *Jut*, p. 201. The identity of the author of this narrative is not given in this source, but he appears to have been an officer on *Spitfire*, which incredibly survived these encounters. The time that he gives for this event is off by an hour and a quarter. The enemy ships identified as cruisers were in fact the battleships *Westfalen*, *Nassau* and *Rheinland* leading the German battle line, all of which had just two funnels. Given all that befell *Spitfire* that night, these minor memory lapses can be forgiven.

17 Ibid, pp. 213–4. 'W/T' stood for 'Wireless Telegraphy', an early name for radio. 'Captain (D)' was the flotilla commander, Captain Wintour.

18 Ibid, pp. 202–3. This is the same narrator as in the first excerpt. He persists in identifying German battleships as cruisers.

19 Ibid, p. 203.

20 Ibid, p. 197. The speaker is *Broke*'s Navigating Officer. The German line was moving eastward, so that the lead German ships were beginning to pass ahead of the flotilla.

21 A note in the original text states at this point that a later examination of engine room telegraph and helm showed that the ratings did not have time to comply with the captain's orders before the salvo landed.

22 Ibid, p. 198.

23 Ibid.

24 Ibid, pp. 208–9.

25 The sun did not rise until 0313 on 1 June 1916, but the first lightening of the eastern horizon could be noticed as much as two hours earlier. At that latitude at that time of year, it is fully dark only for about three hours.

26 Ibid, pp. 199–200.

Chapter 4

Broke *Again – Dover Strait (21 April 1917)*

AFTER THE BATTLE OF JUTLAND, the battered destroyer leader HMS *Broke* was taken in hand for repair and refit. She emerged from the dockyard with an enlarged bridge and a state-of-the-art torpedo controller. She also emerged to a changing strategic situation. Starting in October 1916, the on-again-off-again German U-boat offensive against Allied merchant shipping was on again for the third time, though still with significant restrictions on where and how the U-boats could attack. Finally admitting they would never be able to achieve a sufficiently decisive naval victory by fleet action, the Germans with some reluctance again turned to their U-boats to try to inflict the same kind of privation on the British that the Royal Navy's blockade was causing to Germany.[1]

The Dover Patrol

This, in turn, increased the importance of the Dover Patrol. Denying U-boats passage through the Dover Strait was critical to countering any U-boat offensive. (The best hunting ground for U-boats was in the waters south and west of Britain where merchant shipping converged to enter or exit Britain's main seaports. Denying U-boats the use of the Dover Strait added weeks to their passage to and from these prime hunting grounds, substantially reducing their effectiveness.) However, the state of anti-submarine warfare was still crude in late 1916. Defenders had sinker charges, crude hydrophones and anti-submarine nets. Nets could be highly effective in denying access through narrow waters, such as the entrance to a harbour, but they had never been tried across a stretch of open water as wide as the Dover Strait. Yet this is exactly what the British began building in 1916. The initial barrier, completed in October 1916, was a single line of indicator nets stretching from Goodwin Sands to the Ruytingen Bank near Gravelines. Each section of the net ran between a pair of buoys 457 metres apart and had a depth of between 9.15 and 25.6 metres. Each also had two contact mines attached, which theoretically would be set off when a submarine became ensnared.

This initial net barrage was continuously enhanced as the war progressed, making the nets deeper, adding additional rows of netting and more minefields, yet it proved unable to prevent the passage of U-boats through the Strait. From the beginning, it was necessary to supplement the netting with an increasing number of miscellaneous surface units fitted with the best available anti-submarine sensors and weapons. Originally an odd collection of trawlers, drifters and commandeered yachts, the Dover Patrol was more effective and more feared by the U-boatmen than the net barrage. Not surprisingly, the Germans were unwilling to allow this rag-tag fleet to bottle up their U-boats. In October 1916, the Germans moved two flotillas of destroyers (III and IX Flotillas) down to the submarine base at Zeebrugge, barely fifty miles up the Belgian coast from Calais. The British got wind of this movement and strengthened the Dover Patrol with six destroyers at Dover and eight more at Dunkirk. The first attack on the patrol was on the night of 26–27 October. Despite all the warnings, a German raid of eleven destroyers in two groups surprised the patrol. An old destroyer and seven drifters were sunk before the alarm was raised and the destroyers at Dover and Dunkirk were called out. HMS *Nubian* had her bow blown off by a torpedo in the resulting engagement and had to be beached to prevent her sinking.[2] All the German destroyers returned to Zeebrugge safely. Round one – the first of many to follow – went to the Germans.

Unrestricted submarine warfare

A strong faction in the German navy, led by the Chief of the Naval Staff, Admiral von Holtzendorff, had been pressing for the restrictions on U-boat attacks to be lifted. As successful as the third restricted campaign was, von Holtzendorff calculated that the monthly average of 300,000 tons of shipping sunk between October 1916 and January 1917 would need to double in order to have a decisive effect on the British supply of food and raw materials. He claimed that only unrestricted U-boat warfare could produce results at that level. The political leadership, in the person of the Kaiser, wanted to give diplomacy one more chance to work. When a peace initiative by the Germans was firmly rejected by the Allies at the end of December, the Kaiser finally agreed to a campaign of unrestricted U-boat warfare beginning 1 February 1917.

This decision led to an increase in activity by the German flotillas based at Zeebrugge. The next sortie by German destroyers came on the night of 25

February. The barrage was being patrolled that night by five 'L'-class destroyers. When the German destroyers sighted and briefly engaged HMS *Laverock*, they apparently decided they had had enough and slipped away in the darkness and returned to Zeebrugge. Neither side suffered damage or casualties in that engagement. The next German sortie came on 17 March and resulted in a more serious fight. The British screen on this occasion was four destroyers, three 'L's and one older 'K', each patrolling a two-mile sector in a line running southeast from the Foreland. A few miles up the coast, off Deal, a reserve force was at sea comprising the light cruiser *Canterbury*, the destroyer leader *Faulknor* (a sister of *Broke* and *Tipperary*) and four more destroyers. Finally, *Broke* herself and five further destroyers were waiting in Dover, steam up, in case needed. At 2350, *Paragon* (the 'K'-class ship), in the centre of the screen on the northwest leg of her patrol, sighted and challenged a line of three or four destroyers approaching from the northeast. For her pains, she received a sudden fusillade of gunfire and at least one torpedo, causing her to break in two and rapidly sink. The destroyers on either side of *Paragon* in the patrol line, *Laforey* and *Llewellyn*, under the impression that *Paragon* had hit a drifting mine – always a danger on the Barrage Patrol – were racing to the site of the sinking when *Llewellyn* was also hit by a

Lieutenant Edward Ratcliffe Garth Russell Evans was second-in-command of Robert Falcon Scott's second, ill-fated Antarctic expedition, 1911–12. He was probably the last man to see Scott and the polar party alive. In the late Victorian Royal Navy, glamorous, headline-grabbing adventures were virtually the only way for a young officer to find rapid advancement and relief from the tedium of peacetime duty.

79

torpedo, though she did not sink. The Dover squadron, being closer to the scene than the group off Deal, came racing out, but sighted nothing. The Germans apparently had turned north, because they were next seen at 0235 off Broadstairs, where they sank a single merchant freighter, after which they then returned to port.

It was exactly to counter these kinds of moves that, after completing repairs, *Broke*, along with her two remaining sisters *Faulknor* and *Botha,* had been sent south to beef up the Dover Patrol. The experience with *Swift*, which had been transferred to the south before Jutland, had shown the utility of destroyer leaders in the Barrage Patrol. The larger size of the leaders gave them the ability to better absorb punishment and to carry heavier armament than the standard destroyers of the time. When *Broke* was put back in commission, she was under a new commanding officer, Commander E R G R (Edward Ratcliffe Garth Russell) Evans, one of the more famous characters in the modern history of the Royal Navy. Evans was an experienced destroyer commander before he took over *Broke*, but the origins of his fame date to even before the war.

Commander E R G R Evans in the Antarctic

'Teddy' Evans entered the navy after two years on a merchant marine training ship, being commissioned a sub-lieutenant in 1900. In that same year, Robert Falcon Scott was appointed to lead the Royal Antarctic Expedition. The fates of the two men would be inextricably linked until Scott's death in 1912. At the beginning of the twentieth century, in the midst of the Pax Britannica, there was little chance for excitement or rapid advancement for young officers, and the lure of far-away places was strong. Despite lacking any experience in the Arctic, much less the Antarctic, Scott was appointed to lead the expedition, which set off for the south in the specially built whaler/icebreaker *Discovery* at the end of July 1901. Knowing that the expedition would need re-supplying, a second ship was acquired and stocked with food, coal and mail. *Morning* arrived in New Zealand in December 1902 and immediately set out for Antarctica. Her second officer was a very young Sub-Lieutenant Evans. The plan was for *Morning* and *Discovery* to leave together at the end of the southern summer, but the latter was too deeply embedded in ice to break free and *Morning* sailed alone for New Zealand on 1 March 1903, leaving Scott's party to spend another winter at McMurdo. Evans stayed in *Morning* and returned to the Antarctic the next spring. This time *Discovery* was freed from the ice and left for New Zealand on 19 February 1904.

Evans had been bitten by the Antarctic 'bug'. Back in England, he began campaigning to lead a new expedition south and started raising money. He was only one of many. In England, Scott was considered the natural choice to lead a second expedition, but planning and fund-raising proceeded slowly. Meanwhile, Ernest Shackleton, who had been third lieutenant on Scott's first expedition, was also planning a polar expedition, and others in America, Germany, France and Japan announced plans to head for the South Pole.[3] Shackleton succeeded in getting his expedition to Antarctica in 1908 and managed to get within 150 kilometres of the pole before being forced to turn back. When news reached England the next spring that the pole was still 'unconquered', Scott's planning took on renewed energy. When Evans heard of this, he offered himself and all the money he had raised to Scott, on condition that he be appointed second-in-command of the new expedition. Scott did not know Evans well and he would not have been his first choice for the position, but the money was too much to pass up, so Evans was given the appointment. Despite the opinion of many that he had bought his position, Evans proved to be capable and popular. He took the expedition's ship *Terra Nova* south starting in June 1910; Scott stayed behind to raise more money. He rejoined the ship at Cape Town. Only after arriving in Australia did they learn that the Norwegian Roald Amundsen was also on his way south.[4]

The expedition reached Antarctica on 4 January 1911, equipped with motor sledges, nineteen ponies and thirty-nine dogs. (Amundsen, with much more Arctic experience, brought ninety-seven sled dogs, bringing neither ponies nor motor sledges.) The ponies and motor sledges both proved ill suited for the conditions and gradually broke down. Exactly a year later, on 4 January 1912, Evans and Scott parted company at the top of the Beardmore Glacier, 240 kilometres from the South Pole. Two four-man sledge teams had reached the top of the glacier and were now on the Polar Plateau. The ponies and dogs they had started with had all died by this point, and the remaining distance to the Pole and all the way back would be man-hauled. Scott had to choose four men to finish the push to the Pole. He had already decided that his sledge, pulled by Wilson, Oates, Edgar Evans and himself, would continue, while 'Teddy' Evans and his three men would return to McMurdo.[5]

Before announcing this decision to the men, however, he realised that this division would leave him with no qualified navigator. (The only experienced navigator among the final eight was Bowers on Evans's sledge.) Rather than 'disappointing' any of the three men on his sledge — even though Oates was known to be suffering from fatigue more than any of the other men — he announced that Bowers would join his sledge for the run to the Pole but that he would not be replaced on Evans' sledge. While the ultimate failure of Scott's expedition and the deaths of the five-man Polar party can be blamed on many bad decisions, some made months or even years earlier, this decision by Scott was the proximate cause. It very nearly cost Evans, Crean and Lashly their lives as well. Being one man short, the progress of Evans' sledge was terribly slow. Evans very nearly succumbed to scurvy before reaching McMurdo in late February.[6] The last of Scott's crew died approximately 160 kilometres from base on or around 29 March. Amundsen had reached the Pole on 15 December with seventeen dogs, three sleds and five men.

Evans was in need of rest and recuperation, and he was evacuated when *Terra Nova* departed at the end of February. The rest of the expedition stayed at McMurdo for a second winter. Evans returned to Antarctica in January 1913 to take command of the expedition, but there was little to do but pack up the camp and bring back word of Scott's death. For Evans, resuming a quiet naval career in the immediate future was out of the question. He was feted and honoured, being given, among other awards, the rank of Companion of the Bath (CB). Promoted now to Lieutenant Commander, he was much in demand on what today would be called the 'lecture circuit', but the outbreak of war brought this easy life to an abrupt halt. Unlike others who had gained fame before the war, Evans proved himself to be an able warrior. From the beginning of the war, he was assigned to the Dover Patrol in command of destroyers.

Evans on the Dover Patrol

His first command was HMS *Mohawk*, one of the 'Tribal'-class destroyers initially assigned to the 6th Flotilla in the Channel. The 'Tribal's were the first of the bigger and faster destroyers demanded by Jackie Fisher when he became First Sea Lord in 1904. Most were completed in 1908–9, but by 1914 they were considered too small and short-ranged for fleet duty, so they were assigned to the Dover Patrol in February 1914. It was as *Mohawk*'s commander that Evans began the tradition of nailing a stuffed penguin to the foremast of his ship for good luck. His luck held in 1915, when *Mohawk* encountered an early German minefield. Though seriously damaged, Evans was able to bring her into port for repairs. He then took over another 'Tribal', HMS *Viking,* and was in command when a 6in (152mm) gun was experimentally fitted forward, replacing a 12 pdr. The experiment was not a success, the gun proving unwieldy on such a small hull, and the 6in (152mm) gun and *Viking*'s remaining 12 pdrs were replaced by a pair of 4in (102mm) guns. Evans, now a Commander, left *Viking* to take over *Broke* at the end of 1916.

As a Lieutenant Commander, Evans took over the 'Tribal'-class destroyer HMS *Mohawk* in February 1914. They were the first class of destroyers designed under Jackie Fisher's reign as First Sea Lord, when he conceived of a future Royal Navy composed solely of fast battleships (ie, battlecruisers) and large destroyers. When new in 1907, *Mohawk* was among the biggest and fastest destroyers yet built, but by the time she struck a mine in 1915 (and 'Teddy' Evans left her to take over *Viking*), she was among the oldest still in service. She was the first ship known to have sported Evans' personal emblem, a stuffed penguin nailed to her mast.

By the time of the next German sortie, the Barrage Patrol had been strengthened. It now had two separate components. A western patrol, generally comprising two destroyer leaders, patrolled from the South Goodwin Light Vessel towards the centre of the Strait. The eastern patrol was made up of a division of five or six destroyers keeping a line between the centre of the straights and the shallows off the French coast. Reserve forces, as before, were located at Deal and Dover. On the night of 20–21 April 1917, the western patrol comprised *Swift* and *Broke*. The former, under Commander A M Peck, was in tactical command and led the two ships in line ahead.

On that night, the Germans came out in strength. All twelve ships of the II Flotilla – some of the newest destroyers in the High Seas Fleet – came out of Zeebrugge with the mission to harass Channel traffic and disrupt the Barrage Patrol. Six went south along the coast to Calais, shelled the port facilities and returned to Zeebrugge without incident. The other six went west, briefly bombarded Dover, causing very little damage, and then turned north along the British coast until they reached a point clear of the Barrage and from there started back towards Zeebrugge on a course of east-southeast. Commander Peck, in *Swift*, had every reason to believe the enemy was active that night:

My normal speed was twelve knots; *Broke* was in close order astern and the night being very dark I was burning shaded stern lights. At 11.17 [all times are GMT] we sighted gun flashes bearing about SE, and I went on full speed and steered for them. I reported the same by W/T. The flashes appeared to be a long way off, but I thought they might come from *Nugent*'s Division, which was in that direction.[7] At 11.30, intercepted signal from *Nugent* reporting gun flashed SSE. Finding *Nugent* was not engaged I altered course and proceeded for the South Goodwin to resume my patrol and almost immediately observed gun flashes far away to the westward in the direction of Dover. . . . On arrival near No 3A Light Buoy I eased to fifteen knots and received a signal from the Vice-Admiral to know if I had seen enemy's destroyers, to which I replied 'No.'[8]

All this action over to the southeast and west seems not to have raised much concern on Peck's part. In fact, his main worry was that he might inadvertently run into friendly forces in the dark. He had received word that Captain (D) was out with the Dover squadron and patrolling the section between South Goodwin Sands and the shore. So, as *Swift* and *Broke* were approaching the light ship at the western end of their patrol line, while still about three miles short of the light, Peck had decided to turn away to the east to avoid trouble. Instead, he found it.

At 0.45, when steaming to the westward and about to give orders to turn, a destroyer was reported to me on the port bow and almost immediately a gun was fired from that direction. I immediately put the telegraphs full speed, and about ten seconds later, observing that the boats were steaming on an opposite course, roughly ESE, I put my helm hard-a-starboard with the intention of ramming, and gave orders to commence firing.[9] The flames from the enemy's funnels then began to appear as if they were putting on speed and there appeared to be a division of five or six boats. I since think five.[10]

Evans in *Broke* saw the same thing:

At about 12.45, GMT, I was in station about one and a half cables astern of *Swift* when five enemy destroyers were seen crossing ahead on nearly parallel course. . . . Immediately went to full speed and fire was opened on them immediately in accordance with pre-arranged plan on board *Broke*. In accordance with pre-arranged plan *Broke* held her fire until the second hostile destroyer was nearly abeam, when a torpedo was fired at the order of Lieutenant Despard, in charge of the torpedo control. I had increased to full speed, following the motion of *Swift* and directly the torpedo was reported as fired I put my helm hard-a-starboard in order to ram the second destroyer, should my torpedo miss.[11]

This is the last totally clear 'snapshot' of the positions of the participants that night, as from this point on events happened so fast and the night was so dark, that Peck's and Evan's accounts begin to diverge. The two British destroyer leaders, in line ahead, sighted a line of German destroyers passing ahead on an oblique crossing course. Led by *Swift*, the two destroyer leaders turned to port with the intention of ramming what they took to be the first and second German ships. The Germans kept to a steady course and fired away at the approaching enemy. Peck continues with *Swift*'s story, however he very quickly admits to losing track of everything that was going on:

> The enemy kept up control firing and although I did not know it at the time, we were hit on the port waterline on the stokers' mess deck very early in the proceedings. I suppose we had swung through about ten points before I righted the helm and I find it very difficult to give any connected idea of what happened subsequently, owing to the absolutely blinding effect of the 6in [152mm] gun on the fo'c'sle.[12] My impression is that we narrowly missed ramming one of the enemy boats, probably second or third in line. Just after the action began I was engaging a boat at close range – about 400 yards or less – on my port beam, at which I fired a torpedo, subsequently reported to me as a hit by the Torpedo Gunner, and 6in [152mm] lyddite shell hit the same boat at the same time in her fore end.[13] This hit was reported to me at the moment by the Navigating Officer, the flash of the 6in [152mm] gun having blinded me entirely.[14]

Having broken through the line of German destroyers without ramming any of them, probably passing between the third and fourth ships in the line. Peck believed, but did not personally see, that *Swift*'s torpedo hit the destroyer immediately to port, just before she passed through the line. Now on the other side, *Swift* turned to pursue the leading German destroyers, distinguishable only by the flames from their funnels.

> After about ten minutes action it was reported to me that the main wireless was out of action and shortly afterwards that there was four feet of water in the stokers' mess deck. We continued the chase for about three or four minutes after this firing with the 6in [152mm] gun at flaming funnels, the course then being approximately east. As I had at that time been steaming at full speed for some twelve or fourteen minutes towards the Barrage, I decided to abandon chase in order not to cross it, which I had been given to understand should

not be done, and I was also influenced by not knowing the extent of damage to the stokers' mess deck.[15]

Swift thus pulled away from *Broke*, which was having a more interesting time of it. Evans had just fired a torpedo off to port, probably at the same ship at which *Swift* had also aimed a torpedo, and was trying to decide which enemy ship to ram.

> A hit being reported by the First Lieutenant and the second explosion satisfying me that he was correct, I put my helm hard–a–port to sheer away and then hard–a–starboard and made for No 3 in line.[16] I hit her almost abreast of the after funnel going at full speed and the impact carri[ed] her stern ahead, whilst her fast steaming pulled my bow to port. The next two hostile destroyers were out of station, being abreast of one another, and as we cleared the destroyer that was on our ram, this not being for a considerable interval, I ported my helm to endeavour to ram No 4 again, but she put her helm to starboard and with a small turning circle turned inside me and came down starboard side to starboard side.[17] No 5 passed apparently up my port side and opened a heavy fire, I think with shrapnel, on the bridge and upper works, and with common shell further aft.[18]

At this point, Evans described a torpedo being fired without orders at the destroyer on his starboard side and a hit being obtained. It is unlikely that this hit in fact happened, as only two German destroyers were seriously damaged at this point – the one torpedoed early in the action and the one rammed by *Broke* – and it is highly unlikely that a ship of the size of these destroyers could have absorbed a torpedo hit and continued steaming away at full speed.

He also describes sighting *Swift* and following her for a time. This was also unlikely as the following shows:

> I saw two destroyers after this, but it was not very easy to see as the starboard side of the bridge was on fire with apparently our own cordite that had been exploded, and had been thrown up on to the bridge. Following *Swift* I received a report from the Engineer that he could only steam slow and of injuries in No 3 Boiler room.[19] The ship appeared to have stopped almost. I put my helm over and stood towards flames which came from one of the destroyers we had attacked before. On closing I found two enemy destroyers; the nearest was on fire under the fo'c'sle and flames could be seen through a gaping hole. She was very much down by the stern. . . . More shouting was heard from this ship and as she was obviously sinking and I could not longer manoeuvre my vessel I attempted to close her and take prisoners. However, her foremost gun fired a round, which passed over our bridge and we then

The Germans resisted the tendency to build ever-larger destroyers. The *G.37* class, of which *G.42* was a member, were half the size of *Broke* or *Swift* and carried fewer and smaller guns. A ship of that class is seen cutting through a line of dreadnoughts during manoeuvres.

replied with either three or four rounds, which silenced her fire and the remaining torpedo which hit her aft. After we had silenced her she blazed still more furiously, and I feared that the foremost magazine would blow up before she sank. By this time, my stem was nearly touching her, and the Engineer sent up to say that he could not move the engines more.[20]

Peck described *Swift*'s actions while this was going on.

I then turned, reduced speed, and as I was afraid of having action with *Broke* I switched on and off my fighting lights occasionally. I picked him out of the darkness by his flashing the word *Broke*, to me and his pendants and a signal from him followed to say all his lights were out. I observed a destroyer very badly on fire, which I approached sufficiently near to observe that she was badly listed and sinking, the fire extending practically over the whole ship. Another boat was at this time right ahead of me and stopped. Thinking this might be possibly one of our boats, I challenged her without reply. During this time, there were a lot of cries of help from the water; nothing was seen, as the night was pitch black. I observed the ship that did not answer my challenge to sink by the stern, her bows up in the air, with a few minor explosions. I closed the position she had been in, lowered boats, and picked up survivors.[21]

This brought the action to a close. The ship that Peck saw sink was *G.42*, the one that *Broke* had rammed. The other ship, *G.85*, did not sink until after dawn broke, and even then, there was fire on the surface of the water for at least another hour. It is a bit harder to assign responsibility for the damage that had left this ship afire and abandoned. She was undoubtedly the destroyer torpedoed at the beginning of the action, the one that was third in the German line. Both *Swift* and *Broke* fired a torpedo at her and both claimed a hit. Both reported two large explosions, though Peck, not knowing *Broke* had fired a torpedo as well, ascribed the second explosion to a hit by his 6in (152mm) gun, though he freely admitted to being dazzled by the muzzle flash of his own gun and effectively blind at this point in the engagement. Given the two large explosions reported, it is possible, even likely, that both torpedoes, one from each British destroyer, hit and disabled *G.85*.

Broke was badly damaged and able to make only a few knots of headway. (*Swift* had taken some damage as well, but was in much better condition.) The destroyer *Mentor* from the Dover squadron came alongside *Broke* and pulled her clear of burning *G.85*. *Broke*'s wounded were transferred to *Mentor*, where they could receive better care, and some German survivors *Mentor* had pulled from the water were sent over to *Broke*. The two ships remained in company until tugs came out from Dover and towed *Broke* to port. *Broke* suffered forty-eight casualties, twenty-one dead and twenty-seven wounded. One hundred and four Germans were taken prisoner from the two ships that sank, sixty-nine died.

The Chums *story*

Evans became, if anything, even more famous as a result of this action. He ended his life as Admiral Lord Mountevans, having, among other accomplishments, commanded the Royal Navy's Australian squadron for several years. He was also a popular author, writing a number of best-selling works of fiction, specialising in boy's adventure tales. One of the 'tales' he wrote was a retelling of the Battle of the Dover Strait, which appeared in *Chums,* a weekly magazine for boys, in the issue of 31 July 1927. As with all good stories, it appears to have become better with every retelling. This must have been especially true with 'Evans of the *Broke*' – a man clearly at home with a good story and one who undoubtedly was asked to recount this tale many times. By the time it showed up in *Chums,* it had indeed gained some interesting embellishments. (Some simplification for a one-page article in a boy's magazine is certainly understandable, as is a certain amount of 'amplification', but even with that understanding, the differences from the account given the day after the event are numerous and striking.)

> Suddenly the raiders were sighted retiring at full speed. Fire was opened immediately, and the *Swift* passed down the enemy line, engaging each of the

six vessels in turn. We in the *Broke* held our gunfire as, being a much slower steamer than *Swift,* we rapidly dropped astern, and we prepared to discharge a torpedo at the second enemy vessel, hoping that the *Swift's* would have badly damaged the leader.

Lieutenant Despard, the torpedo control officer, was very deliberate about his shot, and after he had given the order to fire the port foremost torpedo, I held on for a few seconds to give it a chance to clear the tube before altering course to go right in amongst the squadron of raiders. . . .

Despard was watching his torpedo speeding through the water, and quite suddenly he yelled out, 'We've got her!' Our torpedo reached its mark, striking the German destroyer G.85 plumb amidships, and exploding in the most gratifying manner.

My intention to ram this vessel was not necessary now; accordingly I put my helm over and swung the *Broke's* head away for a few seconds, then altered course back and straightened up to ram the next vessel following astern.

Those on board her gathered what our intentions were, but for them it was too late. A cloud of smoke and sparks belched forth from her funnels, and we got a momentary whiff of this as we tore towards her; it all happened in a few seconds, and I can never forget the feeling of exhilaration that came over me as we were about to strike her. We crashed into her port side abreast the after funnel, and our strong bow ground its way into the enemy vessel's flank. In the blaze of gun flashes we read her name, G.42, as her bow swung round towards us whilst we carried her bodily along on our ram.[22]

The *Broke* was steaming at twenty-seven knots at the time, and we whirled our opponent practically on her beam ends so that she could not fire.

It must have been a dreadful moment for those on board as all our guns which could bear with maximum depression were turned on her, and we literally squirted four-inch shell into the helpless vessel.

Anticipating a close action of this description, we always kept loaded rifles with bayonets fixed at each gun and torpedo tube, besides which cutlasses were provided all around the upper deck, revolvers were provided to petty officers, and there were many kept loaded on the bridge, so that when 'Boarders' was piped on the forecastle the weapons practically fell into the hands of the men who were waiting to use them. A deadly fire was poured from our fore part into the huddled mass of men who, terror stricken, were grouped about the enemy destroyer's decks. Many of them clambered up our bow and got on to the forecastle, to meet with instant death from our well-armed men and stokers. Midshipman Donald Giles, RNNR, although wounded by a shell splinter in the eye, took charge on the forecastle and

A dramatic drawing shows *G.42* heeling over after having been rammed by *Broke* during the Battle of Dover Strait, 21 April 1917. Being significantly smaller than *Broke* and having been on the receiving end of *Broke*'s bow, *G.42* came out much the worse for the encounter and sank before dawn.

organised a gun's crew from the survivors of the men there, who had suffered many casualties, and he also repelled the German sailors who climbed on board from the sinking destroyer, freely using his revolver . . .

We had killed everything we could see on board *G.42*, her stern was sinking more and more until we finally steamed right over her, and it was then, when we made to ram the last vessel in the enemy line, that we missed owing to the explosion in one of our boiler rooms which cut our steam pipe.[23]

It is difficult to judge exactly how much credence to give to this version of the story, despite the fact that it was written by one of the principal participants. There are many small differences from the earlier telling of the story, most of them not really critical, but there is one major incident reported here that was never mentioned by Evans or any of the six other officers and men from *Broke* questioned during the original Court of Enquiry, even though all witnesses were asked to fully describe the battle as they saw it. That incident is, of course, the attempted boarding of *Broke* by desperate German sailors, beaten off by *Broke*'s gallant crew. It is impossible to tell at this late date whether the attempted boarding ever took place, and, if it did not, when it was invented. It is possible that it emerged from the imagination of then-Captain Evans, trying to enliven an account of a brief naval battle, ten years in the past, for a 'Penny Dreadful'. Regardless, it must have been retold many times, as it has now become part of the canonical version of the story.[24]

Broke also lived on, for another sixteen years. Repaired yet again, she served out the war without further brushes with the enemy, though she and HMS *Moorsom* mistakenly attacked HMS/M *E33* in 1918. Fortunately, that attack was unsuccessful. She was sold back to Chile in May 1920, where she was named *Almirante Uribe*. She remained in Chilean service until stricken in 1933.

Notes

1 The Germans, in fact, tried another sweep of the North Sea, much like that which led to Jutland, in mid-August 1916. The German fleet was headed for Hartlepool, led by the battlecruisers (reinforced by three of the newest battleships to replace the ships sunk or damaged at Jutland). Jellicoe led the Grand Fleet south along the coast at its best speed. The two forces were only forty-two nautical miles apart when Scheer turned south and then east away from the British. Jellicoe opted not to follow Scheer and the possible repeat of Jutland never happened. Only after this abortive attempt to take on the Grand Fleet did the Germans turn again to U-boats to win the war at sea.

2 When a sister-ship, HMS *Zulu*, lost her stern to a mine the next month, someone had the bright idea of mating the relatively undamaged stern of *Nubian* with the bow of *Zulu*. The resulting ship was christened HMS *Zubian* and served out the remainder of the war.

3 Being the first to reach the South Pole was the goal, whether or not explicitly stated, of all these expeditions. Robert Peary had reached the North Pole in April 1909, and now the South Pole seemed to many to be the last great expeditionary goal on earth.

4 The English always considered Amundsen to be somehow improper and un-gentlemanlike, a serious accusation at the time. For instance, he had raised money to lead an expedition to the North Pole, but, after Peary and Henson conquered that pole, he switched the destination of his expedition to the South Pole without public announcement of the change. The telegram from Amundsen, sent after he had already set out for the south, was the first Scott knew that there would be two parties trying to reach the Pole at the same time. At root, it was the fact that Amundsen was a professional explorer that most irritated the British; Scott represented the Victorian ideal of the amateur dilettante.

5 PO Edgar Evans is sometimes confused with then Lieutenant E R G R 'Teddy' Evans, both in Scott's Polar party. They were not related.

6 Neither Scott's nor Amundsen's teams ate diets with adequate vitamin C, and both were at risk of developing scurvy, a vitamin-C-deficiency disease. The human body stores enough vitamin C to last about three months before the first symptoms of scurvy begin to appear. Amundsen's round trip to the Pole took three months and six days; Scott died almost exactly five months after leaving his base, suffering the classic symptoms of vitamin deficiency. Scott's diet was also deficient in vitamin B, while Amundsen's was not. Scurvy and the various vitamin-B-deficiency diseases, besides causing physical debilities, can cause depression and confusion, perhaps accounting for the increasingly irrational decisions made by Scott after leaving the Pole.

7   HMS *Nugent* was a brand-new war-construction 'M'-class destroyer that could only have been in commission a month or two at the most.

8   *Court*, p. 625.

9   In World War I, indeed until 1933, steering orders in the Royal Navy were given as 'helm' as opposed to 'rudder' orders. To turn a ship to starboard, the helm is put to port and vice versa. Thus, putting the helm 'hard-a-starboard' caused a maximum turn to port. (The US Navy made the change to rudder orders in 1914.) Since those dates, 'port helm' was replaced by 'right rudder' to turn a ship to starboard.

It is worth noting that, as late as 1917, the first instinct of many Royal Navy destroyer captains, when faced with enemy destroyers, was to ram. This was true not only for Peck, but for Evans as well, even in cases such as this, when facing a more numerous, but less well-armed foe, engaging with guns and torpedoes without ramming might have produced a better result. Gordon in *Rules*, particularly in Chapters 16 and 17, makes an interesting point about Royal Navy officers responding to the rapid technological changes immediately before World War I by sometimes finding refuge in a 'romantic' mind set that led some to geographical, particularly polar, exploration and longing for an earlier, simpler age, when ramming would have been a more appropriate tactic.

10   Ibid. Both Peck and Evans actually sighted only five ships. It is likely that the leading German destroyer was well ahead and already past *Swift* when the enemy was first sighted, so that the ship that both Peck and Evans took to be the first German destroyer was in fact the second and so on.

11   Ibid, p. 644.

12   A compass point is 11¼ degrees. In 1916, *Swift* had a pair of 4in (102mm) guns on her forecastle replaced by a single 6in (152mm) gun. As Peck's comments indicate, this was not successful, the blinding effect of the muzzle flash far outweighing any advantage gained from mounting a larger gun. *Broke* retained her 4in (102mm) guns until very late in the war and Evans had no similar problem during this engagement.

13   Lyddite was an explosive filler for artillery shells. It replaced standard gunpowder as the common filling for high-explosive and armour-piercing shells in the late nineteenth century as it was a far more energetic explosive, producing a far larger and more dispersed ring of shell fragments.

14   Ibid, pp. 625–6.

15   Ibid, p. 626.

16   Again, this was almost certainly the fourth ship in the enemy line, the first having escaped notice by either British ship.

17   This sentence is more than a little confusing, but makes more sense if 'again' is understood to modify only the verb 'ram' and not 'No 4', which he hadn't rammed in the preceding action.

18   Ibid, pp. 644–5.

19   It is unclear what Evans means here about 'following' *Swift*. At this time, as far as can be ascertained from Evans' and Peck's narratives, *Swift* was coming back towards the two sinking German destroyers, so she would have been approaching *Broke* from ahead, at least until *Broke* began her drifting turn back towards the two Germans.

20   Ibid, p. 645.

21   Ibid, p. 626.

22   Contrast this with Evans' statement to the Court of Enquiry, when asked if he'd seen any numbers on the enemy ships: "No, sir. I never distinguished any numbers." *Court*, p. 646.

23   *Chums*, pp. 47-8.

24   For example, see the Wikipedia article entitled 'The Battle of Dover Strait'.

Chapter 5

Stumbling to Glory – Narvik
(10–13 April 1940)

DESTROYERS AS A TYPE evolved rapidly in the slightly more than twenty years that elapsed between World War I and World War II. Lessons had been learned from the experiences at Jutland and, even more, in the Dover Patrol. It was easy to reach the conclusion that bigger, more powerfully armed destroyers not only could perform their nominal duties of escorting the main battle fleet better than their smaller counterparts, but that they could also perform many of the singular duties of small cruisers as well. As cruisers grew in size between the wars, larger and larger destroyer classes were designed to fill in as multi-purpose, highly capable warships, big enough to act independently, alone or in small groups, at a distance from the fleet, yet small enough that they could be produced in large numbers and be considered expendable when risks needed to be taken.

The end of World War I left the victorious navies, in particular the British and American, in possession of a large number of relatively small, war-production destroyers. These nations had little impetus to build more of this type in the years immediately following the Armistice. Other Allied nations, those with smaller economies and less need during the war to build up a large fleet of conventional destroyers, were the first to study the lessons of the war and begin designing a new generation of destroyers. This happened more or less independently in France, Italy and Japan beginning in the first half of the 1920s.

Postwar destroyer designs

It started specifically in France, where the six *Jaguar*-class *contre-torpilleurs* were ordered in 1922. These were large and fast – 2126 tons standard displacement, 119 metres overall length and thirty-five knots – and were well armed with five

5.1in (130mm) main guns, two 3in (75 mm) anti-aircraft mounts and two triple 21.6in (550mm) torpedo tubes. This kind of size and capability served as a model for other navies and was followed by the Italian *Navigatori* class ordered in 1926 and the Japanese 'Special Type' authorised in 1923. These latter, which were laid down starting in 1926, were smaller than the French ships, at 1750 tons, but were faster and better armed. As interested as the major powers were in events in the Mediterranean, it took the Japanese to truly alarm them. The British, with the drawing down of the massive navy built for the war, were finding themselves hard put to maintain forces in the Far East sufficient to counter the rapid build up of the Imperial Japanese Navy. The Americans, even more than the British, were keeping a close watch on the Japanese, who were seen as a direct threat to US interests in China, the Philippines and Hawaii. US Navy war planning, in particular after the end of World War I, assumed that the next war would be with Japan.

Except for a couple of one-offs, the Royal Navy only seriously resumed building destroyers with the 'A'-class of 1928–9 and these were straight-forward updates of the late-war repeat 'W'-class design. It was not until the 'Tribal' class of 1936 that the British really responded to the threat posed by large destroyers being built elsewhere. Most British destroyers built well into the late 1930s were smaller. Much more typical were the 'H'-class ships launched in 1936 that displaced 1350 tons and were armed with four 4.7in (119mm) guns and twin quadruple 21in (533mm) torpedo tubes. The US Navy, with its large fleet of 'four-pipers', was not able to convince a parsimonious Congress to build any new destroyers until the early 1930s and even then, the designs evolved slowly, only reaching a size and capability that matched the Japanese 'Special Types' with the *Porter*-class leaders starting in 1935. Like the British, the Americans continued mainly building somewhat smaller destroyers, but by the later 1930s these had grown incrementally to a size very similar to their foreign contemporaries.

It was not just in greater size and greater armament that destroyers changed between the wars. The nature of the threats to warships in general had evolved rapidly during and after World War I, and destroyers had to evolve to protect themselves and the ships they escorted. Destroyers were the natural choice to become the primary anti-submarine platform for the protection of fleets and convoys. The state-of-the-art in ASW (anti-submarine warfare) between the wars centred on sonar for the detection of submarines and depth charges for their destruction.[1] The first operational sonars were deployed in 1923 in the Royal Navy and 1931 in the US Navy. By the outbreak of World War II, they were common in the world's navies. The idea behind depth charges dates back to 1910, but the first practical version was the Royal Navy's Type D of 1916. However, without sonar, depth charges were only marginally effective.[2]

The other new threat introduced in World War I was aircraft. The primitive biplanes of 1918 may not have seemed much of a threat to warships, and AA (anti-aircraft) weapons were still rare at the end of the war, but the rapid evolution of aircraft and aircraft carriers soon made them a major, if not the major, factor in any naval operation. The relatively small size of destroyers, even the larger ones developed between the wars, limited the number of AA weapons they could carry, but not the critical role they could play in AA defence. In the days before radar, destroyers were spread in a wide screen to locate and report incoming aircraft in time for defences to be prepared. Even after radar became ubiquitous, the role of destroyers in AA defence, if anything, expanded. Radar picket destroyers were first widely used in the Okinawa campaign, where they proved to be critical in giving early warning of *kamikaze* attacks, which they drew like magnets.

In general, the growth in size of destroyers reflected the growth in the demands put on the type. From being rather fragile, fair-weather torpedo boats, destroyers evolved between the wars into fast, long-ranging ships, capable of carrying out virtually any job that needed to be done. So useful were they, that many nations found themselves regretting they had not built more of them before the fighting began again.

German destroyers

One nation that certainly had such regrets was Nazi Germany. The once-proud *Hochseeflotte* was emasculated by the Versailles Treaty. That treaty, intended by the victors in World War I as a way of ensuring that Germany could no longer disturb the peace of the continent, in fact guaranteed exactly the opposite. Germany was so humiliated by the treaty that fertile ground was prepared for every form of radical ideology, not least that espoused by Hitler and the Nazis. The post-Versailles navy, known as the *Reichsmarine,* was relatively apolitical, but was not immune to the sense of shame and anger that pervaded the rest of the nation.

The treaty restricted Germany to no more than twelve active destroyers and twelve torpedo boats, and those allocated to the *Reichsmarine* by the victors were hardly the newest and best survivors of the war. The treaty's provisions allowed these old ships to be replaced fifteen years after they were launched by new construction no larger than 800 tons. As all of the twelve destroyers retained by the *Reichsmarine* were launched between 1911 and 1913, this allowed the

A *Typ 1934* destroyer, of which *Georg Thiele* was one, is seen probably at a French port after the defeat of that country by the Germans, sometime later in 1940. These ships were large and well armed, but suffered from a variety of mechanical problems that reduced their effectiveness. She and all the destroyers that took part in the action at Narvik were painted the standard early-war *Kriegsmarine* scheme of medium grey on the hull and a lighter grey above that. (ECPA)

Germans to begin building new destroyers in 1926, but this was hardly an auspicious time in Germany economically or politically, and there was no enthusiasm in the *Reichsmarine* for the construction of new destroyers less than half the size of foreign contemporaries. That situation changed only when Hitler took power in 1933. Suddenly money was available and the political will to rearm extended even to the *Reichsmarine*.[3] More importantly, the new government was willing to ignore the Versailles restrictions, so that when the first new destroyers were laid down in 1934, they were comparable in size and armament to new construction elsewhere. Where the German destroyers suffered in comparison to others was in the reliability of their power plants. The Germans opted to give their new destroyers high-pressure superheated steam propulsion, which would theoretically give improved endurance using a smaller, lighter engineering plant. The Americans pioneered this technology and had success with it, but the Germans, and to a lesser extent the British, had great difficulty perfecting this propulsion system. German destroyers would be continually plagued in the upcoming war by untimely engine failures.

But by far the biggest problem the Germans had with their destroyers, when a new world war broke out in September 1939, was that there were simply too few of them. When Germany entered the war, she had twenty-one operational destroyers. This was nowhere near enough to perform the myriad of tasks at which they would have been useful, anything from escort duties to harbour defence to anti-submarine patrol to a new role that no warship designer could have anticipated – high-speed transport.[4]

The forces gather for invasion

After the occupation of Poland, crushed between her massive neighbours, the new war settled into a seeming routine. The seas were the only venue where the

The Royal Navy's adventures in Norwegian waters in World War II began with the capture of the German auxiliary *Altmark* in Jøssingfjord on 16 February 1940. The destroyer HMS *Cossack* put a boarding party on *Altmark* to free some 300 merchant seaman who had been taken off ships sunk by the raider *Admiral Graf Spee*. The lack of official protest by the Norwegians after this clear breach of that nation's sovereignty and neutrality led in part to Hitler's decision to occupy Norway.

Cheering merchant seamen line *Cossack*'s rail on her return to England after they were rescued from the German auxiliary *Altmark*, 16 February 1940.

two sides regularly took shots at each other. While the French army and the BEF hunkered down behind the Maginot Line and along the Belgian border, the *Kriegsmarine* – the successor to the Weimar *Reichsmarine* – turned to commerce raiding and unrestricted U-boat warfare early in the war.[5] Neither proved as successful as the Germans might have hoped, at least at first. While the pocket-battleship *Admiral Graf Spee* did have a successful cruise in terms of merchant shipping destroyed, she was inevitably cornered and forced to scuttle herself after just three months at sea. The Germans simply could not afford to lose one of a very small supply of capital ships in exchange for nine freighters, regardless of the amount of fear she spread before her destruction. Germany's U-boats were likewise less successful than hoped for a number of reasons, not the least of which was repeated undiagnosed torpedo failures.[6]

Hitler planned to invade France and the Low Countries as soon as the weather permitted in the spring of 1940, but before that could happen, it became necessary to deal with Norway. Officially neutral, Norway was very much on the minds of both the British and Germans. The Germans needed to move iron ore from Narvik down the Norwegian coast; the British wanted to interdict this traffic.[7] In a complex game of cat-and-mouse, both sides knew of the other's concerns and pushed forward plans to forestall each other. The British cobbled up a plan codenamed 'Wilfred', which involved mining those parts of the Norwegian coastal route that were in international waters. The hope was that this would lead the Germans to put pressure on the Norwegians, which would in turn cause the Norwegians to appeal to the British for help. If the Germans instead invaded Norway, the British had a counter–invasion (Operation 'R4') planned. The Germans, who were reading the British codes, knew all this and, convinced the Norwegians were secretly collaborating with the British, simply pushed forward a plan of their own, Operation '*Weserübung*', which called for most of the surface units of the *Kriegsmarine* to be loaded with troops to be put ashore at seven locations in Norway (and another seven in Denmark, which would be occupied at the same time) on 9 April 1940. The force with the farthest to travel was the detachment of 2000 mountain troops under General Dietl, evenly divided among ten of Germany's newest, largest destroyers. The German destroyers were drawn from three different flotillas and had never operated together before. These were:

- 3rd Flotilla – All of newest *Typ 1936* design
  Z17 (*Diether von Roeder*)[8]
  Z18 (*Hans Lüdemann*) – Flotilla commander FK H-J Gadow
  Z19 (*Hermann Künne*)
  Z21 (*Wilhelm Heidkamp*) – Flagship of overall commander Kom Friedrich Bonte
  Z22 (*Anton Schmitt*)

- 4th Flotilla – All of *Typ 1934A* design
  Z9 (*Wolfgang Zenker*) – Flotilla commander FK Erich Bey
  Z11 (*Bernd von Arnim*)
  Z12 (*Erich Giese*)
  Z13 (*Erich Koellner*)

- 1st Flotilla – *Typ 1934* design
  Z2 (*Georg Thiele*) – Flotilla commander FK Berger

Even the oldest of these ships was new by any standard, less than four years old, and all were big, fast and well armed. (The *Typ 1936* ships were 1811 tons, 120 metres on the waterline and carried five 5in (127mm) main guns in single mounts plus 37mm and 20mm AA guns and two quadruple 21in (533mm) torpedo tubes. They were capable of forty knots in calm weather, though they were known to suffer badly in rough seas. (The *Typ 1934* ships were somewhat smaller and slower, but were similarly armed.) In addition to these destroyers, the Germans dispatched four merchant ships, two freighters with the troops' motor vehicles, heavy artillery and extra supplies of food and munitions and two tankers with fuel for the destroyers and the handful of U-boats sent to support this operation. One of these tankers, *Jan Wellem,* was a converted whaler

The first victims in the Battle of Narvik were a pair of Norwegian coast defence ships, the sisters *Eidsvold* and *Norge*. They were old, having been built in 1900, but were considered adequate to defend Narvik in the days before Norway got caught between the two sides in the opening stages of World War II. This photograph shows *Eidsvold* sometime during the 1920s, but she looked no different when she was sunk by *Wilhelm Heidkamp* when Narvik was occupied, 9 April 1940.

sailing from Murmansk; the other supply ships were sailing individually, without escort, from Germany. Protection of a sort for Bonte's destroyers was to be provided by the two battlecruisers *Scharnhorst* and *Gneisenau,* sailing a parallel course further offshore.

Jan Wellem actually arrived at Narvik before the destroyers, but her arrival caused no curiosity, as most of the merchant ships in Narvik harbour at the time were German. The other three support ships would arrive sometime later. The freighters were critical for Dietl's forces, which would land from the destroyers with only the food and munitions they could carry on their backs and a few mountain guns that were strapped to the destroyers' decks. The tankers were even more critical to Bonte's destroyers. After sailing through bad weather at a sustained speed of twenty knots, they would arrive in Narvik with bunkers nearly dry. Bonte's orders were quite clear. He was to refuel as rapidly as possible and get his ships back to Germany. Contact with the Royal Navy was to be avoided if at all possible.

Alerted to the German moves only after the forces started sailing on 6 April, the Royal Navy responded as if surprised by the whole affair, sending ships to

Norway belatedly and in seemingly random order. Fortunately, some ships were already on their way to Norway, as Operation 'Wilfred' had been scheduled to start on 8 April, but the German sailings caused these plans to be delayed and eventually forgotten altogether. These ships at least would be in position to contest the German moves. They included:

- Four minelaying destroyers (HMSs *Esk*, *Impulsive*, *Icarus* and *Ivanhoe*) scheduled to lay a minefield off Vestfjord, the southern entrance to Narvik. These ships were all specially modified for the minelaying role by the removal of half their main guns and all torpedo tubes.

- Four escorting destroyers from 2nd Flotilla (HMSs *Hardy*, *Hotspur*, *Havock* and *Hunter*). Captain Bernard Warburton-Lee had tactical command from *Hardy*.

- HMS *Renown* and two more destroyers (HMSs *Greyhound* and *Glowworm*) were coming up from the south, and several more destroyers were to be posted along the coast as decoys.

All but one of these destroyers were from the identical 'G', 'H' and 'I'-classes launched between 1935 and 1937. They were intentionally designed not in response to the almost universal trend towards bigger destroyers followed by most other navies. These were evolutionary developments from late-World War I designs, smaller (by nearly 500 tons) and carrying one fewer main gun than their German counterparts, but they were excellent weather boats, sturdy and long-legged. And they were converging on the same small patch of ocean as a large part of the German fleet.

First encounters

Inevitably, there was contact between the British ships of Operation 'Wilfred' and the German ships of '*Weserübung*'. On the morning of the 8th, the destroyer *Glowworm*, separated from *Renown*'s escort when she had turned back to search for a man overboard in the rough seas, instead found the heavy cruiser *Admiral Hipper* on her way to Trondheim. In a confused engagement in poor visibility, *Glowworm* was surprised by the big German cruiser, fired a spread of torpedoes that missed and then retired behind an effective smoke screen. *Hipper* passed through the smoke only to find *Glowworm* approaching on a collision course. The two ships scraped each other and then, as if tiring of an annoying game, *Hipper* dispatched *Glowworm* under a hail of gunfire. *Hipper* stopped to pick up thirty-eight of *Glowworm*'s crew before continuing on to Trondheim. *Renown*,

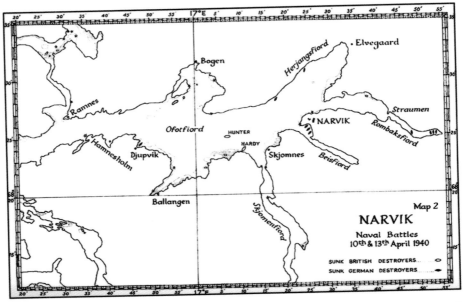

This map shows the waters in which the two Battles of Narvik were fought. The location of the wrecks of the two British and ten German destroyers are shown in white outline and solid black respectively. Most of the action occurred in Ofotfjord, leading up to the town of Narvik from the west and in the three smaller fjords that branch off near the town.

flagship of Vice Admiral W J Whitworth, continued north, accompanied now only by *Greyhound*.

Whitworth arrived off the entrance of Vestfjord and rendezvoused with Warburton-Lee's eight destroyers at 1715 on 8 April. Unknown to him, Bonte's destroyers were perhaps three hours to the south, heading directly for his position. (Whitworth was informed by Admiralty signals that a German force was probably headed towards Narvik, but not exactly where it was or when to expect it. He received a further direct order at 1915 on the 8th to prevent any German ships from reaching Narvik, but he chose, because of the poor weather, to take his ships away from the coast.) The British, therefore, obligingly cleared away to the west for the evening and the German destroyers entered Vestfjord unseen. By 0300 the next morning, Bonte was turning from Vestfjord into the narrower Ofotfjord that leads due east to Narvik. At virtually the same time, *Renown* and her nine escorts turned back towards land and encountered the German battlecruisers. A few shots were exchanged and a few hits obtained, but Vice Admiral Lütjens, commanding the German battlecruisers, well aware that they were his nation's only real capital ships, turned away to the northeast and disappeared into the fog, with *Renown* following at a distance. Warburton-Lee took his destroyers back to Vestfjord, unknowingly blocking the Germans' escape route from Narvik.

When he turned into Ofotfjord, Bonte had nine destroyers in his group. One, *Erich Giese,* had fallen behind due to mechanical problems and was about thirty nautical miles behind the others (but managed to enter Vestfjord before Warburton-Lee took up his blocking position). The others made quick work of two old Norwegian coastal-defence ships guarding the harbour and put Dietl's troops ashore right on time. It did not take Bonte long to realise he would have a much harder time fulfilling the other half of his orders – the rapid return of his destroyers to Germany. Of the four supply ships, only *Jan Wellem* had arrived and she contained barely enough bunker oil to replenish all of his destroyers. Worse than that, she had not been designed to serve as a tanker and could refuel only two ships at a time and those very slowly. It would take eight hours to fill a pair of destroyers. (The other three supply ships heading for Narvik were all captured or sunk. Bonte and Dietl would have to make do with what they had.)

British forces gathered in Vestfjord as the 9th progressed. *Renown* returned from the futile chase after the two German battlecruisers and her sister, *Repulse,* arrived with a strong escort, including four large destroyers (HMSs *Bedouin, Eskimo, Punjabi* and *Kimberley* – the first three were 'Tribal'-class ships and the last was from the 'K'-class of 1938, the first of the larger mainstream ships that would be built with few changes through the end of the war) and the old cruiser *Penelope.* The four 'H'-class ships under Warburton-Lee were posted well up the Vestfjord, now augmented by a fifth, HMS *Hostile,* which had been patrolling down the coast and joined the action to the north on her commander's initiative. The rest of the British ships stayed near the entrance to the fjord.

At noon on the 9th, Warburton-Lee received orders directly from the Admiralty, bypassing Whitworth, acknowledging for the first time that a German warship might have slipped into Narvik and ordering him to 'Proceed Narvik and sink or harass enemy ship'.[9] By the time Warburton-Lee received this order, it was too late to take action that day. (Had he set out right then, he would have arrived off Narvik just as the sun was setting, hardly the ideal time to begin an attack against unknown opponents in narrow, possibly mined, waters.) He wisely opted to postpone the attack until the next morning and to use the available time to gather as much information as he could.[10] He took his squadron up Vestfjord as far as the town of Tranoy, where the pilot station for ships heading for Narvik was located. Warburton-Lee put a German-speaking officer ashore, who came back with a confused message. He reported that at least four and possibly as many as six German warships had passed Tranoy a day earlier, and they were accurately described as being larger than his five ships. At least one U-boat was reported to have passed the town as well. The British now knew the Germans were at Narvik in considerable strength.

Converging on Narvik

Warburton-Lee was now faced with some difficult decisions. He ordered his five destroyers down the Vestfjord to get them into wider waters while he decided what to do. He knew that the Germans had forces at Narvik at least equal to his own. He could have asked Whitworth to put some of the nine destroyers and one cruiser further down the fjord at his disposal, but there were reasons why he may have been reluctant to do so. His orders had come directly from the Admiralty and he had no idea how Whitworth, as officer in command on the scene, had taken being pushed aside by admirals with dry feet back in London. Further, he had every reason to believe that, were other ships assigned

This aerial view of the eastern end of Rombaksfjord shows the narrowness of the waters in which four of the ten German destroyers met their end. Three beached themselves at the far end and the fourth, *Georg Thiele*, ran up on the southern shore towards the bottom in this view. (NHC)

to the mission, they would bring with them a more senior officer who would take over command of the operation. He may also have feared that, having been assigned this task directly, he could be showing career-threatening weakness or hesitancy were he to ask for reinforcements. Whatever the reason, Warburton-Lee did not ask for more ships, nor were any offered by Whitworth. At 2130 on the 9th, his five destroyers turned around and set course for the narrows between Baroy and Tjeldoy Islands, the entrance to Ofotfjord.

As the British destroyers approached the narrows soon after midnight, Warburton-Lee deployed his ships in narrow quarterline to starboard, meaning that rather than being in strict line ahead, each ship would be fine on the starboard quarter of the ship ahead. This would guarantee that, in the narrow waters where they would fighting, each ship could bring its forward guns to bear straight ahead without endangering any other ship. When they reached the eastern end of the fjord, they would find that a pair of headlands split Ofotfjord into three smaller branches. The northern – Herjangsfjord – is the biggest and leads to the small town of Elvegaard at its tip; Rombaksfjord in the middle is extremely deep and narrow; on the right, Beisfjord has a narrow mouth and then widens on its northern side into a broad bight which is Narvik harbour and then rapidly narrows again as it heads off to the southeast. The first three destroyers in line, *Hardy*, *Hunter* and *Havock*, were instructed to head straight into Narvik harbour; the remaining two, *Hotspur* and *Hostile* were ordered to bear off into Herjangsfjord and engage any enemy found there.

At Narvik, Bonte was trying to deal as best he could with the logistical bottleneck caused by *Jan Wellem*'s slow pumps. Four of his ships had completed refuelling: *Georg Thiele* and *Bernd von Arnim* were instructed to anchor in Ballangen Bay perhaps eight miles west of Narvik on the south side of Ofotfjord, *Wilhelm Heidkamp,* Bonte's flagship, was anchored at the southern end of the harbour and *Diether von Roeder* was on patrol in Ofotfjord outside the harbour entrance. Three more of his ships, *Wolfgang Zenker*, *Erich Koellner* and *Erich Giese*, the last in line to be refuelled, were waiting in Herjangsfjord. *Hans Lüdemann* and *Hermann Künne* were tied up on either side of *Jan Wellem* in the harbour and the last of the ten, *Anton Schmitt*, was anchored in the harbour south of those three, waiting for her turn. Bonte wanted as few of his ships inside Narvik harbour as possible, as it was crowded not only with four destroyers and the oiler, but also with twenty-five merchant ships of various sizes and nationalities.

Nature conveniently hid the British from prying eyes as they entered Ofotfjord at twelve knots. Scattered snow squalls often reduced visibility to near zero. The low visibility led to considerable radio chatter between Warburton-

Lee's destroyers as they checked each others' positions, but the Germans were not listening and the British approached undetected. At first light, at approximately 0345, *Diether von Roeder* ended her patrol and set course for the harbour. She was, at the most, a few hundred metres north of, and perhaps a mile and a half ahead of, *Hardy*, but the visibility was such that neither saw the other. Shortly after 0415, *Hotspur* and *Hostile* turned off into Herjangsfjord and the other three British ships bore just south of east towards the harbour. At 0425, *Diether von Roeder* dropped anchor at the northern end of the harbour. Bonte, having been awake most of the preceding forty-eight hours, had retired to his harbour cabin and was sound asleep. No more than five minutes later, *Hardy*, leading *Hunter* and *Havock*, passed the narrows at the entrance to Beisfjord going dead slow, creeping along the southern shore. Visibility had improved to almost a mile, though there remained a thin haze lying on the water. But so many merchant ships filled the harbour, which now opened on *Hardy*'s port bow, that at first Warburton-Lee could see none of the now five German destroyers (with the addition of *Diether von Roeder*) in the harbour, and none of them had sighted *Hardy*. This would not last for long. The first Battle of Narvik was about to begin.

The first Battle of Narvik

Hardy had just passed south of the outermost of the merchant ships, the British ore-carrier *Blythmoor*, when, in a gap between other ships, the two southern-most of the German destroyers, *Anton Schmitt* and *Wilhelm Heidkamp*, were sighted, showing no activity. Warburton-Lee ordered more speed and turned to port so his torpedo tubes would bear.[11] Three torpedoes were fired at a range of barely 1500 metres. As *Hardy* continued to swing around *Blythmoor*, two more German destroyers were sighted, *Hermann Künne* tied up to *Jan Wellem* and *Diether von Roeder*. Four torpedoes were fired at those two and then *Hardy*, now moving at a good clip, exited the harbour near the north shore. The first of *Hardy*'s torpedoes missed *Wilhelm Heidkamp*'s stern and hit a merchantman anchored behind her with a satisfying explosion. But that was quickly overshadowed by the second torpedo's detonation, which hit *Wilhelm Heidkamp*'s port quarter and set off her after magazine, sending three turrets and much of the aft third of the ship up into the air. Bonte was killed in that blast. The rest of *Hardy*'s torpedoes found no targets.

    Hunter followed *Hardy* and then *Havock*. They both curved around *Blythmoor*, firing torpedoes and guns and then exited the harbour. *Hunter* appears to have had some success. She put one 4.7in (119mm) round into *Anton Schmitt* and also

Hermann Künne was in Narvik harbour, tied up alongside the tanker *Jan Wellem* when the British attacked on 10 April. She started backing away from the tanker, but the shock of a torpedo hitting another destroyer in the harbour put her engines out of service. When the Royal Navy returned three days later, her engines had been repaired and she was the only German destroyer in fully operational condition.

appears to have hit her with one torpedo. Most, if not all, of the rest of her torpedoes hit merchant ships. *Havock* likewise loosed a full salvo of torpedoes. One of her torpedoes also hit *Anton Schmitt*, which rapidly settled to the harbour floor. *Hermann Künne* had gotten underway, backing away from *Jan Wellem*'s side, but the shock of the second hit on *Anton Schmitt* damaged her engines and she lost all power. *Hans Lüdemann* pulled away from *Jan Wellem*'s far side and was immediately hit hard by gunfire from *Havock*. Her forward turret was knocked out and a fire started aft that required flooding her after magazine and left her unable to steer. All three British destroyers retired from the harbour unscathed, leaving a scene of devastation in their wake. Two German destroyers were sunk and two more disabled before the battle had hardly begun.

The two destroyers sent north, *Hotspur* and *Hostile*, found nothing and returned just as the other three were leaving the harbour. *Hotspur* lay a smoke screen across the entrance to Beisfjord to protect *Hardy, Hunter* and *Havock* from German gunfire; *Hostile* drifted to a stop near the northern edge of the harbour and began trading gunfire with *Diether von Roeder*. She definitely got the better of the exchange, hitting the German twice and starting a fire in her No 2 boiler room. The three German destroyers still afloat in the harbour fired a total of fourteen torpedoes at the British ships now milling outside the fjord's entrance, but such were the problems suffered by German torpedoes at this stage of the war that not one of them hit. *Diether von Roeder* received several more 4.7in (119mm) hits at this time, one of which required the flooding of her after magazines. Fearing that his ship was sinking and unable to raise his anchor, her captain ordered all power astern and backed his ship up to a pier, where she was lashed in a position that allowed her still working forward guns to bear on the harbour entrance. With all five German destroyers in Narvik harbour either sunk or seriously damaged, a lull now settled over the scene. Warburton-Lee had every reason to be satisfied. Every enemy ship he had seen had been accounted for and all of his ships were completely untouched. It appeared his victory was complete. He pulled away a short distance to the west to weigh his options.

By 0645, a decision had been made and the five British destroyers were again in line ahead, heading back towards the harbour, *Hardy* in the lead, followed by *Havock, Hunter, Hotspur* and *Hostile*. The deciding factor that led Warburton-Lee to order another run in was that, as yet, *Hostile* had fired none of her torpedoes. All five ships took their turn firing at the three remaining German destroyers in the harbour and appear to have achieved no further hits by either gun or torpedo. *Hostile,* on the other hand, received a hit on her forecastle; not serious, but it was the first damage taken by any of the British ships.

Emerging from the harbour for the second time, Warburton-Lee was surprised to see three fresh German destroyers approaching from the northeast. *Hotspur* had reported Herjangsfjord clear, but she had apparently not gone far enough to sight *Wolfgang Zenker, Erich Koellner* and *Erich Giese*, which had now raised steam and were coming up on his starboard quarter. They were under the command of FK Bey in *Wolfgang Zenker*, who, unbeknownst to him, was now the senior German officer afloat. Warburton-Lee turned his line to the west, ordered full speed and made smoke. It was clearly time to make an escape.

Soon four of the British destroyers had cleared the harbour and were blasting away at Bey's three ships. (*Hostile* was lingering in the harbour attempting to find targets for her torpedoes.) But Bey's ships were hardly up to a full-out chase. One of them, *Erich Giese,* was so low on fuel that only two of her six boilers could raise steam, and none of the Germans was capable of full speed, so the British ships, making smoke and weaving their way to the west, appeared to be making good their escape. But there was one more obstacle in their way.

The two remaining German ships, *Georg Thiele* and *Bernd von Arnim,* had been idling at Ballangen, unaware that a battle was going on, when they received word from Bey to make their way home independently. Of the five remaining German ships, they were the only ones with sufficient fuel to reach Germany. As the two ships emerged from Ballangen Bay, they saw the smoke cloud emitted by the British ships approaching at high speed from the northeast and heard the sounds of gunfire. Perhaps they could have turned back into the bay or set a course to the west along the south shore of Ofotfjord and thus escaped notice by Warburton-Lee, but they chose to fight. They put themselves across the course of the approaching British and opened fire on *Hardy,* the only British ship they could see at first.

Hotspur *and* Hunter *collide*

Up to this point, the gunnery on the German side had been uniformly ineffective, but *Georg Thiele* changed that with one salvo. Two shells slammed into *Hardy*'s bridge and at least one more hit her forward gun turrets. In moments, she was left without guidance or the ability to fire back at the German. Both her captain and Warburton-Lee were mortally wounded. She continued on at full speed but on course towards the south shore, followed by the other four (*Hostile* having just rejoined her mates). A junior officer regained

Captain Bernard Warburton-Lee led the force of British destroyers into Ofotfjord on 10 April. He died that day from injuries received when the bridge of his flagship, HMS *Hardy*, was hit by gunfire from *Georg Thiele*. He was awarded the Victoria Cross posthumously, the first to be awarded in World War II.

control of *Hardy* and managed to turn her back towards the west just before she ran ashore. This reprieve did not last long. Another salvo cut her steam pipes and *Hardy* rapidly lost way. She was turned back to port just before she lost the last of her forward momentum and she nosed herself gently on to a shallow beach where she ground to a halt.

Georg Thiele and *Bernd von Arnim* now turned to the west and kept pace with the four remaining British ships, off their starboard beam. (The three other German destroyers had fallen behind and were now effectively out of the fight.) *Havock* now led the British line as the two sides kept up a ragged fire at each other as they raced to the west on parallel courses. Both *Hunter* and *Hotspur*, second and third in the British line, received significant damage in this short-range exchange. Sometimes as little as 1700 metres separated the two lines. *Georg Thiele* took a hit in her No 1 boiler room and had to shut one boiler down. This duel continued for almost half an hour. It came about as close as possible in 1940 to recreating a battle from the age of sail, when lines of ships would attempt to pound each other into submission, iron shot against wooden hulls, unless someone like Nelson came along to break the rules (and the line of battle). Iron shot had been replaced by AP, SAP and HE shells and wooden walls by thin steel plating, but the effect was remarkably similar. The British SAP (Semi-Armour Piercing) shells proved particularly effective, as they would explode only after penetrating the outer shell plating.

At around 0615, disaster struck the British line. It is not clear exactly what happened to *Hunter*, as there were few survivors, but she appeared to stagger, erupt in flames and pull off to starboard mortally wounded. It is likely that she was hit by a German torpedo, as *Georg Thiele*, despite being hit repeatedly, stayed in line and managed to fire three torpedoes just before *Hunter* blew up, but if that was the case, it was one of only two German torpedoes, of the dozens fired in the two battles of Narvik, to find its mark. *Hotspur* followed *Hunter* as she staggered out of line and then, unaware that she was mortally wounded and rapidly losing way, plowed into her starboard side abreast the machinery spaces. *Hostile* and *Havock*, blinded by smoke, continued to the west, unaware of the collision. The Germans, suffering from repeated hits themselves, opted not to follow. Instead, they turned back and began to close in on *Hotspur* and *Hunter*, locked in an apparent death embrace.

For a few minutes the two destroyers remained locked together. Most of *Hotspur*'s guns still worked and one gun on *Hunter* kept firing, and, between the two of them, they convinced the wounded Germans that their part in this battle was over as well. *Georg Thiele* and *Bernd von Arnim* both staggered away to the east. *Hotspur* had been hit seven times and was badly hurt, but she managed to

Seen the day after the first engagement, *Diether von Roeder* has been somewhat patched up, but her power plant was beyond repair and she remained tied up stern-first to the Post Pier in Narvik, so her still operable forward guns could bear on any ship entering the harbour. She fought a gallant, but ultimately futile fight two days later and was finally scuttled next to the pier after firing off all her remaining rounds. (NARA)

wrench loose from *Hunter* and make her way slowly westward. Bey by now had come back on the scene with his three ships and he tried to follow *Hotspur,* but *Hostile* and *Havock* finally noticed her peril and came back to cover her retreat. Bey decided that he had done enough for the day and he led his ships back to Narvik, while the surviving British ships limped out of Ofotfjord. *Hunter* sank some time during these final moves. Bey returned to the scene later and rescued those still alive in the water.

Analysing this, the first Battle of Narvik, is not easy. Tactically, it really fell into two distinct, unrelated halves. The first part, the attack in Narvik harbour, was as complete a victory as could be wished. Just like the Japanese at Port Arthur thirty-five years earlier, complete tactical surprise was achieved when it really should not have been, and the results were similarly one-sided. Five British ships surprised five Germans, sank two and disabled the rest, while emerging virtually untouched. The second half, the fight in Ofotfjord, is far more complicated and less clear cut. The attack by Bey's three ships had little impact and the attackers were quickly left behind, but the two ships from Ballangen Bay managed to make up for what was otherwise a rather poor showing by the *Kriegsmarine*. *Georg Thiele* and *Bernd von Arnim* fought the British to a standstill. While badly beaten up themselves, they managed to sink two and badly damage a third British ship. It is hard to say whether anyone won this part of the battle. There were no victors, just survivors.

Strategically, however, there was a clear winner and loser. The eight surviving Germans were bottled up at Narvik, with a larger British force barring their exit. The only hope for the Germans was that some external distraction would draw Whitworth away, but this was not to be. The only question, then, was what the British would do next, and when.

The second Battle of Narvik

The 'when' was three days later. On 13 April 1940, the Royal Navy entered Ofotfjord again, this time in force. In the meanwhile, significant additional forces had arrived off Vestfjord, allowing the Admiralty to pick and choose what forces they would send in. (The aircraft carrier *Furious* was one of the new ships. Attacks on the 12th and 13th by Swordfish biplanes carrying bombs were uniformly unsuccessful.) For firepower they chose the old battleship *Warspite*. To protect her and lead the way they chose four 'Tribal'-class destroyers (*Cossack, Bedouin, Punjabi* and *Eskimo*), the 'K'-class *Kimberley* and four older, smaller ships (*Hero, Icarus, Forester* and *Foxhound*), sisters or near-sisters of the 'H'-class ships that had fought on the 10th. Whitworth transferred his flag to *Warspite* and would command the force. The formation was designed to sweep the width of the narrow waters they were invading. *Warspite* would head down the middle of Ofotfjord, led by *Icarus, Hero* and *Foxhound* with sweeps deployed to counter any mines the Germans might have laid. *Bedouin, Punjabi* and *Eskimo* would lead ahead and to starboard; *Cossack, Kimberley* and *Forester* would lead to port. It was in this disposition that the British returned to Ofotfjord around noon on the 13th.

(It is more than a bit ironic that *Cossack* should be one of the ships involved in this action, because she had been in Norwegian waters before. On 16 February, she had pursued the German supply ship *Altmark* into Norwegian territorial waters. *Altmark* had been with *Admiral Graf Spee* in the South Atlantic and was carrying approximately 300 merchant seamen, mostly British, taken off the ships sunk by the German raider. *Altmark* was under escort by two Norwegian patrol boats and had already been searched by Norwegian authorities, who found nothing amiss, when *Cossack* drove her into Jøssingfjord.

Erich Giese was barely able to move when the Royal Navy returned on 13 April.
She reached the entrance to Rombaksfjord before being overwhelmed by gunfire
and forced to shore. (via Ken Macpherson)

The Norwegian boats stood aside while a boarding party from *Cossack* overwhelmed *Altmark's* crew and freed the prisoners. It was this lack of intervention by the Norwegian warships and the subsequent lack of official protest by the Norwegian government that helped convince Hitler that Norway was actively collaborating with the British and accelerated German planning for *Weserübung*.)

The Germans were in no condition to fight another battle, much less one at such bad odds. Against one battleship and nine fresh destroyers, Bey had only seven ships capable of movement (plus *Diether von Roeder* tied up at the Post Pier in Narvik harbour). To make matters worse, two ships had grounded while manoeuvering in the harbour two days earlier; one, *Erich Koellner,* was damaged to the point that she could best be used as a stationary gun platform, like *Diether von Roeder.* Bey's plan was to tie her up at the town of Taarstad on the north shore of Ofotfjord west of the harbour. The air attacks on the 12th delayed this movement until the next day and she was still creeping her way westward when the British approached. That left six ships. Only one of these, *Hermann Künne,* was fully operational, with no major damage, all guns and torpedo tubes working and capable of full speed. All the rest were hobbled to some extent:

- *Hans Lüdemann* had one gun out of action, but her flooded aft magazine had been pumped dry and her remaining guns worked.

- *Wolfgang Zenker* had also run aground on the 11th, but she was believed capable of at least twenty knots and still had a full load of eight torpedoes.

- *Erich Giese* also had a full torpedo load and had suffered no battle damage, but her main engines were still under repair on the 13th.

- *Bernd von Arnim* had patched up her five shell holes and all but one of her boilers were functional.

- *Georg Thiele* had been hit hardest in the running gun battle on the 10th, but she had four of five guns working and all but two boilers, and work continued on her powerplant.

Bey's biggest problem, besides being hopelessly outgunned and pinned into a cul-de-sac by the approaching British, was that his ships had fired off much of their ammunition on the 10th and would only be able to fight briefly before they were down to starshells and practice rounds. As the British fleet approached Ramnes, where Ofotfjord turned due east, perhaps twenty nautical miles west of Narvik, they were sighted by *Hermann Künne* patrolling near Taarstad and the alarm was raised. *Erich Koellner,* only halfway to her assigned anchorage, turned south and headed to the less satisfactory inlet at Djupvik. The rest of the Germans were in or near the harbour. *Hans Lüdemann* and *Wolfgang Zenker* had steam up and headed out into Ofotfjord immediately, followed shortly by *Bernd von Arnim*. The other two, *Erich Giese* and *Georg Thiele,* worked feverishly to get underway as well. Such as they were, the Germans came out to fight as best they could.

The result was predictable. Not only were the Germans trapped, but *Warspite's* floatplane was aloft and sending a steady stream of sightings, so that there was no hiding from the advancing British. The only surprise was that the Germans were able to exact a small price before the end.

The first to succumb was the hobbled *Erich Koellner.* The three starboard ships – *Bedouin, Punjabi* and *Eskimo* – put two or three torpedoes and innumerable shells into her and left her sinking at Djupvik. The British came on inexorably, the destroyers weaving so as to bring as many guns to bear as possible, *Warspite* adding 15in (381mm) salvoes, which mostly hit nothing, but added to the pressure pressing the Germans back towards Narvik. By 1350, the German situation was desperate. Two ships had fired off all their munitions and the rest were down to their last few rounds. All that remained was the chance to save his crews, and Bey therefore ordered his six remaining ships (not counting the immobile *Diether von Roeder)* into Rombaksfjord, the narrow, deep inlet just north of Narvik harbour.

Barely able to move, *Erich Giese* was slowly moving out of Narvik harbour when the British caught her creeping towards the entrance of Rombaksfjord.

Looking south along the shore in Narvik harbour after the second battle, all that remained was this scene of devastation. The hulls of two capsized German destroyers can be seen – the nearer is *Anton Schmitt*, the further is *Wilhelm Heidkamp*– as well as the bow of one of the many sunken merchantmen up against the shore in the background. (NHC)

Bedouin and *Punjabi* sighted her and *Diether von Roeder* tied up in the harbour and fired torpedoes, all of which missed *Erich Giese* and ran on into the harbour where they hit and damaged the Post Pier to which *Diether von Roeder* was tied. The two Germans managed to hit *Punjabi* with gunfire and inflict some damage, but this did not delay their fate. *Erich Giese* was hit repeatedly by most of the British ships and was forced to shore off the entrance to Rombaksfjord where she was abandoned. Eighty-three of her crew did not reach shore.

By 1400, four of the Germans – *Georg Thiele, Wolfgang Zenker, Bernd von Arnim* and *Hans Lüdemann* – were inside Rombaksfjord and making their way up to the narrows at Straumen, temporarily out of sight of their pursuers. The other ship, *Hermann Künne,* apparently did not hear Bey's order and proceeded alone up Herjangsfjord to the north after firing off her last rounds. She was run ashore at Trollvik, most of the way up the north shore of the fjord, and her seacocks were opened and demolition charges were set. Before these could explode, *Eskimo* approached and put a torpedo into her. The torpedo must have set off the demolition charges because the resulting explosion completely destroyed the ship, but not before her entire crew had reached safety.

Diether von Roeder continued to resist from her mooring at the Post Pier. *Cossack* nosed her way into the harbour and began trading shots with the immobile German and, somehow, came off much the worse for the exchange. Hit

The same scene as in the previous photograph seen from the south looking north. The sunken freighter carried a small gun at her bow, though it clearly did her no good. (NHC)

seven times in two hot minutes, *Cossack* was left without power or steering and she drifted to the south shore where she beached. *Diether von Roeder* had now expended all rounds and the remaining crew abandoned ship and set charges.

This now left only the four ships in Rombaksfjord. A small shallow beach at the eastern end offered a soft place to abandon doomed ships and two of them – *Wolfgang Zenker* and *Bernd von Arnim* – both without munitions, headed straight there. East of the narrows at Straumen the fjord went straight to the southeast for perhaps three miles and then turned due east for its last few miles. It was at this 'knuckle' that *Georg Thiele* and *Hans Lüdemann* took up position. The former placed herself across the fjord, her bow to the south, so all her remaining guns and torpedo tubes could bear on any British pushing past the narrows. The latter lay near the north shore facing east, her after guns bearing.

Eskimo entered Rombaksfjord at 1424, followed immediately by *Forester* and then, after a pause, by *Hero, Bedouin* and *Icarus*. Creeping along at slow speed due to smoke left by the retreating Germans, *Eskimo* did not reach Straumen until 1445. As soon as *Eskimo* nosed her way through the narrows, *Hans Lüdemann* fired off her last four torpedoes and opened fire with her aft guns. *Eskimo* shot better and soon put the German's remaining guns out of action. Satisfied that all that could be done had been done, her captain rang up slow speed and headed for the beach next to *Wolfgang Zenker* and *Bernd von Arnim. Eskimo* then switched target to *Georg Thiele* and was soon pouring a steady fire into the German. Apparently unsatisfied with the damage being done by his gunfire, *Eskimo*'s captain ordered her turned to port to allow torpedoes to be fired. This move appeared fortuitous, because it was just at that moment that *Hans Lüdemann*'s torpedoes arrived and they all passed harmlessly past *Eskimo*'s stern, which they otherwise would have hit. Unfortunately, the turn moved her into the path of *Georg Thiele*'s last torpedo, which slammed into *Eskimo* under her foremost turret, collapsing her bow.

That was effectively the last shot of the battle. Now out of munitions and rapidly taking on water, *Georg Thiele* was run aground at the knuckle and the last of the Germans was out of action. Fear of German air attack caused the British to leave several of the German ships relatively intact on the beach at the end of Rombaksfjord. The two damaged British ships limped down Ofotfjord and both would be repaired.

An empty victory

The results of this second Battle of Narvik would seem to be a resounding British victory. All eight of the German ships engaged were destroyed against two damaged British destroyers. But strategically, the British gained little from the victory. Troops were put ashore at Harstad, north of Narvik, on the 14th and *Warspite,* supported by cruisers and destroyers, returned to Ofotfjord on the 20th to bombard the German troops at Narvik. Allied forces built up rapidly and eventually numbered almost 25,000. Dietl, reinforced by sailors from the sunken destroyers and some paratroopers, never had more than 5000 under his command. Despite divided command and the daunting geography, the Allies managed to drive Dietl out of Narvik on 28 May. That proved to be the high point of the campaign. The collapse of French and British forces in Belgium forced the British to conclude that a prolonged fight for Narvik was an unnecessary distraction. The Allied forces were withdrawn with little fanfare in early June, and Dietl took Narvik back against no resistance.

Ultimately, it is hard to see the two naval battles at Narvik as being a victory for either side. The Germans sent nearly half their available destroyers on what, in retrospect, can only be seen as a suicide mission. It is virtually impossible to see how, barring a complete lack of response by the Royal Navy, Bonte's ships could have completed their mission and returned safely to Germany. The

What remained of the damaged Post Pier after the battle provided berthing for a pair of Royal Navy vessels. The one on the near side can be identified as a 'Tribal'-class destroyer. The sunken wreck of *Diether von Roeder* juts out at an angle from the far side of the pier.

British reacted, as they had to, and the Germans were trapped at Narvik, where their destruction was unavoidable. The British reaction can only be described as stumbling, particularly at first, but it was sufficient. The Germans were trapped and were destroyed.

There are few lessons to be drawn from this fight. There would be other fights in narrow waters before the end of the war, but none that resembled these battles very closely. When the Japanese sent their destroyers out into the 'Slot' in the Solomons, especially later in the campaign, it was in full awareness of the terrible odds they faced against American technical and numerical superiority. When Bonte's destroyers left Germany on 9 April, there may have been foreboding, but it was doubtful they fully understood the bleak fate that awaited them. The Japanese in the South Pacific harboured no similar illusions.

Notes

1 Sonar, a name invented in the United States during World War II in direct imitation of the word 'radar', was known as ASDIC in the United Kindgom until after that war. It is a myth, albeit an officially sponsored one, that the name ASDIC was an acronym for 'Anti-Submarine Detection Investigation Committee'. In fact, no such committee ever existed. The name derives from the Royal Navy's Anti-Submarine Division (ASD), which began working on the first primitive quartz crystal underwater sound generators in 1916. 'ASDic' was an adjective invented to describe the sounds made by these first generators. It later evolved naturally into the noun.

2 A depth charge, even with 272 kilograms of Torpex as was standard in the US Navy later in World War II, had to explode within five metres of a submarine to guarantee its destruction. Most submarines 'destroyed' by depth charges were in fact forced to the surface due to the cumulative effect of multiple, non-lethal shocks both physically to the submarine's systems and psychologically to its crew, along with battery and/or oxygen depletion caused by a sustained depth-charge attack.

3 It is well known that Hitler had the least interest in and understanding of the navy among the major branches of his armed forces. He visited ships only rarely and never spent a night afloat. Rumours persisted in Germany that Hitler was given to seasickness and would 'turn green' even on ships tied up at a dock.

4 This was a role that most navies involved in World War II found necessary for destroyers to perform. Chapter 8 describes Japanese destroyers pressed into transport duty in the Solomons. The US Navy went as far as converting older destroyers into specialised, high-speed destroyer-transports (APDs).

5 At the very beginning of the war, U-boat commanders were under orders to follow Prize Rules for any merchant ship steaming alone (ships in convoy and belligerent warships could be attacked without warning from the beginning). These restrictions were lifted in gradual steps until, by mid-October 1939, U-boats could attack without warning any ship not specifically marked as neutral.

6 In a story with remarkable parallels in the US Navy, the Germans developed a sophisticated magnetic-influence detonator for their torpedoes between the wars and, being terrified that the secret might be leaked, failed to adequately test the new torpedoes or train crews in their use. German torpedoes were subject to premature detonation and depth-keeping problems that were not completely solved until the spring of 1940. It took the Americans even longer to resolve a similar array of problems with their torpedoes.

7 The ore came from mines in northern Sweden. During warm weather, it could be moved safely down the Gulf of Bothnia to German Baltic ports, but from November through April, this route was blocked by ice and the ore was sent by train over the mountains to Narvik and shipped down the Norwegian Leads, an ice-free route mostly within Norwegian territorial waters.

8 All pre-war German destroyers were initially given a hull number – 'Z' for *Zerstörer* (Destroyer) followed by a one-up number – and were later given the names of martyrs or heroes of the Nazi party. In the rest of this chapter, they will be referred to by these names.

9 *Narvik*, p. 42. The significance of the direct order from Churchill's Admiralty should not be underestimated. It not only bypassed Whitworth but also the Commander-in-Chief Home Fleet, at that time Admiral Sir Charles Forbes, and put Warburton-Lee in a very awkward position. The equivalent in the American command structure of World War II would have been Admiral King sending direct orders to a destroyer division commander, bypassing Nimitz and Halsey.

10 *Repulse* and *Renown* both had a catapult and two aircraft, though they were rarely used. These aircraft could have been used to scout ahead of Warburton-Lee in the same way that *Warspite*'s aircraft was used just four days later, but for unknown reasons this was not done.

11 Unlike German and American torpedoes of the time, the British Mk IX torpedoes of 1940 did not have a course-change feature that allowed them to be fired on one course and then turn to another course after a preset distance. This meant that the torpedo tubes had to point at the target (or the point where the target was expected to be at the end of its run) when the torpedoes were launched. Despite the lack of this important feature, British torpedoes proved far more reliable than the more sophisticated German G7as.

Chapter 6

A Good Day Turned Bad – The Red Sea
(23 June 1940)

What happened to HMS *Khartoum* on 23 June 1940 was probably not the strangest thing to ever happen in the Red Sea. After all, there was that incident involving Moses a few thousand years earlier. But the events that day surely rank right up near the top of the list.

Khartoum was forward based at Aden (now 'Adan) under the command of Commander D T Dowler. Along with her there were the other 'K'-class destroyers of the Royal Navy's 28th Destroyer Division, including *Kandahar, Kimberley* and *Kingston,* plus various patrol craft.[1] Their job was to neutralise the Italian Red Sea squadron based at Massawa. This squadron included seven, mostly old, destroyers, plus an assortment of old torpedo boats, gunboats, patrol

One of the Italian submarines stranded in the Red Sea by the outbreak of war, RMSmg
Evangelista Torricelli was a modern and capable long-range raider doomed by lack of resources
to a brief career operating in the Gulf of Aden. Trapped on the surface by three Royal Navy
destroyers and a pair of sloops, she put up a remarkably stubborn resistance
before being scuttled in the Bab al Mandab.

craft and, most importantly, eight submarines. When war was declared between Italy and the Allies on 10 June 1940, this naval force was effectively doomed. With no land or water connection to 'metropolitan' Italy not blocked by Allied possessions, this squadron would soon run out of all necessary supplies. With the Suez Canal in the hands of the enemy and the southern entrance to the Red Sea blocked by the Royal Navy at Aden, the Italians would soon deplete their stocks of fuel, spare parts and munitions.

The most active parts of the Italian squadron were the submarines, because they, at least, could pass the straits at Bab al Mandab and operate against British shipping and warships in the Gulf of Aden. In addition to the poor material condition of these boats and the low morale of their crews, these submarines had to contend with the constant threat of methyl chloride poisoning caused by vapours leaking from their chronically malfunctioning air-conditioning systems. (Methyl chloride was a widely used refrigerant, but most countries had already banned its use in air-conditioning systems due to its known toxicity. In small quantities it caused effects not unlike alcohol intoxication, but over time, or in greater concentration, it caused paralysis and seizures.)

This was in all likelihood a factor in the sad fate of RMSmg *Galilei*. She had sortied into the Gulf of Aden right after the declaration of war and had sunk the tanker *James Stove* on 16 June, but two days later, her periscope was sighted by the destroyer *Kandahar* and the armed trawler *Moonstone* near the entrance to Aden and she was forced to the surface by two well-placed depth charges. A brief exchange of gunfire with the trawler killed the submarine's commander and eleven more of the crew and convinced the remainder to surrender. The Italians probably assumed *Galilei* would sink, but she was basically intact and largely undamaged and, after the crew was taken off, the British boarded the submarine and towed her into Aden. She was thoroughly examined and even commissioned into the Royal Navy as *X.2*. She was actively employed as a test and training boat throughout the war and not disposed of until 1946. But the most immediately useful items found on the boat were the intact codebooks, operational orders and charts, which had not been destroyed in the crew's haste to surrender.

Knowing the Italians codes and plans resulted in immediate benefit. Five days after *Galilei*'s capture, *Khartoum, Kandahar, Kingston* and the sloops *Shoreham* and *Indus* were waiting across the narrows at the Bab al Mandab as the unsuspecting submarine *Evangelista Torricelli* approached soon after dawn on 23 June.[2] She apparently had been on patrol off the French-controlled port of Djibouti the day before, just inside the Gulf of Aden, and had been damaged there by British aircraft. As a result of this damage, *Torricelli*'s ability to dive was seriously

Torricelli's captain, CC Salvatore Pelosi, would not have been faulted had he chosen to scuttle his boat when first trapped by five British warships, but he chose to fight back and held off the vastly superior enemy force for forty minutes with gun and torpedo. He was feted by his captors and awarded his nation's highest award for valour, even having a new submarine named for him in the postwar Italian navy.

impaired. Now running on the surface and vastly outgunned, CC Salvatore Pelosi would have been excused had he opted to scuttle his boat and save his crew the risk of such a one-sided battle. However, he seems to have decided to put up what resistance he could and even fired the first shot in what was to be a long and confused gun battle. Conventional wisdom is that submarines make poor gun platforms, but in a rare exception to this rule, *Torricelli*'s second shot managed to hit *Shoreham* and damaged her badly enough to force her to retire from the fight. Not satisfied with this success, Pelosi put *Torricelli* on an evasive course that baffled the gunners on the remaining British ships. He even managed to line up shots for his remaining torpedoes, though none of them hit. The running gun battle continued for forty minutes, during which the British fired off at least 700 rounds of 4.7in (119mm) and 4in (102mm) shells before one finally hit *Torricelli*'s tower and wounded Pelosi. Finally satisfied that he had done all that could have been expected, he ordered his crew on deck and the boat scuttled. She settled on the bottom near the western shore of the straits.

The sinking of Khartoum

Some accounts go into considerable detail about how the Italian crew was treated after being rescued and how Pelosi, after he was patched up, was feted at a formal dinner at Aden, attended by the admiral in charge of the Red Sea forces, at which he was praised for his skill and courage. He was considered a war hero by the Italians, being awarded the *Medaglia d'Oro al Valor Militare*, the highest award for valour, and even having a new submarine named for him by the postwar Italian military. In part this was because Italian accounts consistently credit *Torricelli* not only with damaging *Shoreham* during this gun battle, but also with sinking *Khartoum*. According to these accounts, at least one shell hit *Khartoum* amidships and started a fire at or near the after bank of five torpedo tubes or the after deckhouse, which was just aft of those torpedo tubes. The crew's efforts to put out the fire were inadequate and, after some number of hours, the fire reached the after magazines which detonated, sinking the ship. These accounts differ in details, but all agree that the loss of *Khartoum* was a direct result of a shell fired by *Torricelli*.

The only points on which British accounts of this incident agree with the Italian accounts are that: (1) *Torricelli* was sunk in a gun battle with five British ships on the morning of 23 June 1940; (2) a fire started on board *Khartoum* that same day; and (3) some hours later, *Khartoum* sank as a result of that fire reaching and setting off the after magazines. Where the British accounts differ most markedly is that they deny any connection between (1) and (2).

The most authoritative British account is a report by *Khartoum*'s captain, Commander D T Dowler, written the day after the loss of his ship. This account

One of the three destroyers that trapped *Torricelli* was HMS *Khartoum*, seen in this pre-war photograph. Smaller than the 'Tribal's, such as *Cossack*, *Khartoum* and her sisters carried one fewer twin 4.7in (119mm) mount, but compensated with a significantly heaver torpedo battery.

quite noticeably makes no mention whatsoever of there being an engagement earlier that day or any damage to *Khartoum* in the unmentioned engagement. Dowler's account begins just before noon local time, some five hours after the gun battle with *Torricelli*.

3. At 1150 an explosion took place in the starboard wing tube of the after torpedo mounting. The after body of the torpedo was seen later by Mr W J Collier, Gunner (T), Royal Navy, to be forced back against the rear door, while the circumference of the tube abreast the air vessel was blown right out. . . . The air pressure in the torpedo had been taken the previous day.

4. At the same time, the warhead was blown through the officers' galley, cutting the leads from the oil fuel gravity tank on No. 3 Gun Deck, and instantly starting a fire. The warhead then passed through No. 3 Gun Support, through the power unit of No. 3 Mounting, and out on to the quarterdeck, finishing up against the starboard TSDS winch. The warhead did not burst, proving the adequacy of the pistol safety arrangements.

5. The fire spread almost at once throughout the after lobby, with dense smoke, and the efforts to flood the after magazine and shellroom were frustrated by flames and smoke. It is almost certain, however, that the flooding valves in the after lobby were destroyed by the warhead.

6. All fire extinguishers in the ship were used but with only temporary effect. The after rising main was shattered by the warhead, while the hose connected to the starboard rising main abaft the searchlight platform was cut right through, the valve jammed open, and the handwheel blown off.[3]

Dowler then lists the meagre remaining resources for fighting the fire in an attempt to explain why the fire so quickly got out of control. A further, unexplained explosion put all but one fire hose out of commission, forcing Dowler to consider how best to position his ship with a view towards saving his crew and, while acknowledging there might be some risk to innocent bystanders, mainly towards the future salvage of the ship.

7. At the time of the original explosion and immediate outbreak of fire, His Majesty's Ship under my command was in approximate position seven miles 165° from Perim Hight [sic] Light on patrol.[4] Wind was North-west, force 2, Sea 11.[5] The ship was put stern to the wind to reduce the draught, but after thirteen minutes when it was reported to me by the Executive Officer that the fire could not be got under control, and that the after magazine and shellroom could not be flooded, I altered course for Perim Harbour at full speed on one boiler and signalled to the Police

warship with which the nation was seemingly already well supplied, the navy had to find another way to get money to build new destroyers capable of facing potential enemies. The answer was to propose the construction of destroyer leaders. As was well known to the major combatants in World War I, destroyer flotillas benefited by being led by a ship capable of housing a flotilla commander, his staff and the necessary communications equipment. This role was ideally played by a ship of the size and capability of a light cruiser, but these very useful ships were often hard to come by.[5] The British, in particular, responded by building a type of large destroyer specifically intended to have the necessary room and facilities for a 'Captain (D)'. (HMS *Broke* was an early example of the type. See chapters 3 and 4.) The US Navy, even more than most, had failed to build the number of light cruisers needed by a world-class navy. The ten light cruisers of the *Omaha* class, started in 1918, were the first new cruisers built by the United States since 1904, and would be the only ships of the type in the fleet until the first of the large *Brooklyn* class was laid down in 1935. Given that none of the *Omaha*s, needed desperately as scouts for the fleet, could be made available to act as flotilla leaders, the navy found Congress receptive to the idea of funding the construction of purpose-built destroyer leaders as a follow-on to the eight *Farraguts*.

The result was the eight ships of the *Porter* class. To conform to the rules of the London Treaty, the *Porter*s displaced 1834 tons. They were 114 metres long and had a maximum speed of thirty-seven knots. They were originally intended to carry six single 5in (127mm) guns in DP mounts, but it was correctly concluded that this was wasteful of centreline space, so the design was recast with eight 5in (127mm) guns in twin turrets. However, the only twin mounts then available allowed a maximum elevation of thirty-five degrees, meaning the main battery would not be capable of anti-aircraft fire. To make up in part for this deficit, they were fitted with two of the new quad 1.1in AA guns, as well as eight 21in (533mm) torpedo tubes in quadruple mounts. The nicely symmetrical design with super-firing turrets fore and aft and a prominent tripod mainmast gave them the appearance of small cruisers. While not designated as destroyer leaders by the navy, most were employed in this role from the beginning. When TF 16 sailed from Pearl Harbor, the flag of ComDesron 5, Captain Charles P Cecil, flew from *Porter*.

Besides *Porter*, Desron 5 nominally comprised two divisions, each of four *Mahan*-class destroyers. The *Mahan* class directly followed the *Farraguts*, which they resembled in most particulars. They differed most significantly in introducing high-temperature, high-pressure steam power plants that saved weight and room and increased efficiency, resulting in greater range – a very useful

Another destroyer in *Enterprise*'s screen on 26 October 1942 was USS *Smith* (DD 378). This view shows her three months before that battle as she emerged from a brief refit at Mare Island, 28 July 1942. She is in the common Ms 21 overall Navy Blue (5-N) camouflage scheme. She has an SC air-search radar antenna on her foremast, but her Mk 33 dual-purpose director lacks the Mk 4 (FD) fire-control radar that was often fitted at the same time. The fitting of radars during refit depended on the availability of the necessary equipment and the time to install it, both of which were often in short supply at this time in the war. (NARA)

feature for warfare in the Pacific. With two divisions of destroyers of this type, *Porter* provided escort for *Enterprise*, the new fast battleship *South Dakota* (BB 57), the heavy cruiser *Portland* (CA 35) and the anti-aircraft light cruiser *San Juan* (CL 54), as they joined with TF 17 northeast of Espiritu Santo on 24 October and prepared to meet the Japanese.

Zeroes and Avengers

Early morning scouting missions on 26 October found the Japanese fleet and the two American aircraft carriers put up as many aircraft as they could as rapidly as they could. So concerned were they about getting strikes away before the Japanese could react, that the American aircraft headed towards the enemy in three separate groups. This was not the optimal strategy, which would have been to mass all the aircraft into one strike, affording each aircraft better protection and increasing the chances of any one of them reaching the enemy intact. But a piecemeal attack was not automatically doomed to failure, as the experience at Midway had shown, when a long series of evenly spaced attacks had prevented the Japanese from mounting an early counter-strike or from effectively defending against the hammer blow when it came.

The three American strikes were heading northwest towards the last reported position of the Japanese. They totalled seventy-four aircraft, of which twenty were from *Enterprise*. One of the aircraft in the *Enterprise* group was a VT-10 TBF-1 Avenger bomber, *T-11* piloted by Lieutenant (jg) Richard K Batten. *T-11* was one of eight torpedo-carrying Avengers launched from *Enterprise* at about 0800.[6] The Japanese meanwhile had succeeded in getting a sixty-five-aircraft strike away, and they were now heading on a nearly reciprocal course. Not surprisingly, the two groups met in between, closer to the Americans than Japanese, because the latter had started twenty minutes earlier. The first American group passed unseen by the enemy, but *Enterprise's* group was sighted at about 0850 and jumped by a nine-aircraft *Chutai* of Zeroes off the light carrier *Zuiho* approximately sixty miles northwest of the American carriers.[7]

The Zeroes had a 2500-metre altitude advantage, as well as being faster and more agile than any of the American aircraft. The first dive was by a *Shotai* of three Zeroes on the lead Avenger, which was shot down, but the third fighter from that section was itself hit by *T-11's* turret gunner, AM2c Rex Holmgrin, and exploded close aboard, riddling the Avenger's tail with multiple shrapnel holes, fortunately none of them serious. And *T-11's* adventures were far from over.

Porter *makes a daring rescue*

The next pass by the Zeroes concentrated on the two tail-end Avengers, one of which was *T-11*. One of these fighters was shot down as well, also credited to Holmgrin, but the Japanese hit *T-11* hard this time. His port wing holed in multiple locations and trailing smoke, Batten dropped out of the formation and turned back towards *Enterprise*, hoping he could nurse *T-11* all the way home. Even though smoke continued to pour from the wing and the left aileron broke away, Batten managed to locate *Enterprise*, only to find that she was under attack. He circled away from the action until the surviving Japanese departed the area and then, in a lull between attacks, gratefully approached his carrier hoping to get his battered *Avenger* aboard. But when he tried lowering his landing gear only one wheel dropped and he was waved off and instructed to

The destroyer that had the sad duty of scuttling *Porter* was USS *Shaw* (DD 373), a ship that had her own interesting history. In a floating dry dock at Pearl Harbor when the Japanese attacked on 7 December 1941, *Shaw* took three bombs forward, which led to the explosion of her forward magazine, a spectacular eruption caught on film from several different angles. Her bow was rebuilt and she returned to combat in time to participate, along with *Porter*, in the Battle of the Santa Cruz Islands as part of the screen for USS *Enterprise* (CV 6). (NARA)

ditch as close as he could to one of screening destroyers. *Hornet* had been seriously damaged by the first enemy strike; *Enterprise*, as now the only available friendly flight deck, had to be selective about which aircraft to land and which to wave off.

Resigned to a watery landing, Batten circled once more at low altitude and tried to drop the torpedo *T-11* was still carrying. However, this attempt was unsuccessful. His bomb bay doors were jammed shut, probably due to the same hydraulic system damage that caused his landing gear to malfunction. Unhappy at the prospect of ditching with an extra ton of explosive deadweight aboard, he had no choice but to proceed with the water landing. He approached *Porter* at an altitude of sixty metres along her portside. Batten put *T-11* down on to the water in what was described as a near-perfect ditching, about 1500 metres from *Porter* and even closer, perhaps 500 metres, to another screening destroyer, *Shaw* (DD 373).[8] Nevertheless, the Avenger pitched down sharply on contacting the water and came to a sudden stop, so sudden that Batten was momentarily knocked unconscious when his head hit the gun sight. He came to when water started pouring into the cockpit and he joined Holmgrin and the radioman, ARM2c Joe McMullin, in the Avenger's life-raft. As they floated away from their aircraft, which rapidly sank out of sight, they breathed a sigh of relief at having survived the ditching with nothing worse than minor cuts and scrapes and they confidently awaited rescue. The time when *T-11* ditched was approximately 1000.

Rescue, in fact, came quickly – all accounts say that it took less than ten minutes for the three men to be pulled from the water – but it came with serious complications.

> The commanding officer of the *Porter*, Lieutenant Comander David G Roberts, conned his ship in the direction of the plane, ordering 'all engines back full'. The *Shaw*, which was on a parallel course to port, came right sharply, also intending to recover the personnel. The Commander of the Destroyer Squadron, Captain Charles P Cecil, ordered the *Shaw* notified that the *Porter* would recover. The latter, however, lost way more rapidly than expected. While still 100 yards or more from the plane, the *Porter* was practically dead in the water and was no longer closing the three flyers, who were manning their rubber boat.[9]

This left *Porter* stopped some distance from the life-raft while *Shaw*, still with way on, was crossing her bow from port to starboard. Seeing *Porter* slowing, the three aviators paddled towards the leeward side of the ship, its starboard side.

> At that moment the bridge reported a torpedo wake on the port bow. The wake crossed about 50 yards ahead between the *Porter* and the *Shaw*, curving to the left as it went.[10]

This lent a sense of urgency to the rescue effort, but attention was quickly drawn back to the portside by a friendly fighter that, incredibly, seemed to be firing at the destroyer. Reflexively, *Porter's* anti-aircraft gunners started firing back at the aircraft, which banked away and retired to a safe distance. Only then did a lookout on the port bridge wing figure out that the fighter – an F4F-4 Wildcat of VF-10 piloted by Lieutenant Albert D Pollock – had not been firing at *Porter*, but was in fact trying to hit a torpedo even then on course to hit the destroyer. Dead in the water, there was nothing *Porter* could do.

> As the *Porter* was endeavoring to clear the rubber boat on the starboard side, another torpedo was reported approaching on the port beam. It struck, 'shaking the ship violently and sending a column of water at least 100 feet in the air.' The *Porter* took an ominous list to starboard, finally settling on an even keel with a three to five foot increase in draft.[11]

The torpedo hit directly amidships, between the two fire rooms. Eleven officers and men were killed in the blast. The damage to the ship was substantial; the explosion and subsequent flooding put her power plant out of commission. Almost forgotten in the confusion were the three airmen bobbing alongside the ship's undamaged starboard side. Several minutes passed before their shouts attracted the attention of a sailor and a rope ladder was dropped over the side. The time was approximately 1010.

Within five minutes, another air attack was underway, and *Enterprise* and her screen were moving away at high speed, attempting to evade the attackers. Cecil ordered *Shaw* to stand by and instructed the remainder of Desron 5 to maintain their screening stations. The vigil was made more entertaining when *Shaw's* lookouts sighted a periscope 500 metres off her port bow. She proceeded to attack the suspected submarine, dropping two 135-kilogram and four 270-kilogram depth charges without any signs of success. It was soon clear, with *Hornet* mortally wounded and *Enterprise* damaged and exiting the scene at best speed, that there was no chance of saving *Porter*, which was settling towards her bow. *Shaw* was ordered to take off *Porter's* crew and sink her with gunfire, after firing two torpedoes which had failed to hit at point-blank range. This sad task was completed at 1300, and *Shaw* headed south towards Espiritu Santo with *Porter's* survivors and the three airmen.

An own goal?

Still to be ascertained was the source of the torpedo that struck *Porter*. Even today, it is not possible to be 100 per cent certain, but it is generally agreed that the official version of events — which is that *Porter* was torpedoed by a Japanese submarine — is not correct. The evidence on which the official story is based, besides the periscope sighting reported by *Shaw*, was the sighting of a torpedo's wake passing ahead of the ship before she was struck by what was assumed to be a second torpedo. Based on this and little else, it was determined that *Porter* had been torpedoed by the submarine *I-21*, commanded by *Chu-sa*

(Commander) Matsumura Kanji. One serious problem with this claim is that while *I-21*'s location at the time *Porter* was hit is not known with certainty, Matsumura reported no attacks that day, but did report making an attack more than 500 miles away at dawn the next morning, a distance that would have been impossible to traverse in the available time, even at the submarine's maximum surface speed. In fact, a search of records postwar showed that no Japanese submarine was close enough to have made an attack on *Porter* that day.

That leaves only one probable source of the torpedo that sank *Porter* – Batten's *T-11*. The Mark 13 air-dropped torpedo carried in the Avenger's bomb bay was, by the end of the war, a reliable and accurate weapon, but that was not yet true in 1942. At that stage of the war, it was prone to a high percentage of malfunctions, including circular runs. While it cannot be shown conclusively that it was the Avenger's torpedo that sank *Porter*, there are a number of reasons to believe that to be true. First, of course, is that it is the only torpedo known with certainty to have been in the water in that vicinity. Second, had it broken loose when *T-11* ditched, a not unlikely possibility, it would have started running automatically. Third, a torpedo making a circular run would explain how a torpedo's wake 'curving to the left' could be sighted passing ahead of *Porter* minutes before she was hit. Finally, the maximum running time of a Mk 13 torpedo was just under nine minutes. The amount of time that elapsed between *T-11* hitting the water and the torpedo hitting *Porter* varies in different accounts between three minutes (highly improbable given all that happened in that time) and a maximum of eight minutes, all well within the normal running time of the torpedo. None of this proves that *Porter* was sunk by the aircraft whose crew she was trying to rescue, but no other explanation fits the facts nearly as well.

An ingenious manoeuvre

As tragic as the loss of *Porter* was, it was not perhaps the most significant event to occur to Desron 5 that day. As the remainder of the squadron maintained station around *Enterprise* and added their contribution to the largely effective anti-aircraft fire around the carrier, the destroyer *Smith* (DD 378) made her own mark in the history of destroyer combat.[12] At 1125, yet another wave of attackers approached, this one composed of sixteen Kate torpedo bombers.[13] The attackers split into two groups, intent on carrying out a classic 'anvil' attack on the carrier.[14] One group of eleven Kates was broken up by the Wildcats flown by Lieutenant Stanley 'Swede' Vejtasa and his wingman. He splashed one while still five miles from the carrier, then continued firing at the rear of the Japanese

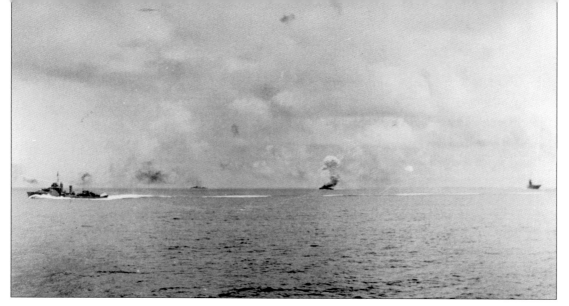

One of a series of dramatic photographs that show *Smith* (centre) immediately after being crashed by a damaged Kate, 26 October 1942. Another destroyer in TF 16 speeds to the left, wreathed in puffs of 5in (127mm) AA rounds fired from her main battery. The main object of the attackers was *Enterprise*, seen to the right in this photograph. (NHC)

formation, claiming three more aircraft. Then he went after yet another of the attackers.

Lieutenant Vejtasa pulled up and tried a low-side attack on a torpedo bomber above him but missed. He followed the plane out of the clouds and discovered that it was too high and flying too fast for an effective drop. Anti-aircraft opened up, and Lieutenant Vejtasa broke away. The enemy aircraft kept going straight and crashed into the destroyer *Smith*. There was a large explosion near No. 1 turret.[15]

The time was approximately 1145. Not only had the Kate demolished the two forward 5in (127mm) mounts, but its fuel tanks ruptured, spreading flaming avgas over the forecastle and the bridge. *Smith's* captain, Lieutenant Commander Hunter Wood Jr, abandoned the bridge and took up station at the after control station. Damage-control crews brought hoses to bear on the fire, but were driven back by a major explosion perhaps ten minutes after the crash, probably the Kate's torpedo warhead cooking off. Her power plant intact, *Smith* continued on at full speed, and Wood had no intention of slowing his ship with an attack underway. However, the wind over the bow fanned the flames and drove them aft. The firefighters were rapidly losing ground. Within minutes, they had been pushed back as far as the forward funnel. Realising he was in

Orange dated from the 1890s and was updated regularly in the years after World War I.[3] However, the navy's pre-World War II plans had not counted on fighting a war with Japan without the benefit of a battle line. America's pre-war plans, not unlike those of the Japanese, had assumed that its navy would advance across the Pacific, protected by aircraft flying from carriers or from islands conquered by amphibious assaults, but always leading up to a confrontation of battleships – a latter-day Jutland – at which the war would be decided.

But Pearl Harbor changed all that. The battle line lay in the mud. There were more ships coming, hundreds, even thousands more, but they would take a year or more to start arriving in useful numbers.[4] In the meantime, there was a war to be fought and only limited resources with which to fight. Limiting resources even more was FDR's determination to defeat Hitler first. As 1942 began, men, materiel and the shipping to transport them were being gathered for an early American involvement in the war in Europe.[5] Likewise, a significant US naval presence was retained in the Atlantic, despite the lack of a serious naval threat, at least on the surface. (Obviously, U-boats were a significant threat, but not one that would be defeated by major surface combatants. The vast US programme of building destroyer escorts (frigates) and escort aircraft carriers for the Royal Navy and for themselves was a more direct response to the U-boat threat.) Stopping the Japanese would, at least at the beginning, be a low-budget operation. So much so that the US landing on Guadalcanal, officially named Operation Watchtower, was known to the Marines on the island as 'Operation Shoestring'.[6]

Certainly, few in any of the Allied navies would have expected to be fighting in the South Pacific over an island with the strange name of Guadalcanal, but, equally, none would have expected the rapid Japanese gains in the early months of the Pacific War or the sharp reversal of that momentum at Midway. With their drive into the Central Pacific blunted, the attention of the Japanese shifted to the South Pacific. Just as the Americans were determined to prevent Great Britain's defeat by Hitler, they were equally firm in their determination to assure that Australia survived as a base from which to start peeling back the layers of Japanese conquests in Indo-China and Indonesia. Though the Allies were constrained by policy and resources to remain largely on the defensive in the Pacific, the moves by the Japanese towards the southern coast of New Guinea and into the Solomons represented a direct threat to the sea lanes to Australia and could not be ignored.

Thus US Marines were put ashore on Guadalcanal and Tulagi on 7 August 1942 and what was to be probably the most violent sustained naval campaign began. Before it was over sixteen months later, there had been two major fleet

One of the first ships to fight and be sunk in the waters that became known as Ironbottom Sound was a World War I-vintage destroyer, converted to a high-speed transport, USS *Colhoun* (APD 2). In this photograph, taken early in 1942, she appears to be painted in a curiously angular version of Ms 12 Mod. *Colhoun* was sunk by Japanese bomber off Lunga Point, 30 August 1942. A second *Colhoun* will become part of this story in a later chapter. (NHC)

engagements and at least eleven surface engagements of sufficient importance to merit a name, almost all of them in the waters christened Ironbottom Sound and the Slot. Every one of those named surface engagements involved destroyers, often playing a central role in the outcome. Three were fought only between destroyers, the rest involved cruisers and, on two occasions, battleships. Almost any of those engagements would make a fit subject for this book on destroyer actions. Since covering them all in any detail would be problematical, out of space considerations if for no other reason, it became necessary to choose a few engagements to represent them all. In the end, two were chosen, one relatively early in the sequence and one late, one between destroyers only and one also involving cruisers, one a clear Japanese victory – at least tactically – and the other also a win for the Japanese, but one that clearly shows how the Americans had learned at least some lessons in the art of destroyer combat.

The significance of Guadalcanal

By the end of November 1942, the battle for Guadalcanal had been underway for nearly four months. The only reason why the Americans were not pushed off the island was that the Japanese were taken completely by surprise, both tactically and strategically. Other than a small force of cruisers and destroyers at Rabaul, the Japanese had few forces in the region with which to repel the Marines. Even worse, they had no plan or even strategy for how to react to this situation. Even after the disaster at Midway, the Japanese were convinced that America lacked the resources to take offensive action in the Pacific, a situation that would not change until mid-1943 at the earliest.

Their analysis was essentially correct. What they had not counted on was the personality of the commander-in-chief of the US Navy, Admiral Ernest King. King was adamant on two points: that the Allies needed to move aggressively against the Japanese before the end of 1942, and that he would not allow General Douglas MacArthur to grab the initiative in the South Pacific. King

An American destroyer screening the heavy cruiser USS *Chicago* (CA 29) on 8 August 1942 moves at high speed as she puts up AA fire aimed at Japanese torpedo bombers attacking the transports that had put troops ashore on Guadalcanal just the day before. One of the attackers, a Mitsubishi G4M Betty, can just be made out to the left, just under the three puffs of flak. (NARA)

was a man of steely resolve and massive intellect, but he was a reserved man who avoided the spotlight. MacArthur, who had commanded the forces in the Philippines before fleeing from Corregidor for Australia in March 1942, could hardly have been more different.[7] Outgoing, flamboyant, publicity-seeking, MacArthur wanted any Allied moves in the South Pacific to be under his control. Only by moving fast would King guarantee that any South Pacific offensive was his and not MacArthur's. Lack of resources or adequate time for planning was not going to get in the way.

The local Japanese forces, based at Rabaul, reacted quickly to the landings. Attacks from the air began the same day and a scratch force of cruisers and destroyers won a stunning naval victory two nights later, but while these attacks succeeded in forcing the Allied assault transports to leave before they had finished unloading, they left the US 1st Marine Division in possession of the airfield at Lunga Point and a small beachhead. Against the 11,300 Marines who landed on Guadalcanal, the Japanese had 2818 men, all but 247 of them construction troops, ill-equipped to defend the airstrip they were building.[8] Possession of the airfield gave the Allies an advantage the Japanese were never able to overcome.

The Tokyo Express

While the Japanese, once they decided that Guadalcanal was worth attempting to retain, built up troop strength to the point that, on several occasions, they had about as many troops on the island as did the Americans – at least on paper – they proved unable to keep them supplied.[9] Several attempts to run supply convoys using large transports proved disastrous. (Before dawn on 15 October, the Japanese had brought six large transports down the Slot to the coast of Guadalcanal, but Marine aircraft sank three of them during the day and forced the rest to leave before they had finished unloading. An even bigger convoy in mid-November, comprising eleven invaluable large transports, was decimated by American aircraft, which sank six, damaged one and forced the Japanese to beach the remaining four near Tassafaronga as a desperate expedient.)

Clearly, a different tactic was required. They had hoped to put in place a series of transit bases spaced close enough together along the Slot that small boats or landing craft could move down from base to base, completing each leg in a single night and hiding out during the day. This was called 'Chain Transport'.[10] However, the first intermediate base, set up at Wickham Anchorage on Vangunu off the coast of New Georgia, was destroyed by aircraft flying from Guadalcanal and the idea was dropped. In its place, the Japanese *Sho-sho* (Rear Admiral)

Already a veteran of action in the South Pacific, USS *Maury* (DD 401) was third in the van group behind *Fletcher* at the Battle of Tassafaronga, 30 November 1942. As was common with US destroyer designs of the 1930s, only the forward main-battery guns had enclosed gunhouses. She is seen passing up Segond Channel at Espiritu Santo, 6 February 1943. (NARA)

Tanaka Raizo, in charge of Destroyer Squadron 2, also known as the Reinforcement Unit, reinstituted the earlier system of resupply known to the Japanese as 'Rat Transport'. The Americans dubbed these regular runs the 'Cactus Express', after the Allied codename for Guadalcanal.[11] However, this name could not be used in news stories for public consumption, so a safe alternative was concocted and almost all reports call these runs the 'Tokyo Express'.

The original 'Rat Transport', which had been operating sporadically since August, involved running fast destroyers, sometimes supplemented by seaplane tenders, down the Slot from the advance base at Buin at the southern tip of Bougainville or from Shortland Island just south of that. These ships would be loaded to the gills with troops and equipment, which inevitably interfered with their fighting capabilities. They would leave early in the day of the intended landing, head southeast at high speed either directly down the Slot or north of Choiseul and Santa Isabel, with the intent of arriving off the northern tip of Guadalcanal, Cape Esperance, an hour or two before midnight. This then gave them several hours of darkness before they had to make a high-speed exit in order to be well on their way back to a safe harbour before the first enemy aircraft could arrive from Henderson Field. During those few hours off the shore of Guadalcanal, they would attempt to unload whatever troops or cargo they carried, transferring them to shore using the destroyers' own boats and a collection of small craft and landing barges collected by the Army units on the island, a slow and inefficient process that often left a sizable portion of the cargo still on board when the time to leave arrived. Since troops were far easier to transfer than cargo, these would go ashore first and then only as much of the cargo as time allowed.

The net effect was that the 'Rat Transport' system was, by the end of November, simply unable to supply the basic needs of the troops that had been delivered to Guadalcanal. Food, medicine and munitions were all in short supply. The Japanese had enough troops on Guadalcanal to challenge the American positions, but barely half of them were in any condition to fight. Tanaka knew that a better system was required and put his considerable abilities towards solving this problem.

The solution he came up with was ingenious. As it was the end of a supply chain, not unexpectedly Rabaul had accumulated large numbers of now-empty shipping containers, including many steel drums used to ship liquids. These drums would be ideal for delivering supplies to the troops on Guadalcanal because, once cleaned and filled to about half-full with foodstuffs, they could hold about 150 kilograms of rice or barley. Best of all, when sealed, they would float indefinitely, so that it would not be necessary to go through the tedious process of loading bushels or crates individually into barges. They could be tied together to form 'rafts' of drums, pushed overboard and then pulled to shore using guide ropes. Each destroyer could carry as many as 240 drums, enough to feed the then 20,000-plus Japanese troops on Guadalcanal for a day. The actual time needed to offload that many drums was just a few minutes. The plan was for each transport-destroyer to stop only long enough to launch a boat and push its drums into the water. The boat would then carry the guide rope to shore, return to the destroyer and be recovered, a process that would reduce the time necessary to deliver supplies to a small fraction of the more conventional method. The main drawback was that this was not a practical method for delivering heavier items, such as munitions, as only trivial amounts could be packed into a drum before it would no longer float. Another disadvantage was that destroyers loaded with upwards of thirty-six tons of supplies needed to remove an equivalent amount of topweight to retain the stability necessary for high-speed manoeuvres. The only available weight was the reload torpedoes, which were landed on those destroyers designated as transports. Nor was that the only problem. A full load of drums made the training of torpedo tubes impossible, restricting the use of their most potent weapon until the drums were offloaded.

Tanaka ventures out

Eager to try out this new method, Tanaka scheduled another run of the 'Rat Transport' for the night of 30 November–1 December 1942. For that mission, the Reinforcement Unit comprised eight destroyers. Three of them were among the newest and best that Japan had to offer. The sister-ships *Naganami*, *Takanami* and *Makinami* had all been commissioned within the last few months. They were units of the *Yugumo* class, each displacing 2077 tons, carrying a main battery of six 5in (127mm)/50 dual-purpose guns in three turrets and two banks each of four 24in (610mm) torpedo tubes and capable of a speed of thirty-five knots. The five remaining destroyers were *Oyashio*, *Kuroshio* and *Kagero* of the preceding class, only marginally smaller than the *Yugumo*s, and *Suzukaze* and *Kawakaze* of the smaller, older *Shiratsuyu* class.[12]

The Japanese knew they entered the war with a navy significantly smaller than the American and that, once a war started, American industrial capability would build new ships many times faster than they could. Any hope for victory, which meant a negotiated peace that left Japan with most of her conquests in hand, rested on their ability to make any advance west of Hawaii or north from Australia so costly that the Americans would decide that the price was too high.[13] Central to this strategy was the use of aircraft and destroyers to wear away the American superiority in heavy ships.[14] To this end, the Japanese built the large 'Special Type' destroyers, of which the *Yugumo* class was the final evolution, designed to carry large numbers of the highly effective 24in (610mm) Type 93 torpedo. (Alone among the world's navies at the time, Japanese destroyers carried a full set of reload torpedoes and the necessary handling equipment. The reloading process could be carried out in less than twenty minutes by a well-trained crew.) This weapon, dubbed 'Long Lance' in postwar histories, was oxygen-powered, which meant it left no telltale trail of bubbles, and carried a large 490 kilogram warhead at thirty-eight knots over a range of almost twenty-two nautical miles or at an incredible fifty knots at half that range.[15] To exploit these ships and weapons, the Japanese developed a doctrine of night attacks taking advantage of a destroyer's speed and relatively small size. They trained their destroyer squadrons to approach at high speed, fire torpedoes at the point of closest approach while turning away and only then illuminate the target. Training emphasised the preservation of night-adaption as much as possible. For example, the Japanese only fired their guns in salvoes at night, so that lookouts could close their eyes before each salvo was fired. In contrast, American doctrine called for continuous fire once a target was found.[16] This would work only if the destroyer sighted the enemy before it was sighted. To this end, the Japanese developed excellent 'light-gathering' night optics that gave them an advantage in night encounters, at least until the quality and quantity of Allied radars tipped the scales decisively in mid-1943.[17] Together, these weapons, equipment and training gave Tanaka and his Reinforcement Unit a fighting chance against any Allied opposition they might encounter.

Tanaka flew his flag from *Naganami*, because his accustomed flagship, the old light cruiser *Jintsu*, had been damaged in an air attack on 25 August. *Naganami*, along with *Takanami*, was assigned screening duties for the remaining destroyers in the unit and therefore neither carried supply drums on their decks. The other six acted as transports. The four newer transport-destroyers carried 240 drums each; the two older ships could carry only 200 each. The four, under the command of *Tai-sa* (Captain) Sato Torajiro, were to drop their load off the coast at Tassafaronga, a small promontory along the nearly featureless northwestern coast of Guadalcanal, and the two others, under *Tai-sa* Nakahara Giichiro, were to do the same at Doma Cove, a shallow indentation perhaps five nautical miles further up the coast.

Tanaka's squadron left Rabaul on 27 November, moving by stages at night to the advanced base at Shortland Island, hoping to avoid detection by the omnipresent American scouting aircraft. They slipped out of Shortland at 2245 on 29 November, forty minutes before moonrise, hoping to be well away before their movement was noticed. Rather than take the shorter, but more closely observed, route straight down the Slot, Tanaka chose to head east into Bougainville Strait and out into the open ocean past Roncador Reef, 150 miles east of Choiseul, and then south to Ramos Island and into Indispensable Strait. This route brought him to Guadalcanal from the north-northeast. His plan was to hold this course until he reached a point southwest of Savo Island and due north of Cape Esperance and then turn toward the drop-off points. At 2245, while still west of Savo Island, *Takanami* split off from the rest of the line. Her role was to sweep ahead, looking for the Americans. The rest of Destroyer Squadron 2 continued on to the south for ten more minutes before turning to the southeast.

All of Tanaka's precautions had been in vain and he knew it. He knew that an observation plane had reported his movements as early as 0800. He did not know for sure, but must have suspected, that even before this his absence from

Shortland would have been reported by a 'coastwatcher'. He fully expected to run into opposition and planned accordingly. As the sun set, the sky was thinly overcast, though visibility was good and the clouds diminished the closer they got to Guadalcanal. The moon would not rise until after midnight. He decided on a flexible formation. The Reinforcement Unit would approach with *Takanami* slightly ahead and about a mile to the port of the remaining ships. These were arrayed in a single column, led by *Oyashio*, the flagship of Sato's Destroyer Division 15.[18] She was followed, in order, by the remainder of his division, *Kuroshio*, *Kagero* and *Makinami* (temporarily attached to Sato's command), then the overall flagship *Naganami* and the two destroyers of Nakahara's Destroyer Division 24, *Kawakaze* and *Suzukaze*. As this formation moved southeast, close in to the coast of Guadalcanal, Nakahara's two ships slowed and then stopped off Doma Cove. Each put a boat in the water to take the guide rope to the troops waiting ashore and had gun crews standing by, ready to push the supply drums overboard. *Naganami*, with Tanaka onboard, slowed just seaward and ahead of *Kawakaze* and *Suzukaze*. The four remaining transport-destroyers, with *Takinami* off their port bow, continued towards Tassafaronga. It was at this point, at approximately 2312, *Takinami* radioed that her lookouts had spotted three ships, what appeared to be destroyers, just south of east from her location. The range was estimated at six miles.

Meeting Task Force 67

The ships that *Takinami* sighted were indeed American destroyers. They were leading Task Force 67 into the middle of Ironbottom Sound. TF 67 could only be described as a scratch force and it was under a relatively inexperienced commander, Rear Admiral Carleton H 'Bosco' Wright. Not that Wright had not earned his stripes – he had come up through the ranks taking the kind of jobs expected of a surface-ship admiral in a peacetime navy – but he had never commanded ships in battle and he took over the task force from its previous commander, Rear Admiral Thomas Kinkaid, only two days before. Kinkaid himself had only been put in charge of the task force on 24 November, so Wright was its second new commander in less than a week.

Under Wright's command were four heavy cruisers armed with 8in (203mm) guns, one big light cruiser with fifteen rapid-firing 6in (152mm) guns and four destroyers. Because he was the senior of the four destroyer commanders, Commander William M Cole, captain of the brand-new USS *Fletcher* (DD 445), was put in charge of the three other destroyers: *Perkins* (DD 377), *Maury* (DD 401) and *Drayton* (DD 366). *Perkins* and *Drayton* were sisters of *Smith*. *Maury* was

Another view of *Fletcher*, Cole's flagship at Tassafaronga, as she completed her post-shakedown
yard availability, 18 July 1942. This shows the Ms 12 Mod camouflage more clearly,
with her hull painted in wavy bands of Sea Blue (5-S) over a base of Ocean Grey (5-O).
(NARA via destroyerhistory.org)

USS *Drayton* (DD 366) was the last of the four destroyers in the van group at the Battle of
Tassafaronga, 30 November 1942. She was a member of the *Mahan* class, which were built with
five main battery mounts, but in this view, taken 14 April 1942, *Drayton* has already had her
No. 3 mount replaced by a pair of 40mm twin mounts in an attempt to upgrade anti-aircraft
defence, while maintaining stability on a small hull. (NARA via destroyerhistory.org)

one of the *Gridley* class that came next after the *Mahan*s, somewhat bigger and
faster, and armed with four more torpedo tubes and one fewer 5in (127mm)
gun. *Fletcher* was lead ship of the main class of war-production destroyers for the

US Navy. They were completely freed of all treaty restrictions, so they were, compared to the *Mahan* class, bigger by more than 800 tons, faster by a knot and a half at top speed and, more importantly, by three knots at cruising speed and had, unlike almost all previous destroyers, a token amount of armour protection. The main armament of *Fletcher* was nominally similar to the *Mahans*, but they excelled in having sufficient reserve buoyancy that they were designed to carry a quad 1.1in and four 20mm mounts, later replaced on most in the class with up to five twin 40 mm and seven single 20 mm mounts.

When Wright inherited TF 67 from Kinkaid on the 28th, he also inherited Kinkaid's operations plan, which laid out how the task force would fight. The plan, completed only the day before, had thus been in effect barely three days when Wright led his task force into battle. It was not a complex plan, taking up just two typewritten pages.[19] The most important parts, in an annex covering ship dispositions during engagements stated that for 'Night Action':

1. Cruisers will form on line of bearing normal to the general bearing line, distance 1,000 yards. Destroyers will form at 4,000 yards 30 degrees on the engaged bow of the cruiser line.

2. Initial contact should be made by radar. One or more destroyer pickets will be stationed 10,000 yards in the direction of the expected contact, in order to obtain early information of the enemy. . . .

3. As soon as possible destroyers will be ordered to form and attack. It is expected that destroyer torpedo attacks will be made early in order to obtain the maximum benefits of surprise. All radar facilities may be used by destroyers, and the attack should be made on radar information insofar as possible. . . . Destroyers must clear expeditiously and in such a positive manner that there is the least possible chance of mistaken identity.[20]

This last precaution was inserted by Kinkaid because it was by then well known that there had been instances in battles already fought in Ironbottom Sound in which US destroyers had been caught between the lines of Japanese and American cruisers and had been damaged or even sunk by 'friendly fire'.[21] The only significant change Wright made to Kinkaid's plan was to rearrange his three cruiser divisions into two, because he had one fewer cruiser than Kinkaid had expected.

At 1752 on 29 November, Wright received a message from Admiral William 'Bill' Halsey, Commander, South Pacific Area (COMSOPAC), to 'Be prepared to get underway as soon as possible with all of your force present and intercept enemy destroyers and transports at Cactus night of 30–1.'[22] Wright reported that he would have five cruisers (in battle order: USSs *Minneapolis* (CA 36), *New*

Orleans (CA 32), *Pensacola* (CA 24), *Honolulu* (CL 48) and *Northampton* (CA 26)), plus the four available destroyers ready to sail at midnight. Wright's flag was in *Minneapolis*; his second-in-command was Rear Admiral Mahlon S Tisdale in *Honolulu*. The van destroyers began working their way out of the narrow Segond Channel at Espiritu Santo at 2310, the cruisers following at 2335. Once clear of the channel, they shaped course at twenty-eight knots to pass north of San Cristobol and then turned northwest into Indispensable Strait. They then proceeded south of Florida Island into the Lengo Channel, the southernmost of the three channels that led into Ironbottom Sound from the east. The uneventful passage brought TF 67 to the eastern end of the channel at 2140 on 30 November.

Coming out of Lengo Channel at the same time that Wright approached from the east was a group of three transports escorted by three destroyers, which had been ordered to clear the area in advance of the expected action. Halsey had ordered two of the destroyers, USS *Lamson* (DD 367) and *Lardner* (DD 487), to detach from the transports and join TF 67. *Lamson* was flagship to ComDesdiv 9, Commander Laurence A Abercrombie, Wright's destroyer commander and senior to Cole, but, because Wright had no opportunity to meet Abercrombie and Abercrombie had not yet seen the battle plan, he ordered the two new ships to fall in behind and conform to the movements of the cruisers, leaving Cole in charge of the van destroyers. The formation slowed to fifteen knots to perform this evolution and to traverse the narrow and treacherous Lengo Channel. The channel widens just east of Koli Point and empties into Ironbottom Sound approximately twenty-three miles east of Tassafaronga Point. The channel was cleared at 2225 and the line turned in succession to the northwest to give it more clearance from the shore to the south. Speed was increased to twenty knots. Thirteen minutes later, satisfied that he had enough leeway, the force turned west-by-north, the van destroyers in succession and the cruisers simultaneously to form a sweep line with the line of four van destroyers approximately two miles ahead and north of *Minneapolis*, which led the remaining cruisers and destroyers in a port quarterline.

Calm before the storm

The night was now clear and eerily quiet, so quiet that a witness on Guadalcanal remarked at the passage of Wright's task force offshore:

> Well, we knew they were coming, and we heard them go by. Sitting there as midnight approached, the night was so still that we could hear them go by, . . .

The SG surface search radar was a vital tool for American commanders starting in 1942, though learning how to use it was not always easy. It was the first S-band microwave radar deployed by the Americans and the first to use the PPI display. It was made possible by the British-designed magnetron tube.

I remember thinking that if we could hear them and recognize the sounds of ships' passage, the whine of blowers, if we could hear them, so also could the Japanese on their side of the island, and surely they will alert their forces. . . .[23]

The Gunnery Officer on *Maury*, third in the line of van destroyers, also remarked on the quiet beauty of the night:

It was a lovely starlit night and we had been able to smell the jungle flowers as we passed close to the Guadalcanal shore. Only the hum of the Forced Draft Blowers and the gurgle of the wake broke the silence as all hands strained their eyes to extract the enemy from the blackness.[24]

First radar contact was made at 2306 by *Minneapolis*'s SG set, when two 'pips' broke free from the background clutter of the Guadalcanal shoreline slightly starboard of straight ahead at a range of eleven miles.[25] Radar gave the Americans a crucial advantage of six minutes before they would be seen by the enemy. The question was whether Wright and Cole would be able to put that advantage to good use.

Two minutes passed while Wright confirmed the contact and then, at 2308, it was reported by TBS to the task force: 'Two Bogies very close to reference point Baker.'[26] At the same time, Wright ordered a turn four points (forty-five degrees) to starboard. Again the van destroyers turned in succession and the remaining ships turned simultaneously, which had the effect of bringing the cruisers back into line-ahead, all now on a course paralleling Tanaka's. Two minutes later, *Fletcher*, the leading destroyer, also picked up the same contact on her SG radar. Cole continued to track these targets for six more minutes as they resolved into five individual returns on his PPI screen, four in a line just over a mile off the shore and the fifth another half mile to the northeast directly abreast the second of the four ships in line. These were Sato's four transport-destroyers – *Oyashio*, *Kuroshio*, *Kagero* and *Makinami* – heading towards Tassafaronga, with *Takanami* further from shore.

It was now 2316.[27] By now, four minutes had passed since the American van destroyers had been seen by lookouts on *Takanami*. These lookouts had by now spotted more of Wright's formation and were reporting seven American destroyers in sight. Realising he was in for a fight, Tanaka ordered the supply operation aborted and all ships to attack. On the six destroyers carrying drums of supplies, this would not be easy. At exactly the same time, Cole, in *Fletcher*, requested permission from Wright to fire torpedoes. His radar showed Sato's Division 15 at a range of three and a half miles and broad on his port bow. A near perfect setup.

A missed opportunity

What happened next is difficult to explain. Wright received Cole's request and consulted his own radar operator, who reported the range to the targets was more than seven miles. To Cole's consternation, Wright replied: 'Range on our bogey is excessive, 14,600 yards.'[28] In the heat of the moment, Wright apparently failed to take into account that Cole was more than two miles ahead of *Minneapolis*, meaning that a distance that appeared excessive from the leading cruiser would be seen as a perfect high-speed setup from *Fletcher*. Wright then queried Cole whether he had the targets on his radar, to which Cole replied: 'Affirmative. Range is all right for us.'[29] Incredibly, three more minutes passed before Wright radioed his permission to fire at 2320. As those slow minutes passed, Cole had watched the firing solution for his torpedoes change from ideal to sub-optimal, as the enemy destroyers passed on the opposite heading. At 2322, *Fletcher* fired a full salvo of ten torpedoes at a target already aft of his beam, meaning it had to be a slow-speed 'overtaking' shot, the hardest kind of shot to hit. The next in line, *Perkins*, fired eight torpedoes at the same time and at the same targets. *Drayton*, the last of the van destroyers, had picked up additional targets to the northwest of those being tracked by *Fletcher* and *Perkins*. These, however, caused considerable confusion because they were tracked as being stationary. Unsure that these were real targets and not a shore feature, *Drayton* fired only two torpedoes. (In fact, *Drayton's* SG was working correctly. Two of the three targets she was tracking were *Kawakaze* and *Suzukaze* which were in fact stationary at that time. The other would have been *Naganami*, which was moving slowly.) *Maury*, the third in line, had no SG radar and was unable to locate a target. She did not fire any torpedoes. Cole reported the firing of torpedoes to Wright with the message: 'Affirm William.'[30] As soon as this was received by Wright, he ordered all ships to open fire. The time was approximately 2323.

Doctrine called for the cruisers' main batteries to be the primary weapon for the destruction of the enemy. The cruisers' secondary batteries were to provide illumination by star shell. Destroyers were to join in with their main guns only when they did not impede the fire of the cruisers. Being well ahead, the van destroyers maintained course, and, once the cruisers opened fire, added their contribution to the cascade of ordnance heading towards the Japanese. This lasted perhaps three minutes. According to *Fletcher's* Action Report:

> The ship stood on at 25 knots, followed closely by destroyers van, and a short opportunity was afforded to observe the battle. No enemy ships could be seen. Illumination was fairly good in front of what appeared to be a wall of splashes from our gunfire. Torpedoes had not yet had time to reach the targets, . . . At about 2326 a salvo of three splashes was seen about 100 yards ahead of the ship, followed by another salvo 200 yards on the port beam.[31]

This was enough to convince Cole that his ships were in danger and he followed doctrine, turning away to a course just west of north a minute later. *Fletcher* was followed by the other three van destroyers. This essentially ended their contribution to the active engagement. Their course was taking them directly towards Savo Island, so *Fletcher* bore left at approximately 2331 so they would clear to the west of the island. Having picked out a target heading northwest away from Cape Esperance, *Drayton* fired four torpedoes at extreme range at 2337. The target could only have been *Naganami*, which was in that general area and heading in that direction at that time. Like all the other American torpedoes fired that night, they missed.

The rear destroyers had minimal impact on the battle. *Lamson*, which lacked an SG, could find no targets and contented herself with firing starshells. *Lardner*, which did have the advanced radar, picked up a target and managed to fire perhaps half a dozen rounds before losing it again. This participation was

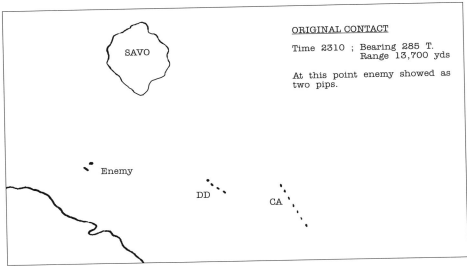

The first of a series of three sketch maps included by Commander William Cole in his action report after the Battle of Tassafaronga, 30 November 1942. On *Fletcher*, which was equipped with SG radar, Cole had as clear a tactical picture as anyone that night. His van group is labelled 'DD', the five cruisers and the two trailing destroyers are labelled 'CA' and the enemy – of which only two have so far been detected – is off to the west. This shows the situation at 2310, when *Fletcher*'s radar first made contact. (via destroyerhistory.org)

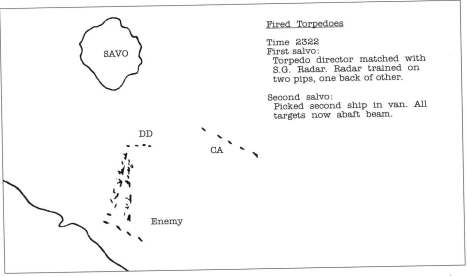

By the time the van destroyers fired their torpedoes, twelve minutes after the first contact, the five enemy 'pips' showing on the PPI were already past *Fletcher*'s beam. This was now an overtaking shot with a low probability of success. (via destroyerhistory.org)

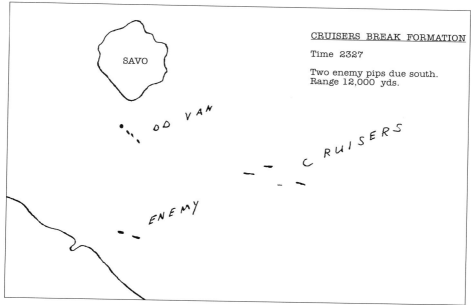

CRUISERS BREAK FORMATION

Time 2327

Two enemy pips due south.
Range 12,000 yds.

SAVO

OD VAN

CRUISERS

ENEMY

Five minutes later, the van destroyers have already disengaged and have begun to pass up the west side of Savo Island. The cruisers are now a confused group of four contacts in no particular formation to the east. Only two enemy contacts are showing up on *Fletcher's* radar. While Cole's orders were clear – to fire his torpedoes and then clear the cruisers' line of fire – it is difficult to understand why he continued up the far side of Savo Island while Wright was actively engaged behind him. (via destroyerhistory.org)

brought to an abrupt end when they were taken under fire by the secondary battery of *Northampton*, the trailing cruiser, and they exited to the east, also playing no further role in the action.

The Japanese response

Takanami, the closest destroyer to the American line, fired a full salvo of eight torpedoes at the largest of the targets she was tracking and then turned sharply away to starboard, towards the shore, away from the American line. As best as can be ascertained, this happened at 2322, exactly the same time that Cole's destroyers were firing their torpedoes and a minute before the American cruisers opened fire. That turn away was intended to move *Takanami* out of harm's way while her crew began the hard work of reloading torpedoes. It did not have the desired effect. Standing, as she did, apart from the rest of the targets, *Takanami* attracted fire from most of the American ships. It is reasonably certain she was fired at by all five cruisers, plus *Perkins* and *Maury*.[32] The effect was rapid and cumulative, as the first hits started fires, which only served to attract even more gunfire. She was soon reduced to a shambles and she drifted, on fire along her whole length, between the two forces. So rapidly had devastation overtaken the destroyer that she was unable to report her condition and Tanaka remained unaware of her plight.

The rest of the Japanese formation was in apparent confusion, but this was more appearance than reality. Japanese destroyer-men were trained to take the initiative and to operate in sub-units or independently, so what might have appeared to be chaos was in fact an effective attack on the American line. It was contrary to doctrine for a destroyer captain to wait for permission to fire. It is simplest to detail the movements of the Japanese destroyers in outline form, all the action starting at 2316 with Tanaka's order to attack:

Naganami – Ahead and to port of Nakahara's transport-destroyers off Doma Cove, Tanaka's flagship turned south away from the Americans and, turning through around 220 degrees and picking up speed, settled on a north–northwest course directly towards the centre of the line of cruisers. She closed to approximately four miles and then turned a point to the left and fired all eight torpedoes, probably at *Pensacola*. The time was approximately 2332. *Naganami* came under heavy fire from the cruisers, particularly *Honolulu*, but was not hit and suffered nothing worse than holes punched in her after funnel by shell fragments. She continued northwest and out past Cape Esperance into the Slot.

Kawakaze and *Suzukaze* – Nakahara's destroyers were stopped when they received Tanaka's order at 2316. Each had a boat in the water, but had not yet started unloading drums. Faced with the immediate need to get underway, they had no choice but to abandon the boats. Both captains decided that it would take less time to push the supply drums overboard than to wrestle them out of the way of the torpedo tubes, so the 400 drums were unceremoniously dumped and the ships got underway as rapidly as they could. *Suzukaze* appears not to have fired her torpedoes, though the reason is not clear.[33] It is most likely that when she was setting up to fire at the American cruisers, at approximately 2328, she was forced to turn away when she sighted *Drayton*'s two torpedoes fired at 2322, and was never able to regain a good firing solution. *Kawakaze*, however, was not forced to turn away and fired a full salvo of eight torpedoes at 2328 at the line of American cruisers. The two destroyers continued to the northwest, somewhat ahead of *Naganami*, exiting Ironbottom Sound.

Oyashio and *Kuroshio* – These two destroyers led Sato's Division 15 down the coast towards Tassafaronga. Sato did not immediately turn when he received Tanaka's order to engage, but continued southeast at slow speed until 2328, when *Oyashio* and *Kuroshio* turned due east in an attempt to get a clear view of the Americans past the burning *Takanami*. Just as they were turning, *Kuroshio* fired two torpedoes at a range of almost seven miles at the cruisers. It was ill-advised, as it was an overtaking shot at a target heading away at twenty knots. *Oyashio* refrained from firing torpedoes at that time. Instead, Sato led the two destroyers in a turn to starboard that continued past 180 degrees until the two destroyers were heading northwest, paralleling the coast. At 2339, after the two destroyers had been on this course for eleven minutes, *Oyashio* fired a full salvo, probably at *Pensacola*. Six minutes later, still on the same course, *Kuroshio* fired four more torpedoes, most likely also at *Pensacola*. The two destroyers then also exited Ironbottom Sound, probably not far behind *Kawakaze* and *Suzukaze*.

Kagero and *Makinami* – These two were in Sato's line behind *Oyashio* and *Kuroshio*, and continued east for another minute after those two turned. They altered course exactly 180 degrees rather than the approximately 225 degrees the others had turned, and they continued west until they approached within half a mile of the coast and only then turned northwest and then again a few minutes later to a course of north-northwest that brought them across the tracks of the other destroyers. At 2352, *Kagero* sighted *Pensacola* and fired four torpedoes at her, but all appear to have missed. *Makinami* was having trouble clearing the supply drums from the way of her torpedo tubes and was unable to fire any torpedoes. The two then continued on past Savo Island and out of Ironbottom Sound.

The departure of these last two ships left the derelict *Takanami* as the only Japanese ship left in Ironbottom Sound. Tanaka gathered his seven survivors northwest of Savo Island shortly after midnight and only then confirmed the absence of *Takanami*. *Oyashio* and *Kuroshio* were sent back into the sound to aid *Takanami* and escort her out or, failing that, rescue survivors. At 0040 on 1 December, they spotted *New Orleans* heading towards Tulagi, and *Kuroshio* launched her two remaining torpedoes, but both missed. At 0115, they came alongside *Takanami*, smoldering and adrift, and were preparing to take off her crew when an American warship was sighted, most likely *Fletcher*, which, along with *Perkins*, was searching for survivors southeast of Savo Island. *Oyashio* and

Kuroshio abandoned their rescue attempt and sped away to the northwest, following Tanaka, who was leading the other five destroyers back towards Rabaul. One hundred and ninety-seven of *Takanami's* crew died. Forty-eight survivors reached shore on Guadalcanal, of which nineteen were captured by the Americans.

A dramatic climax

This leaves only the fate of the American cruisers as yet undescribed. At the time they opened fire, at 2323, they were in a line-ahead formation heading approximately west-northwest (actually 300 degrees, which is eight degrees north of west-northwest). They were led by *Minneapolis* (with Wright on board), followed by *New Orleans*, *Pensacola*, *Honolulu* (flying Tisdale's flag) and *Northampton*. When fire was opened, *Minneapolis*, *New Orleans* and *Northampton* were targeting *Takanami*, with quick success, while *Pensacola* fired at *Naganami*.[34] Lacking an SG, the only one of the cruisers not so equipped, *Pensacola's* gunners believed she had also scored rapidly and her target exploded and sank. Believing they had polished off *Takanami*, the gunners on *Minneapolis* and *New Orleans* switched to other targets, shooting at *Kawakaze* and at a pair of beached transports. *Honolulu* took her time sorting through the confusing radar picture,

The damage that could be caused by a Japanese Type 93 torpedo was truly impressive. The heavy cruiser USS *New Orleans* (CA 32) ran into one at the Battle of Tassafaronga that hit below turret No. 1, ignited the magazine and broke off her bow just forward of turret No. 2. Only the presence of that turret's barbette served to protect the ship further aft from most of the effects of the explosion. (NARA)

Same battle, similar damage, different ship.
This is USS *Minneapolis* (CA 36), which took
a torpedo further forward, so that her bow
collapsed in front of No. 1 turret, but did not
break off as *New Orleans'* had. This photograph,
dated 1 December 1942, shows her after
the collapsed bow has been cut away. (NARA)

waiting a full five minutes after Wright started shooting before she too opened
up on a target, probably also at *Naganami*. Even before she opened fire, though,
dramatic events were occurring further up the line.

At 2327, a huge column of fire and smoke surged skyward from under
Minneapolis's bow, drenching all on her bridge when the plume of water crashed
down. Seconds later a second explosion amidships made the cruiser lurch as if
she had run aground. The first torpedo blew out her bow structure, causing her
forecastle forward of No. 1 turret to collapse, leaving her bow hanging deep in
the water, pushing her over to starboard. The explosion ignited avgas storage in
her bow, starting an intense fire. The second torpedo hit amidships abreast fire
room No. 2, flooding three adjacent fire rooms, dropping her speed to a crawl.[35]
So sudden and unexpected were the explosions that the ships in line aft of
Minneapolis did not comprehend the seriousness of the situation, and, to make
matters worse, for a critical three minutes *Minneapolis* lost all radio
communication, so Wright could not inform the remaining ships of his plight.
New Orleans, immediately aft, saw *Minneapolis* stagger to starboard and slow, and
her captain ordered hard right rudder to clear. The order had barely been given
when she too staggered under a hard blow. A huge explosion under her No. 1
turret caused her bow all the way back to her second main battery turret to tear

away. Almost thirty-six metres of her bow floated free, scraped along her portside, taking chunks out of her shell plating and knocking a blade off her port screw before disappearing into the dark. A torpedo had apparently struck her directly under her forward turret and set off the contents of magazine groups 1 and 3, including a number of 100lb (45kg) bombs intended for her scouting aircraft. *New Orleans*, like *Minneapolis*, staggered out of line, also to the right. The three torpedoes that knocked out two cruisers had been launched by *Takanami* before she was overwhelmed.

The next cruiser aft, *Pensacola*, now had two disabled ships blocking her path ahead and to the right, and did the only thing she could do, turning hard left to avoid a collision and then as quickly back to the base course of west-northwest. It was now approximately 2330, and *Pensacola* was briefly silhouetted against the fires burning brightly on *Minneapolis* and *New Orleans*. That was all the torpedo-men on *Naganami* needed. They were able to get an accurate reading of the cruiser's range and speed and put their torpedoes in the water three minutes later. *Pensacola* obligingly maintained the same course and speed for the next five minutes and at 2338, she staggered under a terrific blow in way of her mainmast. The blow flooded three of four fire rooms and engine rooms, leaving her barely able to maintain steerageway, and, worse, spread a thick coating of bunker oil over her mid-section which began to burn with flames reaching higher than her mainmast. She, too, was out of the fight.

When *Pensacola* had gone to port to avoid *Minneapolis* and *New Orleans*, *Honolulu* had the room to turn away to starboard and she and *Northampton* behind her cleared to starboard on the disengaged side. Rear Admiral Tisdale was now in effective command of the American forces, but he was rapidly exiting the arena hot on the heels of Cole's destroyers. Seeing the havoc to port, *Honolulu* steadied on the base course again after heading north for more than a mile and increasing speed to thirty knots. Unable to find targets with her SG or visually despite firing multiple star shells, *Honolulu* stopped firing at 2336. By 2345, she had cleared the southern tip of Savo Island and turned northwest and then north at midnight.

The last cruiser in line, *Northampton*, followed *Honolulu*'s lead, turning right to clear and then back to the base course somewhat further north than the light cruiser. Unaware of *Honolulu*'s increase in speed, *Northampton* quickly fell behind and, finding herself alone and on course to hit Savo Island, turned left at about 2339 to 280 degrees, west-by-north. She maintained this course for nine more minutes, searching for, but not finding, targets for her big guns. At the same time that she made her last course change, *Oyashio* launched a full salvo of eight torpedoes, most likely aiming at the huge fire just erupting on

Pensacola. If that was her aiming point, she missed her target, but the torpedoes continued on for two more miles and, at 2348, one or two hit *Northampton* in her port quarter, abreast her mainmast. She heeled to port and lost way, but one engine room remained undamaged and she was soon moving at slow speed towards Tulagi.

Thus, of five cruisers, four were now limping eastward in varying degrees of disablement, and the remaining American ships were scattered and had little idea what had transpired, except they knew that it was not good. Typical was the description of events recorded by Crenshaw on *Maury*:

> A volcano erupted astern! A column of fire rose vertically from the water a thousand feet into the sky. A moment later another column of fire rose beside it. Our cruisers were blowing up! We couldn't make out any details, but something terrible was happening. Cole increased speed to 35 knots as we swung around Savo Island and its shadow masked the burning debris from the first two explosions, a renewed 'bridge' of red tracers reached from behind the island toward Cape Esperance – *Honolulu*'s fifteen 6in [152mm] guns, no doubt. At least she was still alive! Then the sky lighted up with the greatest explosion of all. It was behind Savo Island from us, but the sea all around was bathed in the glare. Something big had happened, but it was on the other side of Savo.[36]

As the van destroyers continued around Savo Island, they were largely ignorant of what had happened to the other ships in the task force. Ships had exploded behind them, most likely American cruisers, but they did not know which ones or whether they were still afloat.

> As we came around the north side of the island and headed back to join the fray, Cole divided us into two sections, and turned south towards Guadalcanal. We were in the traditional Search and Attack formation; *Fletcher* and *Perkins* to the east, *Maury* and *Drayton* 3000 yards to the west. We probed southward at a cautious 15 knots searching for the enemy and trying to get our bearings. There were several fires on the water in the direction of Cape Esperance, but we couldn't identify any of them. We were still north of the battle area when, suddenly over the TBS came orders: 'DESTROYERS VAN JOIN HONOLULU'. So at least we still had one cruiser, but where? Cole reversed our sweep to take us north of Savo, but finding no cruiser there, he took us back towards the battle area to make sure there were no Jap ships left there. We still had about 10,000 yards to go to reach the original position of the Jap Force when Admiral Tisdale in *Honolulu*, who had taken over from Admiral

Wright, ordered 'SMALL BOYS STAND BY DAMAGED BIG BOYS'.
Maury and *Perkins* were ordered to stand by *New Orleans*, 'TEN MILES EAST
OF SAVO'. It was a strange order, considering our formation, and from an
unseen commander.[37]

More wrecks for Ironbottom Sound

Besides *Honolulu* and the four van destroyers, Ironbottom Sound was now the
province of the crippled and the sinking. *Minneapolis* had at first headed for
Lunga Point on Guadalcanal because her captain, Captain Charles Rosendahl,
uncertain of her ability to remain afloat, wanted to beach her along an
American-held shore. However, good progress by damage-control parties
caused him to change plans, and, at 0200, he turned her towards Tulagi, eighteen
miles to the north. Able to make three knots and with flooding forward under
control, she crept slowly across the width of the sound. At 0254, she was joined
by *Lamson* and *Lardner*, which had been recalled, and then later was assisted by

Minneapolis had the misfortune to find a second torpedo, which left this gash in her portside
under the narrow armour belt. A torpedo bulge did nothing to prevent the flooding
of three fire rooms. This photograph shows *Minneapolis* under repair, after
most of the damaged shell plating had been cut away. (NARA)

the tug *Bobolink* (AT 131) to Sasapi on the northern shore of Tulagi, where she was secured to coconut trees ashore and covered with camouflage netting. Amazingly, she lost only thirty-seven men.

New Orleans was far more badly damaged and lost 183 of her crew, many of them from the forward turrets. She was able to maintain a speed of five knots and reached Tulagi just before dawn. However, with no bow, she had no way of anchoring, so *Maury* tied up alongside and provided her anchors and stability. *Pensacola* lost 125 officers and men. She was able to steam relatively well and reached Tulagi at 0344, shepherded by *Perkins*. She was still burning when she dropped anchor in the harbour and it was twelve hours before the fire was completely extinguished.

Northampton was not as lucky. With *Fletcher* and *Drayton* standing by, her crew fought progressive flooding without much success. By 0115, her list had reached twenty-three degrees. Worse, she was drifting near enough to Doma Cove that shore-based artillery was getting uncomfortably close. At 0130, all but a salvage crew was ordered off, to be picked up by the two destroyers and those last men were taken off at 0200. An hour later, *Northampton* turned turtle and added her contribution to Ironbottom Sound. Fifty officers and men were lost; 773 were rescued by *Fletcher* and *Drayton*.

The Battle of Tassafaronga should have been a learning experience for the Americans. Certainly, they arrayed a far more powerful force against the enemy and had the advantage of advanced radars that allowed them to fire torpedoes and guns without ever seeing the enemy. Despite this, the Americans came off the loser, at least from a tactical perspective. That very little was in fact learned from the experience was due to two factors. One was the inherent uncertainty involved in any night action. This is true even today, and was definitely the case on the night of 30 November–1 December 1942, despite the excellence of the American radars. (Eight out of the eleven US Navy ships engaged that night had SG radar.) Not having radar, the Japanese had to rely on training, discipline and excellent optics to spot enemy targets. Japanese lookouts did as well as could be expected, correctly noting that they had hit four American ships. Some were misidentified as battleships and all four were claimed as sunk, but those are understandable mistakes. Less easy to understand was Wright's claim, made in his Action Report, submitted eight days after the battle, that the Japanese force had comprised between thirteen and fifteen ships – four cruisers and the rest destroyers – and that the Americans had probably sunk two light cruisers and seven destroyers.[38] When Nimitz got his hands on this report, and was able to compare it to intelligence data unavailable to Wright, he trimmed the claim to four destroyers sunk and two more damaged out of a Japanese flotilla of eight.[39]

Temporary repairs to *New Orleans* at Tulagi allowed her to steam to Sydney, where further work included removing the guns from No. 2 turret to lighten her forward and the fashioning of the new stub bow seen here, sufficient to allow her to steam to Puget Sound, arriving there in March 1943. (NARA)

More distressing was the failure of the Americans to appreciate the quality of the men or materiel they were fighting. It was inconceivable to Wright – and this misapprehension was not corrected anywhere up the 'endorsement chain' – that all four of the American cruisers had been hit by torpedoes fired by Tanaka's destroyers. He accepted that *Minneapolis* and *New Orleans* had been hit by Tanaka's torpedoes, but thought it highly unlikely that the same was true for *Pensacola* and *Northampton*. Instead he hypothesised:

> That undetermined vessels to the westward of our position, perhaps cruisers trying to escape, or perhaps a submarine or submarines fortunately placed, fired long range torpedo shots which hit the PENSACOLA and NORTHAMPTON merely through luck, since the maneuvers performed by those vessels in clearing our damaged ships could not have been predicted when the torpedoes were fired.[40]

The reason he believed this to be true was simple. He could not conceive of torpedoes with the characteristics of the Japanese Type 93:

> . . . the observed positions of the enemy surface vessels before and during the gun action makes it seem improbable that torpedoes with speed-distance

characteristics similar to our own could have reached the cruisers at the time they did if launched from any of the enemy destroyers or cruisers which were observed to be present.[41]

It would be well into 1943 before captured examples of the 'Long Lance' were analysed and their true capabilities understood.

Equally baffling is why the Americans believed they had sunk so many of the Japanese, whether the total was Wright's nine or Nimitz's four. With their excellent SG radar, should not the Americans have been able to accurately determine the effect of their gunfire? The answer, sadly, is no, in part because American radar-men were not yet very experienced with this new and powerful equipment, and therefore they and their commanders were insufficiently aware of the radar's limitations. In practice, the 'God's-eye view' given by the PPI display was seductive, leading operators and officers to believe that what they were seeing was real, but in two critical ways, the SG picture was misleading. Despite having a narrow three-degree beam width with almost non-existent sidelobes, the radar could not discriminate between objects that were close together or were manoeuvering rapidly, so that the radar picture seen by the SG operators tended to under-count the number of enemy ships. This was more than offset by the other problem. As soon as the Americans opened

U.S.S. DENVER P.P.I.
MAR.6-43 TIME 0100½
KULA GULF, NEW GEORGIA
#2

Part of the difficulty in learning to use the SG radar properly was that the PPI display was deceptive, in that it appeared to show more than it actually did, and only an experienced operator could decipher what was really being displayed. An example is this capture of the SG display aboard the light cruiser USS *Denver* (CL 58) in Kula Gulf, 6 March 1943. In narrow waters, it was easy to mistake shore features for groups of ships. (NARA) fire, the screen was filled with the radar returns from shell splashes, which were impossible to discriminate from the returns from ships. Just as a lookout's view of the enemy would be obscured by the splashes of shells falling short when the scene was illuminated by star shells drifting above the battle, the radar operator's view of the scene would be similarly affected by 'shorts'. It was easy to get lured into 'chasing splashes', a situation in which the returns from a shell splash would become the target for the next salvo. Successive salvoes would be targeted at a fixed point while the enemy was moving away. To make matters worse, when the target had moved far enough to show up as a separate return on the radar, it served to multiply the number of enemies believed to be present, and at the point when a ship stopped firing at its own shell splashes and switched to another target, the shell-splash 'target' would magically disappear, leading to the mistaken belief that the false target had been sunk. This explains not only the fact that Americans believed they were fighting and sinking so many enemy ships, but also the fact noted by the Japanese that the Americans were frequently off in deflection, firing at the spaces in between the Japanese destroyers, and not following them as they moved. There were lessons to be learned about the use and misuse of radar, which eluded the Americans at the time and, seen with twenty-twenty hindsight, still eluded them twenty-two years later.[42]

Tanaka emerged from this battle lionised by the Americans, but he was soon transferred to shore duty and never led ships into battle again. Described by Morison as 'foxy', 'tenacious' and 'resolute', his various supply missions in fact failed to keep even a minimal level of sustenance flowing into Guadalcanal and failed to satisfy his superiors.[43] Wright went on to be awarded the Navy Cross for his actions at Tassafaronga and later commanded cruisers again in the Central Pacific. The man who unaccountably was made the scapegoat for the American losses in this battle was William Cole. He was summarily relieved of command of *Fletcher* two weeks after Tassafaronga and was blamed in Halsey's endorsement of Wright's report for many of the mistakes in that battle. He nevertheless went on to command a division of destroyers and retired from the US Navy in 1954 as a Rear Admiral.

Cause for Allied optimism

In the ten months that passed between the Battles of Tassafaronga and Vella Lavella, the world had dramatically changed. By the beginning of October 1943, the situation in Europe and in the Atlantic, which had seemed dire in late 1942, was now showing improvement. The German drive to the east had been blunted at Stalingrad and the Russians were now pushing them back all along

La Vallette, seen sometime in 1944, shows the profile of a typical mid-war *Fletcher*-class destroyer. Besides the five main-battery mounts, she had five twin 40mm mounts (two side-by-side in front of the bridge, one on either side of the after funnel and one on her after deckhouse) and seven single 20mm mounts. Her radar fit was an SC-2 at the top of her foremast, an SG on the small platform just below and a Mk 4 (FD) on her main battery director. (NARA via destroyerhistory.org)

their broad front. The Allies were ashore on the Italian peninsula, and Italy was out of the war. The crucial Battle of the Atlantic had swung decisively in the Allies' favour in May 1943. Less dramatic progress had been made in the Pacific, but still the Allies had reason for satisfaction.

It would have been hard to recognise the naval battle in the Solomons as the same see-saw affair fought by the likes of Wright and Cole in late 1942. Guadalcanal was evacuated by the Japanese in early February 1943, solely because of their inability to keep their troops on the island supplied. The losses in men were appalling – of more than 36,000 Japanese soldiers and sailors to serve on the island, barely 10,000 made it out alive. The Japanese lost eighteen surface combatants during the Guadalcanal campaign, eleven of them destroyers. The Allies lost twenty-five warships, including fifteen destroyers, but they could make up the losses much more easily and, most importantly, now dominated the waters around and the air over the Solomons.

The Japanese tried to build up forces in the Central Solomons, building airfields at Munda on New Georgia and at Vila on Kolombangara, and they established a staging base for barge traffic on the east coast of Vella Lavella. A series of sharp naval engagements were fought in the waters around these islands, starting in March 1943. The Allies continued sending cruisers into these waters, though now they were limited to light cruisers, the losses at Tassafaronga finally convincing Halsey that heavy cruisers were too valuable to send against destroyers. When *Helena* (CL 50) was sunk at Kula Gulf on 6 July and three more cruisers were seriously damaged at Kolombangara a week later, the Allies finally learned that these waters were too narrow for ships of this size and value and tried just sending in destroyers. Finally freed from the necessity to protect cruisers, American destroyers showed that they had learned a few lessons in night fighting at Vella Gulf on 6–7 August 1943. Commander Frederick Moosbrugger, ComDesdiv 12, led his division and a second into the strait between Kolombangara and Vella Lavella to intercept a force of four Japanese destroyers en route to Vila with 950 troops and fifty-five tons of supplies. Moosbrugger used his advantage of radar and an inshore position, which made his ships virtually invisible against the dark background of Kolombangara, to get off a full salvo of twenty-four torpedoes before the Japanese even knew the Americans were there. Only when the torpedoes reached their targets did Moosbrugger give the order to open fire with guns. For once, the Mark 15 torpedo worked as designed. Three of the four Japanese destroyers were hit and sunk; the fourth fled at high speed.

Japanese withdrawal

The Japanese realised that they were again losing irreplaceable destroyers trying to maintain isolated garrisons at too great a distance from their main base and without adequate air cover, and again they decided to pull out. Munda had already been lost, but Vila was evacuated and now, at the beginning of October, the only troops south of Bougainville were a garrison of some 600 men at Horaniu on Vella Lavella, only ninety miles from Buin. The plan devised by Japanese *Sho-sho* Ijuin Matsuji for the night of 6 October was typically complicated. Six destroyers in two separate groups would cover a further three old transport-destroyers and a scratch force of sub-chasers and landing craft tasked with picking up the troops.[44] The destroyers left Rabaul the morning of the 6th and headed south along the eastern side of Bougainville under heavy overcast and intermittent rain showers, but they were tracked by radar-equipped aircraft. Aware that they had been spotted, Ijuin took the four destroyers under his direct command straight on towards the embarkation point, detaching two escorting destroyers under the veteran *Tai-sa* (Captain) Hara Tameichi and the three transport-destroyers to meet the rest of the transport group, which had departed Buin at 1653, south of Shortland and proceed across the fifty-mile-wide Bougainville Strait at nine knots, the best speed the landing craft could make. The whole force was heading towards Marquana Bay, a minor indentation on the northern coast of Vella Lavella where the troops awaited pick-up.

Some of the newest destroyers in the Solomons in the autumn of 1943 were the *Fletchers* of Desron 21. Seen from the flagship, USS *Nicholas* (DD 449), are (right to left): *O'Bannon* (DD 450), *Taylor* (DD 468) and *Chevalier* (DD 451), 15 August 1943. These four, in this order, engaged four Japanese destroyers in an inconclusive engagement off the east coast of Vella Lavella three days later. The three seen here also fought at the Battle of Vella Lavella, 6–7 October 1943. This photograph shows all three in Ms 21, overall Navy Blue (5-N) camouflage. It is possible, but unlikely, that all three ships in this photograph were recently repainted. It is more likely that, because of a quirk of the light and the camera's exposure, the camouflage looks particularly dark, while the unpainted metal of the FD antennas on the Mk 37 directors is reflecting the sunlight very brightly. (NARA)

The four destroyers directly under Ijuin's command were his flagship *Akigumo*, followed by *Isokaze*, *Kazegumo* and *Yugumo*. Of these, *Isokaze* and *Akigumo* were *Kagero*-class ships, the other two were from the most recent class of destroyers, the *Yugumo* class, including the name-ship. Hara commanded two older destroyers, his flagship *Shigure* and *Samidare*, both of the *Shiratsuyu* class, the same class as *Suzukaze* and *Kawakaze*. *Shigure*, in particular, was a veteran of multiple battles in the Solomons and was known as a lucky ship because it had come through all these brushes without a scratch. Hara had equally earned a reputation as a skilled and lucky commander.

Alerted to the Japanese movements, the local commander, Rear Admiral Theodore S Wilkinson, dispatched two groups of three destroyers each to intercept, with the rendezvous to take place at about 2300 off Marquana Bay. The closer group was Desron 4, under Captain Frank R Walker, which had patrolled up the Slot the night before and had retired to Choiseul Bay for the day. Walker flew his flag from *Selfridge* (DD 357), a sister of *Porter*. The other two

In this pre-war photograph, USS *Selfridge* (DD 357), sister to *Porter*, shows the large twin gun houses and the heavy tripod masts that sometimes led ships of this class to be mistaken for light cruisers. The large box structure at the base of her second funnel housed reload torpedoes for her eight tubes, an unusual feature in an American destroyer. (NARA)

A second photograph of *Selfridge*, in the same sequence as the previous, shows her aft end. The large, boxy structure to the left in this view was the aft Mk 35 main-battery director. The *Porter*s were also unusual in having two directors rather than just one. The canvas-covered object just aft of the director was a 1.1in/75 quadruple mount. This gun was so delicate that it was regularly covered to protect it from corrosion when not actually in use. (NARA)

ships in his squadron were *O'Bannon* (DD 450) and *Chevalier* (DD 451), both of the new *Fletcher* class. Alerted by Wilkinson mid-afternoon on the 6th, they headed up the Slot at a moderate twenty knots in order to pass up the eastern side of Vella Lavella after dark and round the island's northeastern point and then turn southwest towards the rendezvous at about 2230.

Part of the reason why Walker proceeded at less than his best speed was to let the other group of destroyers catch up. They were three ships under the command of Captain Harold O Larson in *Ralph Talbot* (DD 390) that had been escorting a convoy south from New Georgia. *Ralph Talbot* was a destroyer of the *Bagley* class, a near-sister to *Maury*; the other two ships in this group were *Taylor* (DD 468) and *LaVallette* (DD 448), both *Fletchers*. With more distance to steam, they came up from the southeast at high speed, passing up the western side of Vella Lavella and coming towards the rendezvous from the opposite direction.

As Walker was starting to turn into Bougainville Strait at 2230, Larson was just entering Wilson Strait between Vella Lavella and Ganongga to the southwest, still at least thirty miles – an hour's steaming – from the rendezvous. Walker tried to radio Larson with his TBS, but, with an island in between, was unable to make contact. Walker's dilemma was easy to understand. He did not know Larson's exact location, but knew, correctly, that the other group was trailing by at least half an hour. He also knew that the Japanese were coming in some strength. The most recent intelligence he had received indicated, again correctly, that at least nine Japanese destroyers were heading towards him. As he turned his short line due west into the heart of the strait, the issue became more than academic. At 2231, his radar picked up a contact ten miles to the northwest. Four minutes later, Walker changed course to 300 degrees.

Difficult command decisions

As he approached from the north, Ijuin had a more difficult problem to solve. Walker essentially had a binary choice to make – engage an enemy force believed to be three times larger than his own or temporarily turn away in order to delay his arrival. Ijuin had more factors to consider. The Japanese also had scout aircraft up that evening and had done a reasonably good job of tracking Walker's approach. However, the pilots completely misrepresented the strength of the approaching enemy, reporting four cruisers and three destroyers, enough to cause Ijuin grave concern for the prospects of his evacuation mission. When he received this information at 2210, Ijuin ordered the three old transport-destroyers to turn back and instructed Hara to join him with his two destroyers as soon as possible. (Hara was approximately eight miles northwest of Ijuin at

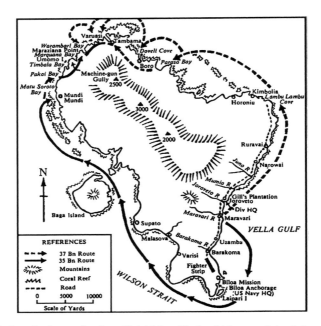

A map of Vella Lavella drawn for the official New Zealand history of the Solomons campaign, showing the movement of New Zealand army units during the campaign. The Japanese had set up a transfer base at Honariu (spelled Horoniu on this map) along the northeastern coast, but they withdrew to Marquana Bay along the northwestern coast for evacuation. The Battle of Vella Lavella took place in the waters off the upper left corner of this map.

this time.) Ijuin did not alter the orders for the remaining transports, which continued their stately progress towards the southeast. While Walker had to worry only about his chances in battle against what he believed to be a stronger enemy force, Ijuin had somehow to shepherd the slow convoy of light craft to and from Marquana Bay with what he had been told were vastly superior enemy forces approaching from the east. Fighting the Americans was a second, lower priority. While by nature a cautious man, Ijuin continued to the south, turning by successive four point turns to the east and then northeast, as he hunted for the Americans he knew to be towards the east and waited for Hara to join up. At 2235, he turned past ninety degrees to the west-northwest in order to close Hara even faster. No sooner had the line turned than a lookout of *Kazegumo*, the third in line to turn, sighted Walker's three destroyers at almost nine miles to the east-southeast.[45]

With probably quite different expectations, the two sides closed rapidly. Walker never hesitated and neither did Ijuin, who turned his line again to port to a course of southwest. Both commanders thought they were facing superior enemy forces, but in fact, the two lines converging north of Vella Lavella were nearly evenly matched, Ijuin's four destroyers versus Walker's three.

At perhaps 2240, seeing that Ijuin was in position to cross his line, Walker turned left to a course of west-by-north and ordered speed increased to thirty knots, hoping perhaps to split the difference between Ijuin's group, now positively identified as comprising four ships, and another, more distant, group. This was Hara's force, just located by radar towards the west-northwest and believed to be made up of two or three larger targets. Walker clearly wanted to leave his options open. Five minutes later, Ijuin turned his line two more points left to south-southeast to again maintain a course perpendicular to Walker's. At this point, the two lines were perhaps six miles apart, well within range for his Type 93 torpedoes. Three minutes later, at 2248, Ijuin made a decision that has been the cause of much misunderstanding. He ordered a simultaneous turn to south-southwest, two points to starboard, a move that put his ships on a course away from Walker and certainly did not appear to improve his tactical position. Hara explains this apparent mistake by observing that Ijuin was mentally exhausted by many months of command and, in his exhausted state, mistakenly believed he was closer to Walker than he really was.[46] This seems to be highly unlikely. If anything, Ijuin may have believed Walker to be further away than he in fact was. Expecting to see cruisers, the apparent size of dim shapes seen in the moonlight could easily cause a smaller ship to be mistaken for a bigger ship further away, but not the other way around.

Then why was Ijuin turning away when it is likely he thought Walker was further away than he really was? Here, Hara gives a useful clue. Ijuin knew that his slow and vulnerable transport group was off to the northeast on a course that would carry them behind Walker, if the Americans held course. His greatest fear was that Walker would launch torpedoes at his ships and then turn back to attack the landing craft. Because the Americans were much closer to the transports than he was, he would be unable to prevent such a move. A turn away might lure Walker further to the southwest, away from the transports. Another factor may also have influenced Ijuin's decision. On his former course of south-southeast, he was about to achieve a classic 'crossing the T' of Walker's line, considered to be an ideal tactical position. Yet he turned away and lost this advantage. Perhaps he did this because 'crossing the T' is an ideal position for gunfire, when one force can bring its broadside to bear on the bow of an approaching enemy, but it is not an ideal position for a torpedo attack, the preferred method of night attack by the Japanese. A bow-on shot has a low probability of success. The ideal torpedo shot is broad on the bow of an approaching target. By turning away, Ijuin was most likely attempting to gain some leeway to port of Walker. This hypothesis is reinforced by his next manoeuvre, which was to turn his line, again simultaneously, 90 degrees to port. Now heading east-southeast, he was diverging by only two points from Walker's approach course.

Battle is joined

It was a nearly perfect setup for both sides to fire torpedoes at each other, with barely five miles between the lines, except that Ijuin's four destroyers were in port quarterline with *Akigumo* leading and *Yugumo* trailing, nearly a mile closer to the Americans. If Ijuin made a mistake that night, it was his failure to reform his ships into line ahead before turning to approach Walker. In port quarterline, only trailing *Yugumo* could fire torpedoes without endangering a friendly ship. Walker had no such difficulty, and at 2250 he ordered a forty-degree turn towards Ijuin. Lieutenant Commander George R Wilson, captain of *Chevalier*, second in Walker's line, later recounted the sequence of events that followed:

2250 – Changed course to 240°T, by head of column movement. The range was closing rapidly and enemy were plainly visible silhouetted DDs or small CLs plus 2 DDs. Received orders by TBS to stand by to execute 'WILLIAM' one half salvo, plus information that group commander would turn to port.

This view of *Chevalier* was taken before she left for the Pacific, at Boston Navy Yard, 24 October 1942. She is wearing the camouflage scheme most common in the Atlantic at the time, Ms 22, Haze Grey (5-H) upperworks and Navy Blue (5-N) hull (up to the lowest sheer line). Like *Selfridge*, she has a canvas-covered 1.1in mount on her after superstructure. She was one of only three early *Fletchers* to go to war with this gun. (NARA via destroyerhistory.org)

This was later changed and word received to turn to starboard.

> 2252 – I ordered 'stand by to fire torpedoes to port, hard right rudder, come to 280°T.'

> 2253 – The ship's head was steady and I ordered 'fire torpedoes one half salvo.' . . . A good solution had been obtained prior to firing.[47]

Walker's three ships put a total of fourteen Mk 15 torpedoes in the water:

> 2255 – Received order via TBS to execute 'DOG' and opened fire on same target. Range 3700 yards. Our second salvo was a direct hit, and we evidently kept hitting.[48]

Apparently all three American destroyers opened fire on the closest target, *Yugumo*, barely a mile and a half distant. Experience and regular training with radar-guided gunnery paid off, and *Yugumo* was hit at least five times by 5in (127mm) shells in the first minute of gunfire. At some point during this minute, her captain turned his ship in a tight circle to port, towards Walker's line, while Ijuin awoke to his danger and turned the rest of his ships ninety degrees to port, reforming his line and showing his stern to the American torpedoes. It has never been clear whether *Yugumo's* turn came before or after she started receiving gunfire. Regardless of the precise timing, within the span of a minute, *Yugumo* turned 180 degrees, launched eight torpedoes at the American line and received damage sufficient to leave her on fire, without steering control and losing way. One or two of the remaining Japanese destroyers (definitely *Kazegumo* and possibly *Isokaze*) fired a few rounds at the Americans before they disappeared to the south. Except for *Yugumo*, none of the Japanese ships had been hit.

The fog of war

Despite the invaluable assistance of SG radar, the Americans again became confused about what they were firing at and grossly overestimated the success of their gunfire. They believed they were hitting every ship in the Japanese line:

> 2256 – Noted a large explosion in number 3 ship in column, evidently a torpedo hit.

> 2258 – The three leading ships were aflame and #3 sank. I directed control to shift targets to #4 which the SELFRIDGE was firing on. #4 apparently was being hit by SELFRIDGE.[49]

At this opportune moment, Hara's two destroyers entered the fray. *Shigure* and *Samidare* had just executed a turn to starboard which put them on a course slightly ahead of and nearly parallel to Walker's, at a range that had shrunk to four miles, an excellent torpedo set-up. Walker now turned his attention away from *Yugumo* and the rest of Ijuin's group. He told his line to be ready to come twenty-degrees further right and light up Hara's group with searchlights. Wilson, however, was being distracted by reports of torpedo boats off his starboard side.[50]

2259 – Received orders via TBS to 'be prepared to illuminate'. Ordered control to be prepared to illuminate. At this time we were informed by CIC that two small high-speed targets were approaching on starboard beam. I swung left to bring the 1.1 machine gun to bear and ordered them to open fire on anything sighted. I did not feel justified in taking the main battery off target since the group commander had just informed us that he was attacking the group of four ships ahead. I noted that he was turning right so I ordered 'right full rudder' come to course 300°T, so as to bring my battery to bear for illumination of his target.[51]

While this was going on, at 2301, Hara put sixteen torpedoes in the water. At virtually the same moment, one of *Yugumo*'s torpedoes, fired five minutes earlier, found a target. The Type 93 hit *Chevalier* abreast the No. 2 5in (63mm) mount, just forward of her bridge. In Wilson's words:

2301 – I was at the center bridge window and was just about to order 'rudder amidships' when the torpedo hit. There were two distinct concussions, the first being the explosion of the torpedo, and the second, almost simultaneously, being Gun 2 magazine. All personnel on the bridge were stunned. I was thrown to the deck and I presume somehow between the compass binnacle and the wheel, since that is where I found myself when I came to. My first thought was to warn O'BANNON that I was out of control swinging right. I saw Crudele, CSM, and directed him to send that message via blinker tube. I did not realize he was injured, but he fainted as he started to call the O'BANNON. In the meantime, still a bit dazed, I inquired as to the extent of the damage. I was informed that the entire bow forward of the bridge had been blown off. All communications were out. I dispatched a messenger, Ensign McQuilkin, to the engine room to order 'back emergency full.'[52]

Her bow was severed aft of the No. 2 mount, sinking rapidly, taking two complete gun crews with it. With everyone on the bridge temporarily incapacitated, the ship continued on without a bow, bearing off to the right and slowing.

Obviously on all-around alert against air attack, *O'Bannon's* five 5in (127mm) guns each point at a different part of the sky, 22 June 1943. In this photograph, her Ms 21 camouflage looks significantly lighter than in the photograph taken two months later. The purple-blue pigment used in US Navy camouflage paints during this period faded quickly to a neutral grey on exposure to sun and salt air. (NARA via destroyerhistory.org)

The smoke from gunfire and then this massive explosion was so thick that neither *Selfridge* ahead nor *O'Bannon* astern were aware of *Chevalier's* plight.[53] Walker continued on towards the northwest, now alone, because *Chevalier* was clearly out of the fight and *O'Bannon*, following at high speed barely quarter of a mile back and effectively blind, came through a cloud of smoke to see *Chevalier* directly ahead. Lieutenant Commander D J MacDonald ordered all aback and tried swerving to the left, but it was too late. Wilson continued:

> By this time, possibly two to three minutes after the explosion, my head had cleared sufficiently so that I knew what I was doing. I ordered the Executive Officer, Lieutenant Hansen, to make a survey of the damage and report to me as soon as practicable. Just then, I felt another shock aft on the starboard side, and presumed it to be another torpedo hit, but was informed that the O'BANNON had rammed us in the after engine room. All light and power were lost, but the ship slowed, stopped and her bow, if such it could be called, came up some. Before, the wreckage of the bow and the hole in the I.C. room and forward fireroom bulkhead had caused the ship to start submerging like a submarine. I believe she would have gone under in spite of everything if the O'BANNON had not stopped our headway. I sent word to the executive and the chief engineer via Hubbard, SOM3C, to attempt to keep power on the

Ralph Talbot (DD 390) was Larson's
flagship as he led *Taylor* and *LaVallette*
(DD 448) up from the western side of
Vella Lavella on the night of 6 October
1943. In this photograph, she is coming
alongside *Enterprise* (CV 6) in April 1942,
probably to refuel. This was always
a tricky operation, as a large ship, such
as an aircraft carrier, caused significant
turbulence even at relatively low speed,
making holding formation alongside
an operation that called for constant
attention and expert seamanship.
(NARA)

ship as I had hopes of backing her in, or at least keeping her pumped until we could be towed in stern first. I received word back that the forward fireroom bulkhead was crumpled and the fireroom had been secured when the water reached the burner level, that the fuel oil suction lines aft had been cut and no oil suction could be obtained, that the after engine room was flooded above the upper gratings and was untenable, that the fresh water tank in the after fireroom and the after starboard bulkhead were ruptured and that we were making water fast in the after fireroom.[54]

Mercifully, *O'Bannon* suffered no casualties, and was unhurt except for having perhaps seven metres of her lower bow plating peeled back. Nevertheless, she too was out of the fight and, once she had separated from *Chevalier*, she hove to and put two boats in the water to start taking off *Chevalier*'s wounded.

Larson's timely arrival

While this drama was being played out, the battle continued both to the south and to the northwest of *Chevalier*. Just two minutes after she was hit, at 2303, one or more of the American torpedoes fired at 2253 found the already seriously damaged *Yugumo* and sealed her fate. Hit on the starboard side, she took on a serious list, and, before any lifeboats could be launched, capsized and sank, no more than seven minutes after the torpedo struck. At least 103 survivors were left to fend for themselves in the water.

Nor was *Selfridge* immune to the many torpedoes criss-crossing these waters. At 2306, three minutes after *Yugumo* was hit, one of the Type 93s launched by Hara's two destroyers five minutes earlier hit *Selfridge* at frame 40, portside under her No. 2 mount, much like the hit on *Chevalier*. But *Selfridge* was luckier. She had fired off much of the contents of her forward magazines, and the detonation of the torpedo vented mainly through the far side of the ship without setting off any secondary explosions. As a result, although she too lost most of her bow, *Selfridge*'s forward structure was more intact than *Chevalier*'s, and she had the added advantage of not being rammed after being torpedoed.

Now would seem to be time for Ijuin to turn his five intact destroyers around to finish off the three damaged enemies in his wake, but this was when Larson's group had its most significant, if unintended, impact on events that night. Still fifteen minutes away from the scene, the three destroyers were sighted by a Japanese scout aircraft and reported to Ijuin as three more cruisers. Unwilling to take on yet another superior foe, especially after having pulled off what he believed to be an incredible victory at long odds, Ijuin ordered his ships to continue on towards Rabaul. His parting shot, at 2313, was to fire off all his remaining torpedoes, twenty-four Type 93s from *Akigumo*, *Isokaze* and *Kazegumo*, in the general direction of the American cripples. None of these torpedoes found a target.

Only one more torpedo would be fired that night. Larson brought his three ships into Bougainville Strait at approximately 2320 and were ordered to search Marquana Bay and the adjacent waters for any signs of the Japanese. Finding nothing, they closed Walker's three damaged ships at 0020. It was now 7 October 1943. By this time, Wilson realised that all attempts to slow the flooding in *Chevalier* were failing:

> The roll of the ship was getting very sluggish and she seemed to have trouble righting herself. The starboard rail was rolling under. . . . I started down the forward fireroom hatch and stepped in the water at the third rung of the

O'Bannon's bow after the Battle of Vella Lavella shows the effects of ramming *Chevalier* after that destroyer had been torpedoed, 6 October 1943. The shell plating at her bow was peeled back with almost surgical precision. This made steering *O'Bannon* difficult, but her survival was never in doubt. (NARA)

ladder. Using a flashlight I could see that this fireroom was almost completely filled and that #1 boiler seemed to be twisted, with the front pointing to starboard. The water in #1 engineroom was about two feet deep over the lower grating. The water in the after fireroom was up to my hips over the lower grating. The after engineroom was completely flooded, and the ship seemed to be working around the hole in the starboard side. I believe that the starboard shaft is the only thing which held her together. After completion of this inspection I decided to make no further effort to save her. . . .[55]

By 0125, 250 out of her complement of 301 had transferred to *O'Bannon* and that ship started her slow progress towards Purvis Bay in company with *Selfridge*, *Ralph Talbot* and *Taylor*. *LaVallette* was left behind to look for survivors and finally, to dispose of *Chevalier*. At 0311, she put a single torpedo into the hulk, which exploded quite satisfactorily – the Mk 15's problems finally having been resolved – and she then dropped a few depth charges on *Chevalier*'s sunken bow

Selfridge was given a new bow after losing her original forecastle to a Type 93 torpedo at the Battle of Vella Lavella, 6 October 1943. At the same time, her original main armament of eight 5in (127mm) guns was replaced by a hybrid of two twin and one single 5in (127mm) mounts, plus a beefed up AA suite. Her old single-purpose directors were replaced by a single Mk 37 dual-purpose director forward. In this photograph taken at the end of her repairs, on 10 April 1944, she is passing under the San Francisco Bay Bridge. She is painted a complex Ms 32/22D deceptive scheme intended to make her difficult to track through a periscope. (NARA via destroyerhistory.org)

to make sure nothing could be recovered by the enemy. She left *O'Bannon*'s two abandoned lifeboats in case there were any more survivors that had been missed in the dark. With that grace note, she departed the scene for Tulagi.

Ijuin's departure did not end the story for the Japanese. At 2340, he had ordered the three destroyer-transports, which had been loitering near Shortland, to join him and also retire towards Rabaul. He issued no further orders to the group of sub-chasers and landing craft which had all this while been making its slow way around the east of the battle towards Marquana Bay. Amazingly, they continued on unseen, or at least unmolested, arriving at the evacuation point at 0110, well after Larson had declared the area free of enemy. They loaded 589 troops and departed at 0305. Despite a near constant Allied presence on the water and in the air over Bougainville Strait, they delivered the refugees to Buin the next afternoon without incident.

Even this does not quite end the story of the Battle of Vella Lavella. A squadron of American PT boats arrived on the scene somewhat after dawn looking for any more survivors. They found no more Americans in the water, but did find seventy-eight of *Yugumo*'s crew willing to be rescued.[56] Twenty-five more of *Yugumo*'s crew, three officers and twenty-two men, managed to find one of *O'Bannon*'s drifting lifeboats and rowed it the fifty-odd miles to Shortland.

The Battle of Vella Lavella was a clear tactical victory for the Japanese, as had been Tassafaronga and Savo Island before that, but as with those battles, the victory gave the Japanese no lasting benefit. Increasingly, they were fighting a war on their enemy's terms, in waters dominated by their enemy's technology and material might. Each side lost a destroyer at Vella Lavella, but while *Chevalier* would be replaced by another *Chevalier* (DD 805), launched a year and a few days after her namesake's loss, there would not be another *Yugumo* for thirty-four years.[57] More importantly, after Vella Lavella, the Japanese would not win another surface engagement in World War II.

Notes

1 The name has stuck. The latest edition of *The Times Comprehensive Atlas of the World* gives that body the name 'Iron Bottom Sound', differing from American usage only by splitting the first word into two.

2 This was particularly clear to Roosevelt's isolationist opponents who wanted nothing to do with Europe's war. They saw the various 'short-of-war' activities of the US Navy in the Atlantic and the Lend-Lease programme as a thinly disguised conspiracy to push the United States into the war.

3 The US Navy, in its war planning, used colours to designate various countries. For example, 'blue' designated the United States; 'orange' designated Japan.

4 At the time of Pearl Harbor, the US Navy had the following ships under construction: eight battleships, five large aircraft carriers, four heavy cruisers, seventeen light cruisers and no fewer than seventy-two destroyers, plus many more escorts and auxiliaries. Many times those numbers would be ordered in the months following Pearl Harbor.

5 The US participated in the landings in North Africa in November 1942 and planned to be ready for an invasion of the European continent in 1943, but that proved to be a more formidable undertaking than originally thought and the Normandy invasion did not take place until June 1944. The landings in Sicily in July 1943 and the subsequent landings in Italy were always a side-show to the Americans.

6 The name Guadalcanal derives from the hometown of Pedro de Ortega, a Spaniard from Andalusia, one of the discoverers of the island. The Melanesian natives who lived on the island long before its 'discovery' call it Isatabu.

7 MacArthur remains an ambiguous figure in American history, with no part of his career more controversial than his actions in the Philippines at the beginning of the war. His supporters claim he planned as well as anyone could for the Japanese attack, that his planning was effective and that his departure from Corregidor was done reluctantly, only after a direct order from the president. His detractors point to the flawed preparations before and slow reaction to the Japanese attack, to his acceptance of large financial rewards from the Philipinos while their country was being overrun and to his seeming indifference to the plight of his troops, whom he visited on Bataan only once during the three months he was on Corregidor, which earned him the unflattering soubriquet 'Dugout Doug'.

8 *Frank*, pp. 50–1. An additional 3000 Marines landed on Tulagi and adjacent islands. They were opposed by approximately 900 defenders.

9 Supplies of all necessities, especially food, were so short that Japanese soldiers dubbed Guadalcanal 'Starvation Island'.

10 *Frank*, pp. 501–2.

11 Guadalcanal was 'Cactus'; Tulagi was 'Ringbolt' and Espiritu Santo was 'Button'.

12 The *Shiratsuyu*s had been designed in an attempt to abide by the tonnage restrictions of the 1930 London Naval Arms Limitation Treaty. Even though they carried one fewer main gun and one fewer torpedo tube than the preceding 'Special Type' destroyers, they exceeded the 1500-ton treaty limit by more than 100 tons. The following classes reverted to the larger size and heavier gun armament of the 'Special Type'.

13 Two factors were the basis of this strategy: (1) The correct belief that the defeat of Hitler was a higher priority to the Allies, and (2) the presumption that the Allies, most specifically the Americans, were unwilling to accept the heavy casualties that would be required to take back the Japanese conquests.

14 Like the Americans, before the war the Japanese saw aircraft carriers and the aircraft they carried as an adjunct to the battle fleet, not as an independent strike force. It was only after the successful attack by Royal Navy aircraft on the Italian fleet at Taranto on 11 November 1940 that the Japanese, specifically Admiral Yamamoto Isoroku, conceived of the aircraft-only attack on the US fleet at Pearl Harbor.

15 These speeds were achieved by the later version of this torpedo with an elongated nose, based on an Italian design; the original round-nosed version was two knots slower. Development of an oxygen-burning torpedo, which left almost no bubbles in its wake because the burning of fuel (kerosene in this case) in pure oxygen leaves only CO_2 as exhaust which dissolves readily in water, was difficult because pure oxygen is dangerous to handle on board a ship. Problems with explosions of the motors when first starting were resolved by starting the torpedo with normal air and switching over gradually to pure oxygen as the torpedo ran. The name 'Long Lance' is credited to the American historian Samuel Eliot Morison and was first used in his postwar multi-volume *History of United States Naval Operations in World War II*. In contrast, the standard American torpedo, the Mk 15, carried a smaller warhead at slower speed over a much shorter range and was far less likely to strike a target due to depth-keeping problems or to detonate once it got there. The Americans were unaware of the Type 93's superior capabilities until some time in 1943.

16 *Crenshaw*, p. 114.

17 In the days before electro-optics, the ability of an optical instrument to gather light was a function of the quality of the lenses and the size of the objective lens – the higher the quality and the bigger the objective, the better an instrument would gather light. The skill the Japanese acquired in making these optical instruments was put to good use after the war in the design of the cameras that came to dominate the world market.

18 Six of the sources consulted by this author gave an order of battle for the Japanese destroyers. The only thing they all agreed on was that *Takanami* was separate and ahead of the other seven. These sources gave four different sequences for the remaining ships. Without any means of resolving this issue, I have gone with the order that seemed to fit best with the subsequent action. I could be wrong.

19 *OpPlan*. The plan also had six annexes taking up an additional sixteen pages covering all possible aspects of formation and communication protocols. The annexes were boilerplate for the most part, the important exception being the first three pages of Annex F, which covered ship dispositions and general conduct during day and night actions.

20 *OpPlan*, Annex 'F'.

21 Probably the best known example of this was the loss of USS *Duncan* (DD 485) at the Battle of Cape Esperance, 11–12 October 1942. In that battle, three van destroyers got caught out of position when Rear Admiral Scott turned his line and were racing to regain position on the engaged side of the American cruisers. When the damage to *Duncan* was inspected before she

sank the next morning, it was obvious that many of the hits she had received were from American guns.

22   *Comp.* Halsey had been put in charge of the South Pacific Area on 18 October 1942 because the Commander-in-Chief, US Pacific Fleet (CINCPAC), Admiral Chester Nimitz, determined that more energy and aggression was needed in this critical theatre. Halsey was, and still is, popularly known as 'Bull', but he always hated the nickname, preferring to be called 'Bill' by his friends. He is quoted as blaming 'some drunken correspondent' for coming up with the nickname 'Bull'.

23   *Mustin*, p. 630. Mustin had been Asstistant Gunnery officer in *Atlanta* (CL 51) until she sank in the 1st Naval Battle of Guadalcanal, 13 November 1942. He was assigned temporary duty as Operations Officer on the staff of Commander, Naval Bases, Cactus-Ringbolt at the time of the Battle of Tassafaronga.

24   *Crest.*

25   The SG was a truly remarkable tool in the hands of operators and commanders who knew how to use it. It was the first S-band microwave surface-search radar deployed by the US Navy and the first to incorporate a PPI (Plan Position Indicator) display. (All previous radars had used an 'A-Scope' display, a simple oscilloscope that showed a target as a spike in the horizontal tracing when the antenna pointed at it.) The SG relied heavily on British research in the form of the Watson-Watt magnetron and experience in developing the Type 271 radar. The SG (often referred to as 'Sail George') was the first American radar able to discriminate a ship against a land background, making it extremely useful in narrow waters.

26   *Comp.* TBS (Talk Between Ships) was a short-wave, short-range (line-of-sight) tactical voice radio used by the US Navy. This message caused some confusion because 'bogey' was a term generally used to refer to unknown aircraft.

27   Not too surprisingly, none of the six main accounts of this battle used to compile this description agree with each other in many of the details. For example, five of those accounts report how many torpedoes the Japanese fired and four list when they were fired. They give four different totals from a low of forty-two to a high of fifty-two, and even the two that agree on the total, do not agree on the timing or sequence. I have done my best to integrate all these accounts.

28   *Comp.*

29   *Ibid.*

30   *Ibid.* Because TBS was an open tactical voice channel, a simple substitution code was used to shorten communications and possibly confuse any enemy listening in. 'William' referred to firing torpedoes, 'Dog' referred to gunfire.

31   *Cole*, p. 2.

32   *O'Hara*, p. 133. According to this account, 180 5in (127mm), 90 6in (152mm) and 155 8in (203mm) rounds were fired at *Takanami*. It is not known how many hit, but even if it was only a tiny fraction of those fired, it was sufficient to disable the destroyer. *Crenshaw* gives totals that are similar, but not identical.

33   *Frank*, p. 509, states that *Suzukaze* did fire eight torpedoes at 2323, but no other source mentions this, and *Long* explicitly states that she did not fire any.

34   *Crenshaw*, pp. 190–1. These pages are a pair of maps that show in exquisite detail who was firing at whom and how many rounds were fired.

35   The *New Orleans*-class cruisers, which included *Minneapolis*, were designed to meet London Treaty restrictions that limited cruisers to 10,000 tons. They were the fourth class of heavy cruisers designed to meet these limits and had been modified by having thicker belt armour, as the preceding classes were considered inadequately protected. To compensate for this added

weight, *New Orleans* gave up the safer, but heavier, arrangement of alternating fire rooms and engine rooms, which is why a single torpedo was able to flood three quarters of *Minneapolis's* fire rooms.

36 *Crest.*

37 Ibid.

38 *Wright*, pp. 9–10.

39 *O'Hara*, p. 136.

40 *Wright*, p. 10.

41 *Wright*, p. 9.

42 Cf., Chapter 10.

43 *Struggle*, p. 83, p. 104 and p. 319.

44 Like the Americans, the Japanese also used old destroyers as transports. The three transport-destroyers involved in this action – *Fumizuki, Matsukaze* and *Yunagi* – were not as extensively modified for the transport role as American APDs.

45 The primary Japanese account of this battle available in English, *Hara*, pp. 202–12, gives times that are two hours earlier than American accounts.

46 *Hara*, pp. 206–7. The following paragraphs are a reconstruction by the author that attempts to explain Ijuin's actions not as mistakes, but rather as a rational attempt to cope with a difficult and confusing tactical picture.

47 *Chevalier.*

48 Ibid.

49 Ibid.

50 There were no torpedo boats at sea that night. It is uncertain what *Chevalier's* SG had detected, but the radar track was clear and consistent. *Hansen* reports twelve minutes earlier: '2247 – . . . Also picked up a third group of indistinct targets bearing 326°T, range 11,600 yards. These targets appeared to be in three close groups and they were definitely made of wood by appearance of the pips. Bridge was informed the these might be PT boats.'

51 *Chevalier.* The quad 1.1in mount was atop the aft superstructure between mounts 53 and 54. By October 1943, this weapon was becoming rare in the US Navy, being replaced by the significantly more reliable and powerful 40mm Bofors. The only problem with the 40mm was that it was also significantly heavier 'per barrel' than the 1.1in mount it was replacing, so that the quad 1.1in was replaced on *Fletchers* by a twin 40mm mount (and a second twin Bofors on the fantail).

52 Ibid.

53 The Americans had switched to 'flashless' powder in 1943, before that using so-called 'smokeless' powder to propel main-battery rounds. Both terms were relative, as 'flashless' powder did produce some flash and 'smokeless' some smoke, but generally 'flashless' powder produced less flash and much more smoke than 'smokeless'.

54 Ibid.

55 *Chevalier.*

56 It was not uncommon for Japanese survivors in the water to refuse and sometimes violently resist what was considered the shame of rescue by the enemy.

57 JDS *Yugumo*, a small destroyer, was launched in 1977 and served in the Japanese Maritime Self-Defense Force until decommissioned in 2005. There was also an *Akigumo* in the same class, also now retired, along with an even older *Takanami* and *Makinami*, launched in 1959–60. However, there would be yet another *Takanami* and *Makinami*. They were launched in 2001 and 2002 respectively, both 4600-ton ASW destroyers currently in commission, as is JDS *Samidare*, a destroyer of the preceding class, which was launched in 1998.

Chapter 9

Fire from the Sky – The East China Sea (6 April 1945)

D ESTROYERS HAD FOUGHT their way, along with the rest of an increasingly formidable Allied armada, ever closer to the shores of Japan. It appeared, in the spring of 1945, that two things, seemingly contradictory, were undoubtedly true. One was that Japan would be defeated. Her navy had been

Probably the most famous American destroyer commander of World War II was Arleigh Burke, who led several different destroyer units during the Solomons campaign, most famously Desron 23 – the 'Little Beavers'. He is seen here on the left as a captain in 1944, while serving as Chief of Staff to Vice Admiral Marc Mitscher (right), the commander of the Fast Carrier Task Force (designated alternately TF 38 and TF 58). He eventually rose to serve as CNO between 1955 and 1961. USS *Cole* (DDG 67), the subject of this book's last chapter, is a destroyer of the *Arleigh Burke* class. (NARA)

reduced to a handful of navigable units stuck in harbour due to lack of fuel. Her merchant marine had effectively vanished from the oceans, obliterated by submarines and omnipresent aircraft. Her army still held large parts of China and southern Asia, but her troops were starving, as were the workers in her war factories and the civilians in her fire-bombed cities. It was plain to everyone, including the Japanese, that this war could end only one way, but what was equally plain was that the Japanese would never surrender. They had fought with unparalleled ferocity for meaningless dots in the ocean, such as Peleliu and Iwo Jima, and had died virtually to a man rather than surrender. On Saipan, the first island to be retaken that had a significant Japanese civilian population, at least 10,000 non-combatants committed suicide rather than surrender. All this made it clear that an invasion of Japan would be necessary to end the war and that it would be a battle of unprecedented savagery and bloodshed.

The kamikaze threat

To lay the groundwork for this invasion, the Allies selected an island in the Ryukyus, the chain of islands stretching between Kyushu, the southernmost of the four main Japanese 'home islands', and Formosa. Okinawa was large enough to serve as an unsinkable aircraft carrier and a logistical base for the ultimate invasion of Japan. Therefore an invasion fleet of unprecedented size gathered in the waters around the island, supporting the landing of the US 10th Army on 1 April 1945. With the Japanese fleet no longer a serious threat, the plans to defend this armada were laid with an eye to protecting the invasion fleet from suicide boats, submarines and attack from the air.

Successive rings of protective forces were arrayed around the landing beaches. From the inside out, they were: a close-in layer of destroyers on anti-submarine patrol; a wider ring of destroyers in a twenty-five-mile diameter semicircle around the landing beaches also on anti-submarine patrol; a roving 'flycatcher' screen of LCIs (Landing Craft, Infantry) backed by a destroyer or light cruiser searching for infiltrating suicide boats, MTBs or barges[1]; a nocturnal patrol of five destroyers protecting the most likely approaches for fast suicide boats; and, perhaps most importantly, a radar picket screen. Even before the actual landings on Okinawa, destroyers were posted at sixteen stations anywhere from fifteen to 100 miles from the landing beaches, each with a fighter-director team onboard and a CAP (Combat Air Patrol) of fighters overhead. They had the responsibility to detect incoming *kamikaze* raids and vector the aircraft from the seventeen escort carriers assigned the defence of the landings.

The steady increase in the use of the *kamikaze* tactic added a scary new dimension to the threat posed by what remained of Japanese airpower.[2] Much as the Japanese navy had effectively ceased to exist by the spring of 1945, the air arms of both the army and navy had been reduced to near impotence by a shortage of trained pilots and the fuel necessary to allow training flights. However, Japan's aircraft factories continued to produce aircraft, so that the Japanese faced the strange situation of having more aircraft than pilots sufficiently trained to fly them effectively. Japanese history and recent experience presented a uniquely Japanese solution to this problem.

From the beginning of the war, navy pilots on both sides occasionally chose to crash into enemy targets if their aircraft was damaged during an attack. This was far truer among Japanese pilots, who from the beginning had had a strong cultural bias in favour of dying honorably and against being captured. It is not possible positively to identify when the first intentional *kamikaze* attacks were made, but it is reasonably certain that the first organised attacks were made in the Philippines, starting on 24 October 1944. In two days of attacks, approximately fifty-five aircraft dived at the Allied fleet off Leyte, sinking one escort carrier and damaging five others. At least two other, smaller ships were sunk in these first attacks. This level of success was due in part to luck and in part to the novelty of the tactic, which caught the Allies by surprise. It encouraged Japanese leaders to believe that *kamikaze* tactics might be able to destroy enough of the Allied fleet to discourage further approach towards the home islands.

If that was the Japanese plan, it did not work, because the success rate of *kamikaze* attacks dropped as Allied defences concentrated on stopping enemy aircraft further from the fleets, and also because the quality of Japanese pilots necessarily continued to decline. As terrible a threat as the *kamikaze*s were, they were unable to stop the conquest of Iwo Jima, needed by the Americans as a base for fighters to accompany B-29 raids on Japan's industrial cities, or the subsequent gathering of forces for the invasion of Okinawa. For every ship damaged or sunk by the *kamikaze*s, it seemed that two more emerged from American dockyards. At no point did the Allies ever consider slowing the pace of the war against Japan.[3] If anything, the threat seemed to emphasise the need to get the job done before the Japanese could increase their inventory of suicide weapons.

Needless to say, as the date for Operation 'Iceberg', the Okinawa landings, approached, the *kamikaze* threat was a very real concern. The sixteen radar pickets took station on 26 March, the day of the preliminary occupation of Kerama Retto, a group of small islands approximately sixty-five miles west of Okinawa. The Japanese reacted immediately, sending nine *kamikaze*s after the assault transports.[4] They clearly understood the importance of the radar pickets to the defence of the invasion fleet, because that same day, *Kimberly* (DD 521) was attacked by two Vals while stationed at picket station No. 9.[5] One of the aircraft was clearly in the hands of a poorly trained pilot, as was the case with most *kamikazes* by this point in the war, and crashed some distance from the destroyer. The other was equally obviously piloted by a skilled aviator as he rolled and slid his aircraft through the destroyer's AA barrage until he turned across *Kimberly*'s wake at perhaps fifty metres' altitude and, overtaking from behind, crashed into her after 40mm mount. The damage was serious, but did not affect her ability to steam or fight, so she was able to remain on station until relieved the next day. Four men were killed and another fifty-seven wounded.

Suicidal chrysanthemums descend on Okinawa

This was just a prelude. A destroyer at station No. 1, just east of due north of Point Bolo, the western tip of the stretch of coast on Okinawa where the main

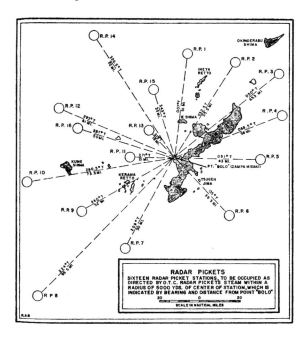

This map shows the positions of the sixteen radar picket stations around Okinawa, all intended to give advanced warning of the approach of enemy aircraft towards the Allied invasion fleet concentrated off the coast of the island south of 'Point Bolo', the centre of the radial pattern. On 6 April 1945, *Bush* was at station No. 1, *Colhoun* was at station No. 2 and *Cassin Young* was at station No. 3. (USN)

landings were made, was attacked and damaged by conventional bombers before dawn on 3 April and later that day, just about sundown, another was attacked by a pair of *kamikaze*s at station No. 4, but not hit.[6] For the first ten days after the landings, until airstrips on Okinawa could be made operational, the picket stations had CAP only during daylight hours. (The escort carriers providing CAP coverage lacked the ability to launch or recover aircraft in the dark, and the fleet carriers of TF 58 had barely enough night-capable fighters for their own protection.) The Japanese found this out very quickly and chose dawn and dusk as the best times to make air attacks. Two days of bad weather kept the attacks to a minimum on 4 and 5 April, but the 6th would bring better weather and the Allied fleet braced itself for an all-out assault.

The Japanese did not disappoint. They launched Operation *Kikusui* (Floating Chrysanthemums), a massive co-ordinated suicide attack that would, before it ran out of steam in mid-June, include more than 1400 *kamikaze* missions. The centrepiece of the operation was a sortie by the few remaining operational units of the Japanese fleet. Fuel was so scarce that the ten ships in the naval attack, Operation *Ten'ichigo*, carried barely enough fuel to reach Okinawa and return.[7] However, no one expected them to return. To cover the opening moves by this squadron, 198 *kamikaze* aircraft took off from bases on Kyushu heading towards Okinawa.

The radar pickets did their job. Of that 198 aircraft, forty-one returned to base for a variety of reasons. Of the 157 that continued on to their targets, the defending fighters vectored towards them by the radar pickets accounted for another fifty-five. A further thirty-five were shot down by anti-aircraft fire. That left sixty-seven aircraft crashing down on the ships of the Allied fleet. Twenty-seven ships were hit, some by more than one *kamikaze*. The best-known target was HMS *Illustrious*, which proved the worth of her armoured construction. She was near-missed by a *kamikaze*, whose wingtip grazed the carrier's island, the aircraft then tumbling into the water near aboard where its bomb exploded. The concussion caused serious structural damage, but the ship never lost speed and continued operating aircraft for two more days before being relieved.[8]

But the brunt of the attack fell on the destroyers of the anti-submarine and radar picket screens. From the anti-submarine patrols and other close-in escorts, fully nine destroyers, destroyer escorts and destroyer-minesweepers were hit by *kamikaze*s, with one of them sinking.[9] The one ship of this group that sank was USS *Emmons* (DMS 22). Originally launched as a *Gleaves*-class destroyer, designated DD 457, she served as such in the Atlantic theatre until late 1944. For part of that time she was attached to the Royal Navy's Home Fleet and was based at Scapa Flow.[10] In November 1944, she began conversion to high-speed minesweeper and was then sent to the Pacific. Her first minesweeping mission was off the landing beaches on the west coast of Okinawa and she was still there, clearing a channel off the northwest coast on 6 April 1945, working with her sister-ship *Rodman* (DMS 21).[11]

A large flight of *kamikaze*s came upon the two minesweepers and attacked. One of the first hit *Rodman* forward and exploded against her bridge, killing sixteen and starting an intense fire. Called to assist her sister, *Emmons* was just pulling alongside when a larger second wave of *kamikaze*s attacked. *Emmons* claimed to have destroyed six of the attackers and believed another twenty were downed by Marine Corps F4U Corsairs, but that did not blunt the attack. *Emmons* was hit in rapid succession by four *kamikaze*s and later by a fifth, and was near-missed by four more. Two hit aft and severed her fantail. A third hit her forward gun mount and holed her bow. The fourth hit the side of her bridge and exploded in her CIC (Combat Information Centre). On fire and settling aft, at least half of her officers dead or wounded, *Emmons* nevertheless fought the fires and managed to keep underway. The crew was making progress, having put out all fires except the one far forward, when, two and a half hours later, a lone *kamikaze* strafed the ship, circled around and crashed into the already-wrecked bridge. With this new damage and the fire forward threatening the magazine, the crew was ordered off after another hour of desperate damage control. Two hours later, the now-derelict *Emmons*, still afloat but nearly burned out and drifting towards a Japanese-held shore, was dispatched by gunfire from another American destroyer.

Intensive swarm attacks

As vicious as that attack was, special fury was reserved for the destroyers at the northern picket stations numbered 1, 2 and 3, manning an arc of forty-five degrees east of north at an average distance of fifty-five miles from Point Bolo. The first to be attacked was USS *Colhoun* (DD 801) at station No. 2. In the early morning hours of the 6th, between 0230 and 0600, *Colhoun* was attacked by eleven aircraft, all of which missed. This early flurry of activity was followed by a quiet morning at all three stations, but that situation did not last. At around 1500, a major attack developed from the north. At least forty aircraft in four waves arrayed at altitudes between 150 and 6000 metres came at *Bush* (DD 529) at station No. 1 and another dozen went after *Cassin Young* (DD 793) at station No. 3. *Bush* had first taken station on 1 April, patrolling for only one day before being relieved by *Prichett* (DD 561) and heading for Kerama Retto for replenishment and minor upkeep. It took a day and a half to get a turn alongside a tanker. Within half an hour of completing fuelling, she was hastily sent back

The new *Colhoun* (DD 801) seen as she appeared probably soon after her commissioning in July 1944. She is wearing an Ms 32/6D camouflage scheme. She was damaged off Iwo Jima by shore-battery fire and was repaired at Saipan, where she was probably repainted in Ms 21. (NARA via destroyerhistory.org)

to station No. 1. *Prichett* had been holed aft by a 250-kilogram bomb the night before and needed to be relieved.

The success rate of these *kamikazes* was low, the result of a combination of ferocious defence and questionable pilot skill. All twelve of the aircraft that went after *Cassin Young* missed, but the forty-plus aircraft that attacked *Bush* were simply too many to fend off. With the help of the four fighters in her own CAP and four more from *Cassin Young*'s, she was able to fight off the first three waves, but one attacker from the fourth wave got through.

At about 1513, a single-engined enemy plane was sighted dead ahead low on the water and headed straight for the ship. Since the ship was in a turn to the left, rudder was increased to full in order to bring the enemy abeam to starboard as quickly as possible and speed increased to 27 knots. The 5in [127mm] battery opened fire on the target at a range of 7000–8,000 yards. The plane employed rollercoaster tactics, climbing and dipping, combined with a slight weave during its approach. Its altitude varied from 10 to 35 feet. All batteries were firing at maximum rate and despite heavy and what appeared to be accurate 5in [127mm] and 40mm gunfire, the plane kept coming in. At the time it seemed unbelievable that it could do so. At a range of 2000 yards when it appeared as if a suicide crash were probable, the rudder was shifted hard right in an attempt to swing the stern clear. The plane, (a 'Jill' carrying a large bomb or torpedo), however, changed course to the right at the same

The third destroyer to be involved in the battle of the radar pickets on 6 April 1945 was
Cassin Young (DD 793). A dozen *kamikazes* went after her that day, but all missed.
Her camouflage at the time of this photograph, taken off San Pedro on 13 January 1944,
was Ms 32/7D. (NARA via destroyerhistory.org)

instant and at 1515 crashed with a terrific explosion at deck level on the
starboard side between No.s 1 and 2 stacks. The bomb or torpedo appeared to
have exploded in the forward engine room. An idea of the force of the
explosion may be gained from the fact that a six-foot section of engine room
blower weighing 300–500 pounds was blown into the air high enough to
knock off the SC-2 antenna and land on the port wing of the bridge.[12]

The damage, as might be expected, was serious. The shell plating was blown in
amidships, causing flooding in three of four engineering spaces and a ten-
degree list to port. Main power was lost and emergency power lasted only long
enough to get out a distress call. After that, flooding in the diesel generator
room shorted out the main switchboard and the ship went dark.

Despite the extensive damage, there were reasons for optimism onboard
Bush. Steam escaping from the damaged boilers had suppressed most of the fires
amidships and sailors manning handy billies managed to control flooding on
either side of the damaged mid-section. The diesel generator was restarted and
electricians were working on restoring current through the main bus. Topweight was reduced by putting the gig in the water and jettisoning torpedoes,
depth charges and all 5in (127mm) rounds in the upper handling rooms. Four
fighters maintained a continuous CAP presence during this period. Word was
gotten through to *Colhoun*, which departed station No. 2 at high speed along
with her own CAP, though it took them more than an hour to close *Bush's*

position. Aid stations were set up forward in the wardroom and aft on the fantail to treat the many wounded. At 1655, *LCS 64* came alongside to take off the wounded and any crew not needed for damage control or to man the anti-aircraft guns.[13]

All this was positive and led *Bush's* captain, Commander R E Westholm, to believe the ship could be saved, but there were also some serious threats to her survival. The seas were rising and the two halves of the ship began working, threatening to break the ship in two, though the captain was confident that, if *Bush* did break, the two halves would each remain afloat. More serious was the pair of Vals that began circling the small flotilla just before 1700. As seen from *Bush*, these two were just the beginning of another major attack, but they managed to do their share of damage.

> At about 1700, the two 'Vals' previously mentioned split up and one started a run on the BUSH from starboard. The starboard 40mm forward and the after 40mm fired on this target and caused him to turn away and pass astern. The plane circled until in vicinity of the COLHOUN, then three to four miles southeast of BUSH, and then dove on that ship, hitting her amidships. She appeared to have way on after the crash and continued on an easterly course until about five or six miles away. Observers claim that there were 15–20 planes in sight at this time.[14]

As seen from *Colhoun*, the *kamikaze* that hit her was not one of the first pair of Vals, but was part of the second, larger group of aircraft seen from *Bush*. This group appeared to be composed mainly of Zekes (more commonly known as 'Zeroes') which were coming initially after *Colhoun*. One overshot *Colhoun* and was headed towards *Bush* when it was splashed.

> At about 1710, the leading top Zeke peeled off and started a run on *Colhoun*. . . . Opened fire at 9000 yards . . . motor started smoking at about 1000 yards off. Plane released bomb at about this point, but continued his strafing and glide. He passed over the ship . . . no damage to ship . . . Plane apparently headed for *Bush* . . . *Bush* was in line distant about 4000 yards, 40mm and 20mm continued to register hits . . . plane hit water about midway between *Colhoun* and *Bush*.[15]

Colhoun's crew had no time to celebrate this small victory as more attackers swarmed in. Her captain, Commander George R Wilson – the same officer who commanded *Chevalier* at the Battle of Vella Lavella (see chapter 8) – is reported to have commented: 'This left one down, eleven to go.'[16] A second Zero was destroyed by a round from one of the 5in (127mm) guns at 4000 metres. A third dove from off *Colhoun's* starboard bow, but was hit and splashed fifty metres off her beam. At the same time, a fourth Zero came in from the port bow, escaping detection until it was too late to shoot down or evade.

> . . . received report that plane on port bow was about to crash us, ordered full left rudder but too late . . . Plane hit in flames on main deck at No. 44 40mm mount, part of flaming fuselage swept across ship, engine and bomb penetrated main deck exploding in after fireroom . . . also setting fire to handy billys which had been placed in readiness for going alongside *Bush* . . . Gun crews of 40mm mounts 3 and 4 were either killed or badly burned, mounts destroyed by crash and fire and ready ammunition on fire. Gun crews of 20mm guns 1 and 3 were all severely burned but guns not badly damaged.[17]

The bomb carried by this *kamikaze* penetrated *Colhoun's* after fire room and exploded there, rupturing the main steam line. Only quick action by the seriously wounded engineering officer redirected steam from the forward fire

USS *Bush* (DD 529) is seen at Mare Island Navy Yard, during a refit, 11 June 1944. She is painted in a fairly common 1D variant of the Ms 32 medium-pattern scheme, which generally employed Dull Black (BK) as the darkest tone, Light Grey (5-L) as the lightest and Ocean Grey (5-O) as the middle tone, though the exact colours used varied by yard and by paint availability. It is possible she was still carrying this camouflage when she was lost, 6 April 1945. However, if the opportunity presented itself, all ships still in a deceptive pattern scheme in early 1945 were repainted in overall Navy Blue (5-N), Ms 21, as this was more effective against observation from the air. (NARA)

room around the break and allowed *Colhoun* to maintain a speed of fifteen knots for the moment. Despite the loss of the handy billies, progress was rapidly made on the fires amidships and *Colhoun* appeared able to continue the fight. However, neither *Colhoun* nor *Bush* would be given much respite. Barely five minutes after the crash on *Colhoun*, *Bush* was again being swarmed.

At 1715 a group of three enemy planes (single-engine, believed 'Zekes') was sighted circling the ship at a range of about ten miles going in and out of the clouds. At 1725 one of these three peeled off and went into the sun, which was dead ahead of the ship at the time. He did a wing-over and commenced a 25–30 degree dive from ahead, strafing as he came in. The forward 40mms took him under fire and personnel on the forecastle went over the side. The Jap crossed slightly from starboard to port, dipped his left wing, and at 1730 dove into the ship, just missing the bridge, crashing the port side of the main deck between 1 and 2 stacks starting a large fire. The crash almost cut the ship in two. It is believed that bottom and keel were the only things holding it together. Personnel started to come back aboard and the repair party was able to get water on the fire with the two handy-billies still operative and had it almost under control. There was no passageway aft from the forward part of the ship.

About ten to fifteen minutes later, a second plane (also a 'Zeke') from the circling group peeled off and started a shallow dive on the starboard beam, weaving on his run in. He too was strafing. The 20s and 40mm took him under fire and registered some hits. At the last minute he pulled out of his dive and cleared the ship amidships by about five feet. The plane traveled some distance beyond, gained altitude, did a wingover, and headed for the forward part of the ship. The forward port 40mm took him under fire. He came in fairly low and at 1745 crashed on the port side just above the main deck in the vicinity of gun No. 2 and the wardroom, starting a very large fire. Casualties being treated in the wardroom were killed or burned to death. The water stream from the forward handy-billy was shifted from amidships to this fire but the area became untenable as 40mm ammunition and remaining 5in [127mm] ammunition started to explode.

It is believed that this plane must have been carrying extra gasoline for incendiary purposes as it seemed as if the entire forecastle were enveloped in flames. The forecastle was abandoned and the gig sent to pick up the badly wounded.[18]

Ships beyond saving

Even with damage this extensive, Westholm refused to give up the prospect of saving *Bush*. The two halves of his ship were barely hanging together and the forward half was untenable, but the aft half was intact and he believed the fires forward would burn themselves out, allowing that part of the ship to be reclaimed during the approaching night.

Though rightly concentrating on saving his own ship, Westholm was able to observe that *Colhoun* was being swarmed at the same time. Wilson was able to identify one Zero and two Vals circling *Colhoun*, obviously planning a co-ordinated attack.

> The Zeke came in on starboard bow, one Val on port and one on port quarter. Again all three came in at about a 45° dive very slow . . . All guns opened fire when attack started on port bow targets . . . hit Val square with first 5in [127mm] salvo thereby splashing him off port quarter about 200 yards. Guns 1 and 2 obtained hits early on (estimated 6000 yards) Val on port bow and he appeared out of control . . . Shifted to plane on starboard bow. Here our luck failed . . . and plane crashed through starboard motor whaleboat and into forward fireroom, where bomb exploded, breaking keel, piercing both boilers, putting hole about 20 feet long and 4 feet wide in starboard side below water line . . . All communications lost with after part of ship.[19]

At this point, *Colhoun* lost all way and drifted to a stop. With the remaining CO_2 extinguishers and foamite canisters, the crew fought back the fires until the next attack developed.[20]

> 1725 another attack commenced . . . the Val on starboard bow caught his port wing on the after stack bounced off gun 3 knocking off his gas tank which flamed to the main deck by gun 4, flaming and taking 45 director bath tub along, bounced off main deck into water where bomb exploded putting a hole below the water line about three feet square in compartment C-205, but so deluging the after part of ship with water that all fires started were extinguished. The water however washed most of after 20mm crews and a few of the torpedomen over the fantail. They were in most instances able to swim back, one was rescued by Enyon, Coxswain, and four by ship's port motor whaleboat.[21]

That was nearly the end of the attacks, but not the end of the efforts to save the two devastated destroyers. Neither effort would be successful. Neither ship survived very long. *Bush* was the first to succumb.

A photograph taken five days later shows *Bush* alongside a pier at the busy Mare Island Navy Yard at the northern end of San Francisco Bay. This is where most destroyers and submarines in the US Pacific Fleet underwent their refits and repairs. Besides the three single 20mm mounts directly aft of Mount 55, she has depth–charge racks and tanks for her smoke generator (which do double duty as the tie-downs for a clothes–line) at her fantail. (NARA)

At 1830 an unusually heavy swell rocked the ship. A loud tearing and crunching noise was heard as the swell passed. The ship started to cave in amidships, the bow inclined about 15 degrees above the stern. As each swell passed, this angle increased until at the point at which the angle forward by the two halves reached 135 degrees, the stern section was abandoned. The commanding officer was the last to leave.[22]

Colhoun did not survive much longer. She suffered one more attack, being clipped by a *kamikaze* that then wheeled into the water. This aircraft spilled fuel over the bridge structure, but the avgas failed to ignite and no further damage was done. But the damage already sustained was enough to doom the destroyer. By 1900, Wilson concluded that the battle was likely lost and had all wounded and all but a skeleton crew of four officers and seventeen men taken off by a pair of LCSs. These last continued to fight the fires and flooding on into the evening. At 2320, a fleet tug arrived from Kerama Retto, but when it was discovered that the tug had no additional pumps or fire extinguishers to offer, Wilson reluctantly conceded that the fires could no longer be controlled and decided to take the last men off *Colhoun*. For the second time in a year and a half, he ordered his ship abandoned. At 2355, Wilson ordered her finished off by gunfire from *Cassin Young*. Between *Bush* and *Colhoun*, 129 officers and men were lost, surprisingly few considering the beating the two ships had sustained.

Bush and *Colhoun* were by no means the last destroyers to be lost to *kamikaze* attack as the war drew close to the shores of Japan. They were replaced at the picket stations by two new destroyers. The role they played warning the fleet of approaching attacks was too vital to be discontinued. *Mannert L Abele* (DD 733) was lost on 12 April. *Pringle* (DD 477) was at picket station No. 14 on 16 April when she was sunk. *Morrison* (DD 560) was at station No. 1, the same one previously occupied by *Bush,* when she was overwhelmed on 3 May. Nor was this the end of the losses. The list grew as destroyers were sent to man the picket line, but it grew less rapidly over time as the size of the protective CAP over the pickets was increased and as the skill of the *kamikaze*s continued to decline. Destroyers, as always, were big enough to do almost any job and small enough to be sacrificed, if necessary, to accomplish it.

Notes

1 *Shinyo* (Sea Quake) suicide boats were one-man fast motorboats, most often loaded with a pair of depth charges, designed to be piloted alongside an enemy vessel and then detonated. More than 6000 were built towards the end of the war, of which approximately 400 were deployed to attack the Allied fleet at Okinawa. Almost all the rest were retained in defence of the 'home islands'.

2 The word *kamikaze,* which in Japanese means 'divine wind', was, in fact, never used by the Japanese during the war to describe suicide attack units. They were generically called *tokkotai* in an abbreviation of the Japanese words for 'Special Attack Units'. Navy *tokkotai* units were sometimes called *Shinpu,* which is the Chinese pronunciation of the *kanji* characters for 'divine wind'. These were mispronounced by American translators using the indigenous Japanese pronunciation *kamikaze* for the *kanji* characters.

3 Which is not to say that the *kamikaze* threat did not give Allied naval commanders pause. While the abandonment of the Okinawa invasion was never seriously proposed, the withdrawal of major naval units, particularly aircraft carriers, from relatively static positions near the island was considered.

4 *Victory*, p. 124.

5 The Aichi D3A Type 99 Carrier Bomber was given the codename 'Val'. It was an effective dive bomber early in the war, roughly comparable to the US Navy's Douglas SBD Dauntless, though the latter was somewhat faster and could carry double the bomb load. By 1945, any surviving Vals were obvious candidates for *kamikaze* duty.

6 It is important to note that, while the *kamikaze* threat absorbed the attention of the defenders, the Japanese continued to make 'conventional' attacks in which the pilot attempted to return to his base.

7 Virtually the only remaining active units of the Japanese fleet – the battleship *Yamato*, the light cruiser *Yahagi* and eight destroyers – sailed for Okinawa on 6 April. They were sighted late in the day and attacked the next morning by US carrier aircraft. Of this force, only four destroyers survived the overwhelming attacks and managed to return to Japan. None came within sight of the Allied landing forces.

8 It is interesting that, based on wartime experience, the US Navy followed the *Essex* class with the three *Midway*s, which featured armoured flight decks and enclosed hangars like HMS *Illustrious*, while the Royal Navy designed, but did not build, the *Malta* class, which would have foregone flight-deck armour and would have featured an open hangar.

9 The damaged ships were USSS *Leutze* (DD 481), *Newcomb* (DD 586), *Morris* (DD 417), *Howorth* (DD 592), *Hyman* (DD 732), *Mullany* (DD 528), *Witter* (DE 636) and *Rodman* (DMS 21).

10 Among other missions while attached to the Home Fleet, *Emmons* escorted HMS *Duke of York* on a sortie to and from Iceland in July 1942.

11 *Victory*, pp. 193–4.

12 *Bush*. This is from the section of the report titled 'Brief Summary (Day of Loss)'. The use of a hyphen in describing the weight of the forced-draft blower sent skyward by this explosion is misleading. It is certain that the writer meant to use a comma, as the weight of the blower is described in other accounts as being greater than 4000lb (1.8 tonnes).

13 An LCS (Landing Craft, Support) was a fire-support craft based on the hull of an LCI (Landing Craft, Infantry). It displaced 250 tons and generally carried one 3in (76mm) gun, along with two twin 40mm and four single 20mm anti-aircraft guns. At this time, two LCSs were assigned to each radar picket station off Okinawa to support the destroyer on picket duty.

14 Ibid.

15 *Colhoun*.

16 *Victory*, p. 187.

17 Op. cit. The US Navy identified gun mounts on destroyers by calibre and by a numerical sequence from bow to stern. If mounts were paired port and starboard, the starboard mount was numbered first. A shorthand designation used the first digit of the calibre followed by the mount number. Thus mount No. 44 was the fourth 40mm mount, amidships on the port side. A 'handy billy' was a portable water pump.

18 *Bush*.

19 *Colhoun*.

20 Foamite was a soy-protein powder which, when mixed with a water stream created a foam that floated on water, which was effective in fighting chemical fires, such as a gasoline-fed fire. The effect was to allow a film of water to be maintained long enough on the burning liquid to smother the fire. It was the predecessor of modern AFFF foams.

21 Ibid.

22 *Bush*.

Chapter 10

The Cold War Gets Hotter – The Gulf of Tonkin (2 and 4 August 1964)

THIS WAS MOST definitely not war as usual. Not the kind of war for which the officers and men had trained or for which the ships had been built. They had all emerged from World War II, the victors in what many Americans consider 'the last good war'.[1] These included officers such as Captain John J Herrick, who had joined the US Navy during World War II and had fought off the shores of Korea, rising to command of Desdiv 192 by 1964. His flagship, USS *Maddox* (DD 731), was herself a veteran of both of those wars.

She was a *Sumner*-class destroyer. This class was an evolutionary, mid-war development of the very successful *Fletcher* class. The *Sumner*s shared the same hull and machinery as the *Fletcher*s, but substituted three twin 5in (127mm)/38 gun houses for the five single mounts on the earlier class. This twin mount was developed just before the war. It became the standard medium-calibre dual-purpose mount on all large war-construction US warships. The space saved by putting three main-battery mounts in the place of five was used to increase AA weaponry, generally two quad and two twin 40mm mounts and up to eleven single 20mm Oerlikons. All this added topweight affected the *Sumner*s' stability and reduced both top speed and range compared to the *Fletcher*s, but the strong AA battery made them very popular as escorts for fast carrier groups.[2]

Maddox *arrives in Vietnam*

Maddox was active from the time she arrived in the war zone in October 1944. Hit by a *kamikaze* while on picket station off the coast of Formosa, she had spent three months at Ulithi under repair, but had returned to fight, providing escort and bombarding shore facilities on the southern Home Islands until Japan surrendered in August 1945.[3] *Maddox* remained in the Pacific, and in commission, continuously after the war. She was at Hong Kong when the Korean War broke out and was one of the first US warships on scene a day later.

USS *Maddox* (DD 731) was put in service in time to see combat in World War II. She was a member of the *Sumner* class, destroyers built on the hull of a *Fletcher,* but with three twin main-battery gun mounts in the place of five single mounts. This change was made to allow even more medium and light AA guns to be mounted, but when the full battery was fitted, the *Sumners* were found to be slower and less stable than the *Fletchers* they were supposed to improve upon. This photograph shows *Maddox* in the company of a light cruiser somewhere in the Pacific sometime in 1945. (NHC)

She was active throughout the war, but naval activity was always secondary to the land campaign in that war, as the North Koreans and their Chinese allies never seriously attempted to oppose Allied control of the waters around the Korean peninsula. *Maddox* had patrolled the Taiwan Strait, provided escort for aircraft carriers whose air groups were active in the war over Korea, and occasionally bombarded North Korean positions ashore. After that war ended without much satisfaction, she continued an active career in the western Pacific. She spent two years operating off the west coast of the United States between March 1962 and March 1964, and then again headed west across the Pacific for assignment in the Far East. From mid-May, she was assigned patrol duty off the coast of Vietnam.

As with the rest of her surviving sisters, *Maddox* had not been extensively modified at this point. Most of the changes from her as-built condition involved the removal of all her light and medium AA guns and both of her quintuple torpedo-tube mounts. Fleet defence now required that enemy aircraft and surface ships be engaged at ranges far beyond that of these weapons and they were therefore considered redundant. In their place, two twin and two single 3in (76mm)/50 mounts, capable of firing a shell with a VT proximity fuse, were fitted. However, the greatest threat to the fleet was considered to be the vast fleet of Soviet submarines, and *Maddox* had become primarily an anti-submarine platform, with two triple Mk 32 12.75in (324mm) tubes for ASW torpedoes and twin Hedgehog mounts. The net effect of these changes was, if anything, a decrease in stability and speed, as the new 3in (76mm) AA mounts weighed significantly more than the weapons they replaced.

Vietnam — the story so far

The war, if that term could be used, that *Maddox* and John Herrick found off the coast of Vietnam was different as well. The Americans, so far, were not actively involved in the fighting on the ground, but they had already done everything possible short of that in support of one side in an already long and ugly war. From the American point of view, it was yet another episode in a struggle against Communist aggression that had been underway since the end of World War II. To the Vietnamese, it was also part of an ongoing struggle,

Seen in profile as she was observing a test firing of a Polaris missile in the Pacific, 6 May 1962, *Maddox* shows some of the many changes made to World War II-vintage destroyers over the intervening years. The most obvious change is the addition of many more sensors, requiring a massive tripod foremast to hold the heavy SPS-6B air-search radar antenna on the foretop and an SPS-4 surface-search set, successor to the SG, at the masthead. The radomes mounted on the second funnel are for ECM systems. The large Mk 4 (FD) antenna on the main-battery director (or its successor the Mk 12/22) has been replaced by the circular antenna of a Mk 25. All 40mm mounts have been replaced by single or twin 3in (76mm)/50 automatic weapons and all 20mm mounts deleted, as were the two quintuple banks of torpedo tubes. (NHC)

between the French-influenced, affluent and Roman Catholic southern part of the country and the more isolated, poorer and Buddhist north.[4] The government in the north, led by Ho Chi Minh, were the direct heirs of the Viet Minh guerillas who had fought the Japanese and later the French in an attempt to gain independence. Having beaten the French decisively at Dien Bien Phu in 1954, the Viet Minh agreed to the Geneva Accords, which left Ho in charge in the north and set up what was to have been a temporary state in the south under Ngo Dinh Diem, dividing the country at the 17th parallel. Elections were to be held in 1956 to determine the nation's future.

The Americans had provided early support to Ho when he was fighting the Japanese, and appeared at first to sympathise with his nationalistic goals, but when the French returned to re-establish their colonial government in 1946, the Americans were already too focused on containing communism to care much about earlier hints of support for a leftist leader in a far-away country. Propping up the French was more important. By 1950, American 'advisors' were on the ground in Vietnam, arming and training forces to fight the Viet Minh. This help did not prevent the defeat of the French and their subsequent agreement to the Geneva Accords. The Americans never signed that agreement and rapidly became the main support of Diem's government in the south. The French were happy to leave the stage.[5]

In 1956, the northern government authorised a low-level insurgency, led by Viet Minh cadres who had stayed behind in the south when the country was split. At first the tactics were restricted to the assassination of village officials appointed by Diem, but this campaign was so successful in creating havoc in the southern countryside that Ho agreed to allow more organised military operations in 1959. American support for Diem increased after the election of John F Kennedy in 1960. There were many reasons for this; the fact that Kennedy and Diem were both Catholics was seen by some as significant, but was certainly less important than Cold War politics. America had suffered a number of perceived losses and humiliations at the hands of communists in the 1950s and Kennedy decided that Vietnam was the place to make a stand.

It was, however, a long way from making that decision to actually having success against the Viet Cong on the ground.[6] Despite ever-increasing aid and the presence of ever-larger numbers of US 'advisors', it was clear by 1963 that the south was losing the war.[7] Corruption and incompetence in the southern government and military made the Viet Cong's programme of land reform and simple nationalism sound appealing to the rural population. There are signs that President Kennedy had grown wary of the southern regime and was planning a phase-out of American military and financial support when Diem was assassinated. This happened, apparently without Kennedy's knowledge, though with the full support of the CIA, on 2 November 1963. Diem was replaced by a succession of short-lived military governments. It is impossible to know what course the American involvement in Vietnam would have taken had Kennedy not been assassinated in Dallas, Texas, on 22 November, just three weeks after Diem. The first priority of the new president, Lyndon Johnson, was addressing the serious domestic issues facing America at the time, particularly racial integration and poverty.[8] He had no natural interest in foreign policy and was content to let the American commitment in Vietnam continue as before.

OPLAN 34A and 'Desoto'

Two programmes emerged during this period that combined to make *Maddox* the target of North Vietnamese torpedo boats in August 1964. One was OPLAN 34A. This started as an effort by the CIA to employ South Vietnamese

The cause of much of the trouble that led to the Gulf of Tonkin Incident was the small fleet of *Nasty* boats nominally operated by the South Vietnamese under the auspices of the CIA to harass North Vietnamese shore facilities and coastal forces with the hope of convincing the Viet Cong to cease operations or, failing that, to provoke a major incident that would justify US intervention. This photograph shows five of the OPLAN 34A boats at Da Nang in 1965. The boat on the right is *PTF 7* and the two in the centre background are *PTF 1* and *PTF 2*. The two boats to the left of these, seen just above the parked Jeep, are also *Nastys*. In the centre foreground are a pair of river patrol boats, similar in appearance to the later PCF *Swift* boats. (Dan Withers/www.ptfnasty.com)

assets to infiltrate commando teams into the north and attack high-value North Vietnamese military installations. Part of this effort involved seaborne attacks on coastal facilities. At first, these missions were mounted on junk-type coastal craft that appeared identical to hundreds of other boats plying their trade (and often smuggling people and goods) along the coast. As the fortunes of the southern government waned, the pressure to mount more effective attacks against the north increased, and the CIA turned the operation over to the US Defense Department at the beginning of 1964. A cover organisation called the Studies and Observations Group (SOG) was set up under the Military Assistance Command, Vietnam (MACV) to manage OPLAN 34A. At the same time, new and much more capable boats were acquired – *Nasty*-class patrol boats built by Batservice Verft A/S of Mandal, Norway. These were state-of-the-art fast patrol craft armed with a single 20mm and single 40mm gun and powered by diesel motors capable of reaching forty-five knots in calm water. They were retrofitted with various grenade launchers, flame-throwers and rocket launchers, as the original tactic of landing small raiding parties proved less than successful and the *Nasty*s increasingly just stood offshore and lobbed ordnance at North Vietnamese coastal installations.

The idea behind OPLAN 34A was to put sufficient pressure on the northern government to convince them to cease their effective material support for the Viet Cong. As 1964 progressed, it was becoming increasingly obvious that this tactic was not working, that the naval attacks were not having any serious impact on the North's willingness to continue the war. Indeed, rather than backing off, the North Vietnamese acquired fast patrol boats of their own to counter the raids from the south. They actually acquired two different types of small boats. Most were of the larger *Swatow*-type designed in Russia and built in China. These displaced sixty-seven tons, were twenty-five metres long and carried twin 37mm and 20mm mounts at a top speed of forty-five knots, making them very close equivalents of the *Nasty*s they were intended to counter. To support the *Swatow*s, the North Vietnamese also acquired a number of smaller Soviet-built *P*-4-class MTBs (Motor Torpedo Boats) that displaced twenty-five tons, were armed with a pair of heavy machine guns and two single 17.7in (450mm) torpedo tubes and could reach a top speed of fifty knots. In addition to these patrol boats, the North Vietnamese also requested and received coastal radar installations and defensive weaponry from Russia and China. As these facilities and forces came into service in the early 1960s, the ongoing OPLAN 34A raids became more difficult and the pressure on the Pentagon and military intelligence units to provide effective support increased.

One result of the pressure was an operation, codenamed 'Desoto', mounted by a covert US naval intelligence unit known as the Naval Security Group (NSG). This operation involved lashing a van-sized container to the deck of a destroyer. Called a DSU (Direct Support Unit), the container was filled with electronics, including receivers dedicated to the interception of voice and manual Morse communications and other radio frequency emissions, such as radars.[9] The van also contained equipment that allowed it to send and receive classified radio traffic connecting it to other NSG units in South Vietnam and the Philippines.[10] The idea was that a Desoto-equipped destroyer would move along an enemy coast just outside the territorial limit. This was designed to provoke the enemy into activating its radars and initiating bursts of communications, all of which would be captured and analysed by the twelve to eighteen officers and men who manned the van.

At first the US Navy was reluctant to associate Desoto, which was a perfectly legal and legitimate activity, with the technically illegal OPLAN 34A raids. The first Desoto mission in the Tonkin Gulf (there had been others elsewhere) was supposed to be carried out by USS *Radford* (DD 446) in January 1964, but was cancelled because an OPLAN 34A raid was scheduled for several weeks later and NSG wanted there to be a clear separation of the two activities. The postponed mission was then carried out by USS *Craig* (DD 885) in late February and concentrated mainly on the border area between Vietnam and China, west of Hainan Island. As her route approached the coast of North Vietnam only briefly, there was no particular reaction from North Vietnamese coastal forces or radar sites and it was not clear whether they were even aware of *Craig*'s presence or mission. Another series of OPLAN 34A raids was planned for July, targeting the islands of Hon Me, Hon Nieu and Hon Matt off the coast of central North Vietnam, south of where *Craig* had operated, which were believed to be the sites of radar installations and bases for coastal patrol boats. MACV specifically requested additional support and, with assurances from General Westmoreland that there would be no interference between the two activities, CINCPAC (Commander-in-Chief, Pacific) agreed to another Desoto mission to start in late July 1964.

Maddox *makes a Desoto sweep*

Maddox was tapped for this second Desoto mission off the coast of Vietnam. She was based at Yokasuka, Japan, but stopped at Keelung, Taiwan, near the northern tip of the island, to pick up the Desoto DSU and sixteen analysts. This mission, unlike the first one carried out by *Craig*, would sweep the entire length of the coast of North Vietnam. The instructions to Herrick were to remain

Captain J J Herrick (left), ComDesdiv 192, and Commander H L Ogier, CO USS *Maddox,* pose just in front of that ship's forward funnel, August 1964. It was Herrick who first reported and then questioned the presence of North Vietnamese torpedo boats during the critical second 'attack' on 4 August 1964. (NHC)

eight miles from the coast, though he was allowed to approach within four miles of offshore islands.[11] Informed that an OPLAN 34A raid against Hon Me and Hon Nieu islands was planned for the night of 30–31 July, *Maddox* headed out to sea south of Hainan to clear the area. The raid was only partially successful. *Nasty* boats manned by South Vietnamese sailors and assorted mercenaries, mainly Taiwanese, attempted to put a commando team ashore on Hon Me, but were driven off before a landing could be made, and resorted to shelling installations there from offshore. Other *Nastys* shelled Hon Nieu. In neither case was the shelling particularly effective, and the North Vietnamese reacted by sending out *Swatows* and the smaller and faster *P-4s* in an unsuccessful attempt to catch the escaping *Nastys.* These patrol boats were still astir the next morning when *Maddox* approached the coast again and began a slow run up the coast starting near the DMZ (DeMilitarised Zone) that separated the two halves of the country, allowing the Desoto unit to gather a rich harvest of SIGINT.

While the US officially considered the OPLAN 34A raid and *Maddox*'s Desoto sweep to be entirely separate and unrelated activities, despite the obvious co-ordination, the North Vietnamese did not and presumed that

Maddox's continued presence in disputed waters off their coast to be the preliminary to yet another OPLAN 34A raid. Therefore, it is not surprising that the North Vietnamese monitored *Maddox's* progress up their coast, or that NSG units intercepted and decrypted this traffic. A message reported at 2300 local time on 1 August indicated that the North Vietnamese had determined to attack *Maddox*.[12] At the time, she was approaching Hon Me. Herrick decided to suspend the Desoto mission and headed first south and then east away from the coast at ten knots. When no attack materialised, Herrick decided at 0500 the next morning, 2 August, to return to the coast and resume the intelligence operation.

NSG's analysis of North Vietnamese intentions had been essentially correct. It is not clear whether an attack would have happened the night of 1–2 August had *Maddox* not moved away from the coast, but it is likely that the Gulf of Tonkin Incident would not have occurred – at least not at the beginning of August – had *Maddox* really broken off the Desoto mission that night and not resumed her patrol the next morning. However, it is evident that as she headed north the next morning, she was being tracked and patrol boats, both *Swatows* and *P-4s*, were gathering near Hon Me as *Maddox* was passing south-to-north, barely ten miles east of the island. At that point the two sides were on a collision course.[13] An NSA analysis was distributed at 1000 that morning predicting an attack on *Maddox* that same day, but, intentionally or not, the message was not sent to *Maddox*. The message acknowledged North Vietnamese concern about *Maddox's* proximity to Hon Me, given the OPLAN 34A raid just three days earlier:

> . . . THE INDICATED SENSITIVITY ON PART OF DRV AS WELL AS THEIR INDICATED PREPARATION TO COUNTER, POS[SI]BLE THE DRV REACTION TO DESOTO PATROL MIGHT BE MORE SEVERE THAN WOULD OTHERWISE BE ANTICIPATED.[14]

Certainly, had any of the recipients of this message wished to prevent this attack, including CINCPAC and 7th Fleet, both in Herrick's chain of command, it would have been a simple matter to order *Maddox* away from the coast. This was not done. The reason given later for public consumption – that *Maddox* was exercising her right of free passage in international waters – was technically correct, given the American interpretation of maritime law at the time, but does not explain the actions of Herrick's superiors that day. Simply put, American leadership from the White House on down was looking for an excuse to expand the US role in the Vietnam War. To their immense relief, the North Vietnamese were about to provide that excuse.

The North Vietnamese give chase

By noon on 2 August, *Maddox* had approached within visual range of Hon Me and had sighted five North Vietnamese patrol boats: two *Swatows* (*T-146* and *T-142*) and three P-4s (*T-333*, *T-336* and *T-339* – which comprised Section 3 of Patrol Boat Squadron 135). Now at the proper distance offshore to continue her Desoto mission, *Maddox* turned to the northeast and headed away from the island and the patrol boats at eleven knots. At this point there seems to have been confusion on the part of the North Vietnamese. According to intercepted messages, different parts of the command structure sent contradictory orders to Section 3/135, but because the P-4s lacked the necessary radio equipment to receive these orders directly, all messages had to be retransmitted to the P-4s by one of the *Swatows*. This clumsy communications set-up bears some of the blame for the attack taking place when it did, and perhaps for it taking place at all. This is because a message ordering Section 3/135 to attack was received by *T-142* at almost the same time as a message ordering the boats to head for shore and then back to Hon Me. The sequence of the sending and receipt of these messages certainly confused the radio crew on *T-142* and, in the event, only the attack message was retransmitted to the three P-4s of Section 3/135. Even if, as it appears, the North Vietnamese naval command had decided to postpone or completely call off the attack, it was too late.[15] *Maddox* was kept apprised of each of these communications.

At 1400, radar on *Maddox* detected three boats approaching from the southwest. This was the three P-4s of Section 3/135. *Maddox* immediately turned first to the east and then southeast and increased speed to twenty-five knots. Although the P-4s were equipped with radar, they did not appear to be using them, and they were slow to react to *Maddox's* course changes. Rather than 'cutting the corners', the patrol boats followed the destroyer's wake and found themselves in a poor attack position, well astern of *Maddox*.[16] Even with a twenty-knot speed advantage, they would need at least half an hour to pull ahead and achieve an optimal position for launching torpedoes. At 1430, Commander Ogier ordered the crew to General Quarters. Ten minutes later, Herrick sent a broadcast message stating he was being trailed by hostile torpedo boats and that he intended to open fire if necessary to prevent an attack. The nearest support was the aircraft carrier *Ticonderoga* (CVA 14), which had four F-8E Crusaders aloft on patrol.[17] These were vectored to the site and the destroyer *Turner Joy* (DD 951) was also dispatched to aid *Maddox*.

The chase continued, with the P-4s gaining ground and beginning to pull up on the destroyer's starboard quarter. At 1500, Herrick gave Ogier permission to

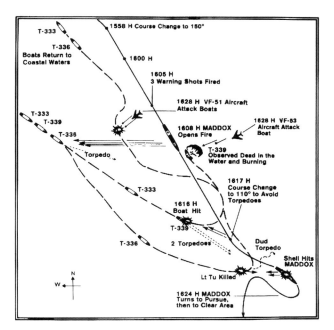

The official US Navy map of the first half of the Tonkin Gulf Incident, when three North Vietnamese torpedo boats approached *Maddox* with clear intent to engage. This chart shows the events quite accurately, because the events depicted here actually happened in the afternoon of 2 August 1964. The times on this map are shown in time zone Hotel (GMT or Zulu plus eight hours), which was one zone east (and one hour ahead) of the true local zone, Golf. (USN)

open fire if the torpedo boats came within five nautical miles. Five minutes later, *Maddox* fired three warning shots ahead of the *P-4s*.[18] After three more minutes, at 1508, *Maddox* resumed firing and continued lobbing shells at the three boats gaining on her starboard beam, but without effect. Over the next few minutes, at least one torpedo was launched at *Maddox*, but it was a long–range overtaking shot and was not even noticed by the destroyer. The three torpedo boats then split, with the lead boat, *T-336*, swinging to starboard in an attempt to loop ahead of the destroyer, while the other two, led by *T-339*, continued to close. At around 1516, a number of events occurred at the same time. *T-339* was hit by at least one shell from *Maddox* and at least two torpedoes were fired at *Maddox* by the two nearer boats. Seeing these torpedoes hit the water, *Maddox* turned slightly to port to present the smallest possible target. All torpedoes missed. The two nearer boats, *T-339* and *T-333*, turned away and started heading northwest. Soon after making the turn, *T-333* swung around *T-339*, which was on fire and losing way, and left the stricken boat behind.

One of a series of photographs taken from *Maddox's* starboard quarter that show the attack by the three North Vietnamese *P-4* motor torpedo boats, 2 August 1964. This would appear to have been taken at around 1508, just before *Maddox* opened fire, just after the lead torpedo boat, *T-336* (left), split away from the other two boats. (NHC)

One of the three attacking *P-4s* speeds to the left as a shell splash subsides in her wake, 2 August 1964. Her 'Skin Head' radar is mounted on a short mast aft of her low bridge. It is impossible to tell which of the three boats this is. (NHC)

Three shell splashes rise aft of a speeding *P-4* with several others subsiding further to the right, as seen from *Maddox*, 2 August 1964. Being small and fast, these boats proved to be difficult targets for the gun-control radar of the day to track. Another boat, almost certainly *T-339*, burns to the left, which means that the boat to the right on the receiving end of all this attention is probably *T-333*, following her as they turned to the north. (NHC)

T-336 now attempted an attack, but her torpedo misfired and she too was hit by a shell from *Maddox*. After this, she also turned to the northwest and fell in astern of *T-333*. *Maddox*, which at this time received its only damage – a slug from a large-calibre machine gun fired by *T-336*, probably 14.5mm, which lodged in her superstructure – briefly turned to pursue, but then thought better of it and turned again to the south, away from the site.

At this point, at about 1528, the four Crusaders from *Ticonderoga* arrived on the scene. Two of the aircraft went after *T-339*, which was on fire and drifting to a stop. They fired Zuni 5in (127mm) FFARs (Folding Fin Aircraft Rocket) and their internal 20mm cannons at the small boat, claiming they saw it sink as they were leaving the area. The other two Crusaders took on the two remaining torpedo boats heading northwest at high speed. They claimed to have heavily damaged one of them. As the jets headed back to *Ticonderoga*, the two torpedo boats and *Maddox* also exited the scene, each in a different direction. The one thing they all agreed on was that *T-339* was either sunk or sinking and her twelve-man crew lost. *T-333* had been hit three times, but was described in a post-action report as being 'lightly damaged'. *T-336* suffered more serious damage and two wounded crewmen.[19] There had been no casualties on the American side.

The initial reaction in Washington was surprisingly subdued. President Johnson opted only to send a note of protest to Hanoi, asserting the right of US warships to navigate in international waters. In part this mild reaction was due to understanding by the Americans that the attack that day may well have been an error caused by bungled communications on the part of the North Vietnamese. This was knowledge derived from SIGINT and therefore not information that could be made public. To emphasise the American insistence on navigational freedom, the Pentagon ordered *Maddox,* now accompanied by *Turner Joy,* to resume the interrupted Desoto mission the next day.

Ghosts in the water

The daylight hours of 3 August were tense but passed without further incident. The two American destroyers arrived on station south of Hon Me in the early afternoon and resumed their slow patrol off the coast. The North Vietnamese had spent the day shepherding the two damaged *P-4*s to port and, when they realised the Americans had resumed their patrol, shadowed the two destroyers with *Swatow* boats from a safe distance. President Johnson stated publicly that were US forces again attacked, they had instructions to destroy any attacking forces. Other than that, the US refrained from further provocation until that night.

Lieutenant Commander Dempster M Jackson, executive officer of *Maddox*, looks very serious as he shows off the only damage received by the destroyer in her encounter with the North Vietnamese torpedo boats, 2 August 1964. A hole was punched through one of the supports for the ship's Mk 56 director by a round from a large-calibre machine gun, probably a Soviet-made ZPU 14.5mm AA weapon or a Chinese-made copy. The photograph was taken eight days later. Considering the pristine appearance of the bullet, it was most likely added later for dramatic effect. (NHC)

At nighfall, *Maddox* and *Turner Joy* turned away from the coast. They were tracked for a while by the *Swatows,* but these boats soon had other concerns and lost contact with the two destroyers. At 1510 that afternoon, another OPLAN 34A raid had left Da Nang headed north. It is doubtful that Washington was aware, as the president and his top aides were exhorting restraint from the North Vietnamese, that four *Nastys* were heading for a radar site at Vinh Son, about 100 miles south of Hon Me. Shortly after midnight on 4 August, they shelled the facility and then headed back south, pursued briefly by a North Vietnamese patrol boat. Needless to say, by the time the two destroyers arrived back on station at 1300 on the 4th, their presence had again attracted continual radar and visual surveillance.

Despite this active surveillance, no North Vietnamese craft were sighted during the day and the two American destroyers ended their patrol at 1600 and again headed away from the coast. At 1815 and again at 1840, Herrick received warnings issued by NSG stations that another attack by North Vietnamese torpedo boats was imminent. The second warning was quite explicit, reporting that three boats had been told to 'make ready for military operations the night of 4 August' and that the likely target was the Desoto mission.[20] Quite alarmed,

The next day, *Maddox* was joined by a second American destroyer, *Turner Joy* (DD 951).
A member of the postwar *Forrest Sherman* class, they were half again bigger than the wartime
Fletchers and were the last American warships to be designed primarily as gun platforms,
being armed with three fully automatic 5in (127mm)/54 mounts
and two twin 3in (76mm)/50 AA mounts. (NHC)

Herrick sent a message an hour later to CINCPAC indicating that he had changed course to the southeast and increased speed to twenty knots to avoid, if possible, what appeared to be an imminent attack.

It certainly appeared that Herrick's concern was well founded. At 2000, *Maddox* reported two 'skunks' (surface contacts) and three 'bogies' (air contacts) on her radar.[21] The surface contacts were seen at forty to forty-five miles to the northeast, meaning they were coming from the direction of Hainan and were well over 100 miles away from the coast of Vietnam, a fact which seems to have raised no doubts in Herrick's mind. He reported the contact and four jets already aloft over *Ticonderoga* were vectored towards the destroyers. *Maddox* tracked the two 'skunks' for forty-five minutes, during which time they closed to within twenty-seven miles. Then, inexplicably, the two contacts disappeared, and for more than half an hour the two destroyers steamed now south-southeast without any further excitement.

That period of relative calm ended at 2108, when *Maddox* reported a radar contact fifteen miles to the southwest approaching at more than thirty knots. The four A-4 Skyhawks from *Ticonderoga* now loitering over the two destroyers checked out the contacts, but found no sign of any other craft in the water. At 2131, this contact also disappeared off *Maddox*'s radar screens as suddenly as it had appeared. Three minutes later, yet another contact popped up, this one even more threatening. This time, both ships reported radar contacts, but, curiously, they were at different range and bearing. This did not seem to bother anyone on the two ships at the time (or anyone in the American command structure later), who all agreed that these must be the same contact. *Maddox* acquired the target at just under five nautical miles and tracked it until it turned away at just over three nautical miles, a manoeuvre that was interpreted as a torpedo launch.[22] A sonar contact was reported, which was assumed to be a torpedo in the water, and the two ships reacted accordingly. Both destroyers opened fire on their contacts, but since the contacts were at different bearings, each fired in a different direction. The contact *Maddox* was engaging continued away until it disappeared at approximately five nautical miles; *Turner Joy*'s target continued to approach until it disappeared at two nautical miles.

Quiet settled over the Tonkin Gulf, but again this was not to last long. Fifteen minutes later, at 2201, *Turner Joy* picked up multiple targets to the west and again opened fire. More than two dozen torpedoes were reported and the ships took evasive courses, dropping depth charges in the path of the torpedoes in an attempt to force them off course. The radar contacts were discontinuous, far from ideal, but this did not stop either ship from keeping up an intense fire. *Turner Joy* fired more than 300 5in (127mm) rounds during the engagement.

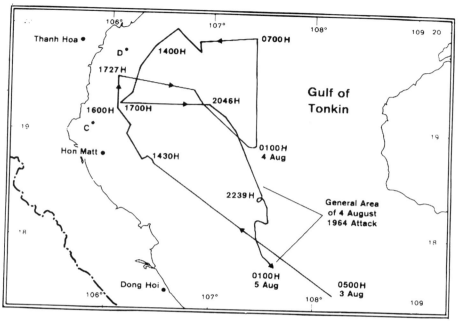

The course taken by *Maddox* and *Turner Joy* starting the morning of 3 August 1964 is shown on this official map. Entering the Gulf of Tonkin from the southeast, they swept up the North Vietnamese coast until late afternoon and then headed to more open water for the night. They returned to the coast the next morning and followed it southwards until again turning away in the later afternoon. It was after they had steamed due east for almost four hours and turned towards the southeast that the second, critical 'incident' occurred. (USN)

One of her officers commented: 'We were getting blotches on the radar screen – nothing real firm, so we were whacking away at general areas with proximity fuses, hoping to get something.'[23]

These contacts were reported to the orbiting aircraft and star shells were fired to illuminate the enemy. The Skyhawks repeatedly investigated the contacts, dropping their own flares, but failed to find a single attacker. This melée continued for an hour and a half, the last of the contacts disappearing at 2335. Despite the apparent intensity of the attack, both destroyers emerged un-harmed. Herrick's first after-action report claimed two patrol boats sunk, though he conceded that one of them might have been sunk accidentally by another North Vietnamese boat.

However, almost immediately, doubts began to threaten Herrick's certainty about what had just happened. On top of the failure of the aircraft to sight any boats, there was the fact that *Maddox*'s radar failed to pick up any contacts during the second and more serious encounter. Further, the sonar operators on both destroyers reported their doubts that they had actually heard any torpedoes in the water. Investigation revealed that the first torpedo reports had come from radar tracking what appeared to be a torpedo attack manoeuvre. Only after the ships began evasive manoeuvres did sonar pick up the sound of high-speed screws, and this could be explained by the sound of the destroyer's own screws reflecting off their own rudders.

Sufficient doubts had accumulated that, within an hour after the first report, Herrick sent another, more sobering, message, though he was unwilling to give up entirely the thought that his destroyers had been attacked.

ENTIRE ACTION LEAVES MANY DOUBTS EXCEPT FOR APPARENT ATTEMPTED AMBUSH AT THE BEGINNING. . . . NEVER POSITIVELY IDENTIFIED A BOAT AS SUCH.[24]

He requested an aerial reconnaissance of the site at first light to check for debris.

The excuse long sought

These doubts should have been enough to inspire caution in the American leaders who were following the action in close to real time, had they arrived in time. However, despite – or perhaps because of – Washington's restrained response to the skirmish two days earlier, this time there was a clear desire to react aggressively and quickly to what appeared to be a clear provocation. Lyndon Johnson had been alerted when the first warnings of a possible attack had been broadcast and was informed as news of the apparent attack came through the Pentagon. Within three hours, by 1400 Washington time, two fateful decisions had been made – to bomb North Vietnamese naval facilities starting at 1900 (0700G on the 5th) and to submit the fateful Gulf of Tonkin Resolution to Congress two days later, which authorised the President to 'take all necessary steps, including the use of armed forces' to protect South Vietnam and other Southeast Asian allies. Thus, these decisions were made less than three hours after Herrick dispatched his first after-action report and less than two hours after his more doubtful follow-up.

It is not clear at what point the President or his advisors saw these messages, if ever, but it was irrelevant once the retaliatory air strikes had been ordered. Lyndon Johnson was in the midst of a campaign for re-election and was opposed by the very hawkish Barry Goldwater, so any sign of wavering or indecision would have been used against him. North Vietnamese protests that no attack had taken place on the 4th were dismissed as typical Communist

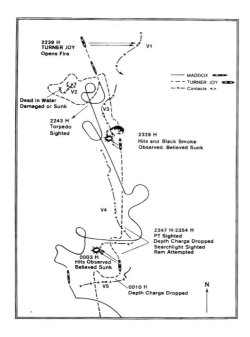

The tracks followed by *Maddox* and *Turner Joy* late on 4 August 1964 are shown in this official chart. The gyrations of the two ships, particularly *Maddox*, as they tracked radar contacts, make it appear they were involved in a fierce struggle against a determined foe. Later examination of intelligence data strongly supports the conclusion that no North Vietnamese (or any other) attackers were in the vicinity that night. (USN)

disinformation.[25] Any doubts within the Administration were dismissed the next day.

> On the first attack, the evidence would be pretty good. On the second one the amount of evidence we have today is less than we had yesterday. . . . This much seemed certain: there was an attack. How many PT boats were involved, how many torpedoes were fired, etc. – all this was still somewhat uncertain. This matter may be of some importance since Hanoi has denied making the second attack.
>
> Douglass Cater, sitting in at his first staff meeting, raised a question about the Congressional resolution on SE Asia.[26] He said he had not thought it through completely, but the logic behind the resolution troubled him somewhat. . . . The logic that troubled him was how an attack on US forces specifically justified a resolution in favor of the maintenance of freedom in SE Asia. Bundy, in reply, jokingly told him perhaps the matter should not be thought through too far.[27] For his own part, he welcomed the recent events as justification for a resolution the Administration had wanted for some time.[28]

The fallout from the increased American involvement in South Vietnam is well known. It is, in the cold light of hindsight more than forty years after these events, hard to decide which is more disturbing, the fact that America was pushed into the nightmare of the Vietnam War with laughter or the fact that, in light of all available evidence, the second, critical attack never in fact happened. The radar returns at which first *Maddox* and later *Turner Joy* fired that night were most likely nothing more than reflections off waves kicked up by a rising wind. Vietnamese records make it clear that no boat strayed far from the coast that night.[29] It is indeed tragic that so many deaths and so much destruction came from such an insubstantial cause. America is in many ways still paying the price.

Notes

1 It is probably impossible to pin down the origins of this description of World War II. It obviously must have its origins in reference to the experience of later wars that were less than 'good', such as the Korean and Vietnam wars. The phrase refers mainly to the spirit of the United States, which entered World War II with unanimous resolve and accepted the sacrifices necessary to achieve what was universally seen as a righteous victory. No war since then could claim those attributes.

2 A further wartime development was the *Gearing* class, which added four metres to the length of the hull, which addressed nearly all the complaints about the *Sumner*s.

3 Formosa, of course, is now called Taiwan, and remains in legal limbo, not quite part of China and not quite independent.

4 Roman Catholics were always a minority, even in the south, but they represented a disproportionate share of the educated and moneyed classes, the bureaucracy and the officer corps, which made them disproportionately influential in the south.

5 Neither regime, Ho's or Diem's, was popularly elected or particularly benevolent. Ho instituted Maoist agrarian reforms that killed many landowners and displaced more. Diem purged all leftist or Buddhist opposition groups with hardly any less brutality. For a while, the border between the two halves remained open and it is estimated that 450,000 northerners, mostly Catholics, moved to the south, and that 52,000 southerners moved north.

6 'Viet Cong' was a term originally coined by Diem to refer to communists operating in the south, but became the most common name for anyone fighting with the National Front for the Liberation of South Vietnam.

7 While there were not any US ground troops officially committed to the war at this point, there were American pilots flying American aircraft carrying South Vietnamese markings and Special Forces ('Green Beret') teams accompanying South Vietnamese army units on patrol.

8 It is the tragedy of Lyndon Johnson's presidency that, had he not got the nation bogged down in an unwinnable guerilla war in Vietnam, he likely would have gone down in history as one of the most important and effective of American presidents, as he was a consummate politician and a man with a true concern for the less fortunate in society. Many programmes and policies he instituted continue to pay dividends more than forty years later.

9 The use of radio frequency information is grouped together in the branch of intelligence called Signals Intelligence (SIGINT). Even if the contents of signals cannot be immediately exploited, much can be determined from the location, frequency, structure and addressing of messages in a process known as traffic analysis. The more specialised analysis of non-communications emissions, specifically radars, is called Electronic Intelligence (ELINT).

Knowing where enemy radars are located and when and how they are used can be exploited to reveal enemy intentions in real time. The Desoto DSU van had dedicated SIGINT and ELINT positions.

10 For details of the NSG and other US intelligence deployments in the region, see *Skunks*, pp. 4–7.

11 *Skunks*, pp. 6–7. The North Vietnamese claimed a twelve-mile limit for its territorial waters. At that time the United States acknowledged only a three-mile limit.

Captain John J Herrick was ComDesdiv192 and was OTC (Officer in Tactical Command) on board *Maddox*. The ship's captain was Commander Herbert Ogier. Herrick reported to Rear Admiral George S Morrison in command of US naval forces in the region. Morrison was, incidentally, the father of legendary rock singer, Jim Morrison.

12 Local time is given in time zone Golf, which is Zulu (GMT) plus 7 and Hotel (the time zone used by *Maddox* that day) minus 1.

13 It is clear the North Vietnamese never intended to use the *Swatows* to attack *Maddox*. Their lack of torpedoes made them unsuitable for such an attack, but their superior radio equipment made them useful as communications links with the smaller, torpedo-armed *P-4s*.

14 *Skunks*, p. 14. 'DRV' stands for Democratic Republic of Vietnam, the official name of North Vietnam.

15 *Skunks*, p. 15.

16 Both *Swatows* and *P-4s* were equipped with the standard Soviet small-boat radar, which had the NATO codename 'Skin Head'. This was essentially a copy of the American World War II-era SO radar, given to the Russians as part of wartime military aid. This radar was a 10cm-wavelength lightweight unit capable of picking up aircraft at fifteen nautical miles and a ship the size of *Maddox* at ten nautical miles.

17 The Vought F-8 Crusader was a supersonic carrier fighter developed in the early 1950s. The 'E' version was the last major production variant, boasting a bigger engine and better radar. It would be phased out later in the 1970s in favour of the McDonnell-Douglas F-4 Phantom.

18 Reports of these initial warning shots were not forwarded to the White House at the time, and Lyndon Johnson repeatedly stated over the next few days that the North Vietnamese had fired first.

19 *Skunks*, p. 18.

20 Ibid, p. 22.

21 Ibid, p. 22. Both US ships in this incident had radar deficits that may have affected the night's activities. *Maddox* reported that her air search radar (AN/SPS-40) was sporadically inoperable; *Turner Joy* reported that her fire-control radar (AN/SPG-53) was likewise out of commission.

22 North Vietnamese tactical doctrine for *P-4s* specified that torpedoes should be launched at a range no greater than 1000 metres.

23 Ibid, p. 23.

24 Ibid, p. 24.

25 The significance of this protest was never emphasised by the Americans, because the North Vietnamese had never denied making the attack on the 2nd.

26 S Douglass Cater was Special Assistant to President Johnson.

27 McGeorge Bundy was National Security Advisor to Presidents Kennedy and Johnson.

28 *Memo*, pp. 1–2.

29 This conclusion does not sit well with some. In a letter to the editor published in the April 2008 issue of *Naval History*, Commander William Buehler, USN (Ret.), operations officer on *Maddox* the night of 4 August 64, states emphatically that the enemy his ship and *Turner Joy* tracked that night was real.

Chapter 11

A War Over Very Nearly Nothing –
The Falklands (May 1982)

THE FALKLAND ISLANDS are a pleasant enough place if you can stand the weather and the near total isolation. The weather is grey and damp summer or winter. The closest mainland is nearly 500 kilometres away. Sheep outnumber humans by almost 200 to one. The landscape is certainly reminiscent of the Hebrides or the Orkneys; not surprisingly, most of the islanders are of Scottish descent. There are believed to be oil reserves offshore, but the weather would make them hard to exploit. Besides sheep ranching and fishing, there is little else to the islands' economy. It would hardly seem to be the sort of place that two civilised nations would fight over in the late twentieth century, but the willingness of human societies to go to war for the most trivial of reasons should never be underestimated.

For reasons that go back to nineteenth-century jurisprudence and geo-politics, it turns out that both Argentina and Great Britain lay claim to the Falklands (or Islas Malvinas). In fact the islands were first 'discovered' by the Dutch and settled by the French, but they were formally 'claimed' by the British in 1765. A year later, the Spanish took over the French settlement and in 1767 set up a colonial governor on the islands. A brief skirmish in 1770 drove the British off the islands and almost brought on a war between Spain and Great Britain, but a treaty signed in 1771 allowed British settlement to resume. Sadly, the issue of which nation owned the Falklands was left undecided by that treaty. By 1811, both the Spanish and British governments had, for similar reasons, removed their colonial governors, leaving the islands to the few settlers and the visiting whalers.

When Argentina gained independence in 1816, it laid claim to the islands as a former Spanish possession administered from Buenos Aires and sent a governor to the islands ten years later. In 1833, the British returned in force, kicked out the Argentinian governor and began construction of a naval base at Stanley on the largest island, East Falkland. With the coming of steam navigation, the islands gained some strategic importance as a coaling station. At the beginning of World War I, they lured von Spee's cruisers to their destruction by a superior Royal Navy squadron.

That should have been the high point of the islands' importance in international affairs. As oil replaced coal as the fuel of choice for warships, the Falklands' strategic significance rapidly declined. With no obvious natural wealth to attract outside interest, there seemed to be little to disturb the islanders' peaceful isolation. But the Argentinians did not forget their claims, and after World War II, they periodically reiterated their case at the United Nations. The two countries talked about the issue from time to time in a perfectly civilised manner, though the British showed no inclination to surrender sovereignty. Despite signing on to the various UN resolutions calling for divestiture of colonial possessions, the British pointed out that every poll of the islands' inhabitants showed them nearly unanimous in wanting to remain a British colony.

Internal Argentinian politics ended that peaceful state of affairs. Like many of the nations that grew out of the collapse of the Spanish Empire in South America, Argentina's hold on democracy was tenuous at best. These countries had established their borders and their national identities by internecine fighting, and in many of those countries, the military had political power far greater than in more 'mature' nation states. Many of the same factors that led to the rise of Fascism in Europe in the 1920s and 1930s – economic depression and the fear of communism by conservative upper and middle classes (which included the military) – fostered the rise of military dictatorships in South America, but often with a somewhat different flavour.[1] Perhaps the best example of this strange amalgam of militant fascism with leftist populism was the tumultuous reign of Juan Perón in Argentina.[2]

Perón died of a heart attack in 1974, being succeeded by his wife, Isabel, who had a hard time holding his coalition of supporters intact. A right-wing coup in 1976 ended her troubled rule, but replaced it with a military junta that found itself equally incapable of dealing with the nation's social and economic problems. Losing popular support and fearing accountability for the many 'disappearances' that had occurred under their rule, the junta played their final trump card – a distracting little war.

Provocation

It appears that the war over the Falklands was not so much planned by the junta as stumbled into. The war began not in the Falklands at all, but rather on South

The lessons on how to build a modern warship were sometimes hard won. Along with other navies, the US Navy began to use increasing amounts of light metals, particularly aluminum, in ship superstructures to save weight and allow the mounting of multiple missile launchers and advanced sensors well above the waterline. The danger inherent in this practice was brought home dramatically when USS *Belknap* (CG 26) collided with an aircraft carrier during night manoeuvres, caught fire and burned down to her steel hull, 22 Nov 1975. (USN)

Georgia Island, some 750 nautical miles east-southeast of the Falklands, but then considered part of the Falklands territory (and also claimed by Argentina). An Argentinian merchant had purchased the abandoned whaling station at Leith Harbour on South Georgia in 1979 with the intent of salvaging the scrap metal in the rendering plant. He tried several times unsuccessfully to hire the British auxiliary ship based at South Georgia to haul away the metal. Finally he turned to the Argentinian navy, which agreed to his use of the troop transport ARA *Bahía Buen Suceso* to carry his forty-one workers to the site and then return with the salvage. On 19 March 1982, the party of Argentinian salvers landed and ran up the Argentinian flag.

It is unclear whether raising the flag was a spontaneous act of patriotism by the workers or whether it was a deliberate attempt by the merchant or the Argentinian junta to provoke a response from the British. It is quite clear that, at least at this stage, it was not the intent of the junta to start a war at that time. It is known that General Leopoldo Galtieri had initiated planning for an occupation of the Falklands when he took over leadership of the junta in December 1981, but it is also known that he believed that the British would react to this occupation by accepting the *fait accompli*.[3] But his calculations had failed to take into account the personality of the then British Prime Minister, Margaret Thatcher. Of all the prime ministers of Great Britain since Winston Churchill, the 'Iron Lady' was the least likely to allow a foreign flag to be raised over British soil, no matter how remote.

Within days, the local patrol boat, HMS *Endurance,* had shown up and, with great ceremony, hauled down the Argentinian flag. This was all the excuse Galtieri needed. A contingent of marines was loaded on the assault transport ARA *Bahía Paraíso* and on 3 April 1982 landed at King Edward Point, South Georgia. They captured the dozen or so scientists of the British Antarctic Survey and the small contingent of Royal Marines who comprised the sole 'permanent' inhabitants of the island. The day before, Argentinian commandos had landed at Stanley in the Falklands and by day's end had captured the town and accepted the surrender of the British garrison. The war about almost nothing was up and running.

Great Britain's ability to respond

As determined as Thatcher was to respond swiftly to this provocation, there was a very real question as to whether Great Britain had the ability to recapture these islands. By 1982, the Royal Navy, which would have to be the lead service in a campaign to retake the Falklands, was a mere shadow of its former self. In 1918, it was arguably the most formidable military force of any kind ever assembled. Amassed under Beatty's command were no less than thirty-four battleships and eight battlecruisers, supported by seemingly innumerable cruisers and destroyers and even the first rudimentary aircraft carriers. But much of this apparent strength was illusory. By war's end, many of those capital ships were effectively obsolete compared to the newer, bigger, better-armed battleships being built by the United States and Japan, and neither of those countries had sacrificed anything like the same degree of national wealth to achieve victory. The British were only too happy to sign the naval arms–limitation agreements worked out at London and Washington between the wars, which guaranteed them parity with the United States and superiority over Japan. Long gone were the days when the Royal Navy was expected to be as large as the two closest rivals combined.

By the end of World War II, the power balance had shifted again. The United States now possessed by far the world's largest navy; the Royal Navy was now significantly smaller and Great Britain had neither the ability or necessity to challenge America's position. As the British Empire gradually transformed into a Commonwealth, the Royal Navy no longer needed a global reach. As a member of strategic alliances dominated by the United States, Great Britain had become a regional power with a navy now ill suited to project power across nearly 8000 miles of ocean.[4]

By 1982, the force that the British could muster to send south to the Falklands comprised two aircraft carriers (HMSs *Hermes* and *Invincible*) plus a container ship modified to act as a base for the Sea Harriers, which were the only available tactical aircraft. The rest of the task group was composed of transports, landing ships, submarines and destroyers (or frigates, which in modern parlance, are small destroyers).

Typical of those destroyers was HMS *Sheffield*. The first of a class of sixteen Type 42 destroyers, the design to which she was built came about more from political and economic decisions than from military requirements. By the beginning of the 1960s, the Royal Navy was facing a crisis. The remaining war-construction units were at retirement age and there was much disagreement about what, if anything, would replace them. The most important replacement program was the CVA-01, planned to replace the multiple aircraft carriers built (or at least started) during World War II. The plan called for two large aircraft carriers to be escorted by a fleet of four large 'destroyers' of a new type designed to provide anti-aircraft defence.

These Type 82 destroyers, the first of which was ordered in 1966, stretched the limit of the type.[5] However, the Labour government then in power decided that Great Britain did not need two large aircraft carriers and the orders for the three remaining Type 82s were cancelled. (The one Type 82 that was built, HMS *Bristol,* was commissioned in 1973 and is still in service at the time of writing as a static training ship moored at Portsmouth.) Even though the need for which *Bristol* was built had largely disappeared, she still served a very useful function as a trials platform for the multiple new weapons and sensor systems introduced in her design. These included the Sea Dart surface-to-air missile system, the Mk 8 4.5in (114 mm) semi-automatic gun and the ADAWS-2 targeting system designed to take inputs from all the ship's sensors and provide a uniform threat picture and weapons control capability.[6]

For all this capability, *Bristol* was considered something less than a success because she was too big, expensive and manpower-intensive for her capabilities, and she lacked sufficient anti-ship capability to operate independently. So, when design began on the Royal Navy's next generation of general-purpose escort ships in the mid-1960s, the requirements called for a ship that was both significantly smaller and less expensive than *Bristol* and, at the same time, more capable. This was certainly a difficult set of requirements to satisfy and, if the resulting Type 42 destroyers were less than totally satisfactory – at least in their first two iterations – it was not for lack of trying.

HMS *Sheffield,* the first of the Type 42s, was packed with all the major weapons and sensors carried by *Bristol,* plus the hangar and landing pad for a Westland Lynx helicopter that gave it anti-ship and anti-submarine capabilities, all on a displacement barely two-thirds that of *Bristol.* Unfortunately, it was not possible to reduce the ship's complement as much as her size, and the first two batches of Type 42s were notoriously cramped. The last four Type 42s, known as Batch III, were sixteen metres longer and displaced 1000 tons more, which went a long way towards resolving the overcrowding and made them better sea boats. The 'short-hulled' Type 42s, including *Sheffield,* were also famously wet in any seaway, which not only made them uncomfortable, but also adversely affected the reliability of their primary weapons, which were located on the forecastle. The Sea Dart launcher was particularly susceptible to mechanical and electrical problems due to repeated inundation with salt water. However, none of the Batch III ships were ready in time to send to the Falklands. When the Falklands Task Group sailed from Great Britain in mid-April 1982, its 'backbone' was five Type 42 destroyers – HMSs *Sheffield, Coventry, Cardiff, Glasgow* and *Exeter.*

The routine of war

The principal role of the Type 42s was to provide air defence for the two aircraft carriers and that is what *Sheffield* was doing on 4 May. The task group had only just arrived in Falklands waters, but was rapidly settling down to the 'routine' of war. Harriers operating off the carriers had begun attacking Argentinian positions in the islands. The week before, commandos had recaptured South Georgia, and on 2 May, the Argentinian cruiser ARA *Belgrano* had been sunk outside the 200 nautical mile TEZ (Total Exclusion Zone) declared around the islands. This act caused outrage in Argentina and unease elsewhere, as war had not been officially declared between the two countries. Any Argentinian shipping, even warships, outside the TEZ should have been safe from attack. Except for that one glitch, however, everything seemed to be going well for the Royal Navy.

Perhaps things were going a bit too well. The first day they had been on station – 1 May – everyone had been on edge. On that day, *Sheffield* and most of the other ships in the task group had gone to 'Action Stations and State 1, Condition ZULU' on numerous occasions, as Argentinian aircraft were detected at ranges as great as 160 nautical miles.[7] However, on that day Argentinian aircraft actually attacked only a few times, and then without much apparent skill or co-ordination. Based on this experience and the belief that

When Great Britain went to war with Argentina over the Falklands, the greatest danger to the Royal Navy units sent south seemed to be represented by the small force of French-built Super Étendards armed with Exocet AM 39 second-generation anti-ship cruise missiles. An Argentinian Super Étendard is seen many years later, on 17 June 2004, launching off the US Navy aircraft carrier *Ronald Reagan* (CVN 76) during an international exercise. It is doubtful the irony of Argentinian aircraft operating from a ship named for the American president who most openly admired Margaret Thatcher was lost on anyone. (USN)

shipboard ESM (Electronic Support Measures – a general term covering systems that analyse sensor inputs and attempt to mislead enemy sensors) was mistakenly reporting Mirage III radars as the similar Super Étendard radar, the decision was made that this extreme state of alert would only be called if the enemy approached much closer and then only if called by the anti-aircraft controller (AAWC) for the task group.[8] For the next two days, this more relaxed routine worked as planned.

However, intelligence had made it clear that the Argentinians had the ability to strike at the task group.

> CTG and TG ships had been provided with a large amount of intelligence data. On the crucial question of whether Argentinian SUPER Es had Air-to-Air Refuelling and EXOCET (AM 39) capabilities, and hence whether ships were liable to AM 39 attack on 4 May, CTG and SHEFFIELD had much the same information, showing that such an attack was quite possible. However SHEFFIELD rated the AM 39 danger lower, and the submarine threat higher, than did CTG.[9]

It was difficult for the British to correctly gauge the threat posed by the Argentinian military. The sinking of the *Belgrano* had the salutary side-effect of causing the remaining Argentinian naval units, at least the surface units, to head back to port. They would play no further role in the conflict. They had three remaining submarines, two of them relatively new and difficult to detect with passive sonar. (They had started the war with four submarines, but one, the World War II-vintage *Santa Fé,* had been lost when South Georgia was recaptured.) It was these submarines that most concerned *Sheffield's* captain, Captain J F T G Salt.

Super Étendards and Exocets

The threat from the air was easier to analyse. The Argentinian air force had historically been supplied primarily by the United States and still flew a large number of A-4 Skyhawks, a subsonic strike aircraft known for its simplicity and reliability, but this had been the last aircraft supplied by the United States, which cut off military support to show disapproval of the military regime takeover. Thereafter, the Argentinians had bought their aircraft from other sources, primarily France and Israel, or had made their own. The most dangerous of these, from the British point of view, was the French-built Dassault Super

The combination of Super Étendard and Exocet proved fatal for the first time on 4 May 1982, when a single missile hit HMS *Sheffield* amidships on her starboard side. Externally, the damage did not seem major. The hole in her shell plating was well above the waterline and extended only 1.4 x 3 metres.

Étendard (the 'SUPER Es' referred to in the above quote). This was a supersonic attack aircraft capable of carrying a single Exocet AM 39 air-to-surface missile. At this time, this missile was still an unproven weapon, having never been fired in anger, but its potential was recognised and the fleet had been warned to keep particular watch out for the Super Étendard launch platforms. Fortunately for the British, another side-effect of the premature beginning of the war was that only five aircraft and five missiles had been delivered to Argentina before the war began.[10] When the war started, the French stopped further shipments and ordered their training personnel in Argentina to stand down.

The Exocet AM 39 represented a new kind of threat. The first primitive missiles and guided-bombs had emerged at the end of World War II, and development continued after the war, but the first operational anti-ship missiles were large and slow and generally not very effective. Their first use in combat was in October 1967, when three Styx missiles hit the Israeli destroyer *Eilat,* which sank two hours later.[11] The Styx was essential a small unmanned aircraft and proved to be relatively easy to track and defeat using the same technology that defended against aircraft. But the success of the Styx in 1967 spurred a number of developments of 'second-generation' anti-ship missiles that would be harder to counter. One of these was the Aérospatiale Exocet.[12] Originally developed as a surface-to-surface missile (MM 38), the Exocet improved upon the Styx by being significantly smaller and by flying a low altitude 'sea-skimming' flight profile that combined to make it much more difficult to detect and therefore defeat. The air-launched AM 39 version began development in 1974 and entered service, first in the French navy, in 1979.[13] Argentina was an early adopter.

'Pop-up' manoeuvres

On the morning of 4 May 1982, *Sheffield,* along with the Type 42 destroyers *Glasgow* and *Coventry* was providing forward air defence for the task group some twenty miles to the west of the two aircraft carriers. Her position was approximately seventy miles southeast of Stanley. *Sheffield* was the southernmost of the Air Defence Screen. The weather was cool and the sea calm with only a light swell. The ship was at 'Defence Watches', a state short of 'Action Stations', and in 'Damage Control State 2, Condition YANKEE', meaning that all non-essential watertight closures were shut, but regularly used hatches and doors were left open.[14]

An Argentinian P-2 Neptune patrol aircraft was aloft that morning and detected electronic emissions consistent with a Royal Navy warship about 100 miles south of Stanley and 380 miles east of the Rio Grande naval air station on Tierra del Fuego, the base of operations for the five Argentinian Super Étendards.[15] A pair of these aircraft, each armed with a single Exocet, set off from their base. The lead aircraft was piloted by CC Augusto César Bedacarratz. Fifteen minutes into their flight, they refuelled from a KC-130H Hercules airborne tanker and then settled into a low-level straight-in approach to the coordinates supplied by the Neptune. The weather closed in, soon reducing the ceiling to 150 metres and visibility to less than 100 metres. In another half an hour they received a target update from the Neptune. The target was described as three ships approximately 155 miles ahead of the two aircraft.

At a point approximately fifty miles from the target, at approximately 1050, the two aircraft performed a 'pop-up' manoeuvre. For aircraft carrying Exocets and similar missiles, which rely on inertial guidance to deliver them to the vicinity of the target after which an active seeker provides terminal guidance, it is necessary for the aircraft's own radar to acquire the target so that initial course data can be downloaded to the missile's guidance system.[16] A 'pop-up' is a brief excursion from the low approach altitude – which is generally less than 100 metres – to an altitude sufficient to acquire a target. In this case, the 'pop-up' was to 160 metres. (The advantage of a low-altitude approach is that it makes an attacking aircraft difficult to detect against a background of environmental clutter, but that works both ways. The aircraft's own radar will generally not be able to acquire targets when at that altitude. Thus a 'pop-up' is required, but it is kept as brief as possible because at the same time it allows target location, it also makes the attacker more liable to be detected.)

The two Super Étendards needed only a few seconds to realise that they were beyond the effective range of their radars and had to get closer to their targets. They dropped down again and continued on another five minutes and, now another twenty-five miles closer, repeated the 'pop-up' manoeuvre. This time the Super Étendard's Agave I radar was able to acquire all three targets detected by the Neptune. The middle target appeared to be the largest and this was the one Bedacarratz locked on to.

For several reasons, the few seconds the Super Étendards were at higher altitude did not allow *Sheffield* to detect the attackers. First, her Type 965 air search radar was obsolescent at best – there were plans in place to replace it with a more modern Type 1022 – and had particular difficulty identifying low-altitude targets (though, as will be seen, *Glasgow,* fitted with the same radar, did detect the two aircraft). Second, her satellite communications were in use, which on Type 42 destroyers required that the ESM system be shut down. Ironically, the satcomm was being used

However superficial the damage to *Sheffield* may have seemed, the havoc created by the high-speed impact of the heavy missile and its rocket motor with considerable unburned fuel was major, even though it appears that its warhead did not explode. Fires and the resulting acrid black smoke soon drove damage-control crews from the entire midships section of the ship.

for local communications for fear the enemy would be able to detect regular ship-to-ship communications.

Even though *Sheffield* failed to find the two aircraft, they did not go undetected. *Glasgow*, north of *Sheffield*, located the two Super Étendards during their first 'pop-up' at a range of more than forty miles. Radar on *Invincible*, which was serving as the AAWC, also sighted the attackers. But these detections turned out not to help *Sheffield* in any way.

GLASGOW reported the raid on AAWC HF and AAWC UHF . . . and called the racket as 'CONDOR 245'. GLASGOW went to Action Stations and fired Chaff D. Paints had been seen in INVINCIBLE at 50 and 30 miles which correlated with GLASGOW's CONDOR report. CAP were told to investigate but found nothing. The AAWC did not accept GLASGOW's classification of the raid and declared the contacts to be spurious. ZIPPO 4 was not called by the AAWC and Air Warning remained YELLOW.[17]

Sheffield *is hit*

Glasgow did everything possible to protect herself and warn the task group. But it was not enough to alert *Sheffield* to the approaching danger. If anything, between her actions and *Invincible*'s, it only served to increase the threat to the destroyer, because she was relying on coverage by other ships in the task group while her ESM suite was shut off.

Once the target was acquired, the two Super Étendards returned again to low altitude. In the case of Exocets of that time, launch could occur as far away as thirty-five miles from the target, though the likelihood of a hit increased considerably if the launch was delayed until the range was half that or less. Bedacarratz, aware of how few Exocets Argentina possessed, did everything he could to make sure he had a good chance of scoring a hit. He decided to wait a few extra minutes after the second 'pop-up' manoeuvre before launching his missile.[18] It was just as well that he did because the Super Étendards were still some twenty miles from the targets when *Glasgow* began her defensive manoeuvres.

By firing chaff, *Glasgow* managed to effectively disappear from the attackers' radars. Chaff is one of the oldest and still one of the most effective ways to spoof a radar. Its first use followed not too long after the introduction of radars in the early 1940s. Codenamed 'Window' by the RAF, its original form was strips of metal foil dropped from attacking bombers to confuse German radars by causing spurious, diffuse returns. Over the years, the principle has remained the same, the only difference is that the metal foil has been replaced by metalised synthetic fibres that tend to remain airborne much longer before falling to the surface. By firing chaff, *Glasgow* suddenly appeared to the Super Étendard's radar as an impossibly large target and was filtered out by the radar's noise suppression circuits.

Glasgow, north of *Sheffield* and in the middle of the formation, had been the original target of Bedacarratz and his wingman, but the attackers, now less than twenty miles from the British ships, turned to starboard and turned their attention to *Sheffield*. As soon as the new target data was downloaded to his Exocet, Bedacarratz fired his missile and turned away. The time was 1104.

Exactly what happened in the next few minutes is unclear.[19] At some point in the five minutes or so it took for the first Exocet to cover the distance from launch to target, it was detected by *Sheffield*'s sensors. Most accounts agree that her Type 965 picked up the incoming missile when it was at most a few miles away and under the control of its terminal guidance radar seeker. Even had appropriate action been initiated, it was far too late for those actions to have had any effect. The contact showed up on her ADAWS display as an unidentified threat. The ship's Operations Officer had time to alert the Missile Director, but then time ran out. The missile was apparently sighted visually by someone on *Sheffield's* bridge, because there was a loudspeaker warning alerting the crew to the impending impact.

Less than ten seconds later, the Exocet hit *Sheffield* amidships on her starboard side. The impact was approximately two and a half metres above the waterline and tore a hole 1.4 by 3 metres adjacent to the bulkhead that separated the Galley from the Forward Auxiliary Machinery Room (FAMR) and Forward Engine Room (FER). As far as can be ascertained, the missile's warhead did not explode, but that had no impact on *Sheffield's* fate.[20] Unlike bombs or torpedoes, which tend to cause little damage if they fail to explode, the Exocet was able to inflict significant damage regardless of the detonation of its warhead. Massing more than 600 kilograms at launch, the missile had lost some, but not much, of that mass before it hit the destroyer, and much of the damage was caused by the impact of that amount of mass moving at close to the speed of sound. It is believed that the destruction caused by the missile's body tearing into the ship's vitals was sufficient to effectively disable the ship's damage-control capabilities.

10. The missile's impact . . . caused widespread minor shock damage, typically the buckling of doors and collapse of ladders. . . . Large fires broke out immediately in the FAMR/FER area. The overwhelming initial impression is of the very rapid spread of acrid black smoke through the centre section of the ship and upwards, as far as the Bridge. This smoke very quickly forced evacuation of the Machinery Control Room, Main Communications Office, HQ1 and the Bridge, followed after a few minutes by the Ops Room and later the complete Forward Section of the ship and forward superstructure. Missile propellant and burning Dieso from FAMR Service and Ready Use Tanks were the main source of this smoke, which was responsible for the early and almost complete loss of the ship's fighting capability. Smoke clearance was unsuccessful forward and only partially successful aft.

11. The Firemain was breached at impact. Pressure was lost immediately and was never restored. . . . The lack of Firemain pressure was crucial, as it removed any real chance of tackling the fires. Fire fighting was largely restricted to external boundary cooling, using portable pumps and buckets, and this had little or no effect on the fires raging within the ship.

12. The fires gained quickly, soon embracing most of H, J and K Sections

from 4 to 2 Deck and subsequently spreading forward and aft. Re-entry attempts were made along the starboard 2 Deck passage, and later at 1H Starboard Cabin Flat and at 1J Starboard Access Hatch. These were well-briefed, determined attacks by men wearing fearnought suits and BA, but all were beaten back by heat and smoke.[21]

Behind this dry account in the records of the Court of Inquiry there is much left unsaid or, at best understated. There is hardly any mention of casualties.

> 15. Twenty Officers and Ratings died. Some personnel, in the Galley area, were killed on impact. Others asphyxiated, later, either attempting to escape, re-entering the ship or staying at their quarters to try and restore the ship's fighting capability.[22]

This smoothes over the hellish scene inside the ship in the moments after the missile hit. Over the preceding thirty years since destroyers had last been in serious combat, much had been forgotten about how to build and equip warships. Ignoring the brief, disastrous experiment with using aluminum to save weight in the superstructure, ships were still more lightly constructed and more lavishly fitted out than their more robust and austere forebears.[23] By the time *Sheffield* was built, crew comfort had become a major element in the recruiting and retention of sailors, so living spaces were filled with furnishings and other materials that would have been unthinkable thirty years earlier. Unfortunately, many of those items were flammable and only served to further feed the fire that started with diesel oil ignited by solid rocket propellant.

Some of the deaths were mercifully quick, off-duty crewmen in the galley or engineers in the machinery spaces. Others succumbed to the smoke, some showing extraordinary heroism, such as the computer crew who died at their posts while attempting to restore the ship's control systems. Some displayed black humour, such as the bucket brigade that reportedly kept its rhythm by singing Monty Python's *Always Look on the Bright Side of Life*. Some of the dead and injured no doubt fell due to poorly managed damage control. The official report was terse, but clear in its assessment of the leadership by many of the ship's officers.

> 13. The control of fire fighting and other activity after impact lacked cohesion. No emergency HQ1 was established, it was not clear where Command of the Ship was located, the control of personnel was unco-ordinated and, in particular, inadequate checks were made on which Quarters had been abandoned and which were still closed up.[24]

Yarmouth's lifesaving manoeuvres

While the fire spread with incredible speed throughout *Sheffield's* mid-section, the war continued around her. As several miles separated each of the units in the screen, it was not immediately clear to the remaining ships how seriously *Sheffield* had been damaged. As soon as word of the attack was received, the frigates *Arrow* and *Yarmouth* were ordered to assist in any way possible and they both made towards the destroyer at best speed. No sooner had they set course towards *Sheffield*, than sensors picked up a second Exocet approaching from the west.[25]

It is not clear why almost exactly fifteen minutes elapsed between *Sheffield* being hit and the approach of the second Exocet. Argentinian accounts consistently report that Bedacarratz and his wingman fired their missiles simultaneously, but this would make the arrival times of the missiles as reported from *Yarmouth* impossible to explain. (*Yarmouth* and *Arrow* were some distance further from Bedacarratz' aircraft than *Sheffield* at the time of his launch, perhaps as much as fifteen nautical miles, but that distance would be covered by an Exocet in less than two minutes.) Add to this the fact that it was widely reported that one of the two Super Étendards, but not both, approached within a mile of *Sheffield* before slowly turning away, as if inspecting the damage done.

HMS *Yarmouth* was ordered to close *Sheffield* and help with fighting the fires. This photograph, taken by Peter J Green, shows *Yarmouth* crewmen pouring water and foam into the starboard side of the burning destroyer, 4 May 1982. The effort was ultimately unsuccessful and *Yarmouth* began receiving *Sheffield's* survivors that evening. (Peter J Green)

These various accounts make more sense if it is assumed the second pilot delayed his launch by five or even ten minutes, approached within visual distance of *Sheffield*, confirmed that the first missile had hit, and only then, after looping around, launched the missile detected from *Yarmouth*.

Regardless, the second launch was detected by *Yarmouth* at 1137 and confirmed by *Glamorgan* a minute later.[26] The missile appeared to be headed straight for *Yarmouth*. Because of the timely warning, some four minutes before the missile would have impacted, the frigate was able to take defensive measures. She turned towards the oncoming missile to reduce her radar signature and fired chaff. These measures worked. The missile obviously lost its lock on *Yarmouth* because it started to gain altitude, as it is programmed to do under the circumstances, and passed directly over the frigate, continuing on to the east. It eventually fell harmlessly into the sea.

This ended the attack, but not *Sheffield*'s agony. All attempts to control the fire failed. The ship's own firefighting capability was limited at best by the destruction of the firemain by the initial impact. After that, her firefighting capability was limited to that provided by portable pumps and bucket brigades. *Yarmouth* and *Arrow* did their best to help, but they were also limited in what they could do:

14. Much external help was provided. To port, ARROW did an excellent job of boundary cooling, supplying hoses and general support. Conditions for YARMOUTH, to starboard, were less easy. Both ships' efforts were bedevilled by frequent spurious submarine and torpedo alarms.[27]

The best the two frigates could do was pour water or foam on *Sheffield*'s superstructure. The damage caused by the Exocet was perhaps unique in naval history in that there was very little disruption of the outer structure of the victim; the damage and fire were almost entirely contained within the still-intact shell of the ship. There was little that could be done from outside and not much more with *Sheffield*'s own resources. The end was inevitable.

16. At 041750Z there was still no Firemain, the fires were spreading, the Sea Dart Magazine was thought to be at risk and the ship's fighting capability had been largely destroyed. With the tactical situation in mind, the Captain ordered hands to abandon ship. Most climbed over to ARROW, a few went to YARMOUTH by Gemini, some were flown to HERMES.[28]

When her fires had burned out and she showed no signs of sinking, *Yarmouth* took *Sheffield* under tow five days after the attack and headed east away from the battle zone. The tow lasted a day and night, but rising seas caused water to enter the ship through the hole in her shell plating and led, on 10 May 1982, to the tow being cast off. She foundered that morning.

The abortive salvage of Sheffield

At first there was some confusion about what to do with the abandoned *Sheffield*. Word spread on *Yarmouth* later on the 4th that *Arrow* had been instructed to sink the hulk, but concern that not all of the crew had got off delayed any action until the next morning. Daylight on the 5th showed *Sheffield* still burning fiercely, but showing no signs of sinking. As she was not endangering any other ships or obstructing any activities, and as she was in no danger of falling into enemy hands, it was agreed that there was not any rush to decide her fate. She was allowed to drift and burn undisturbed for two more days. On the 6th, it was noticed that the smoke coming from Sheffield had abated considerably and by the 7th the fires appeared to have burned themselves out.

By the 8th, now four full days after the attack, *Sheffield* appeared quiet and still rode on an even keel and at her normal draft. It was then decided that the hulk could perhaps be salvaged. *Yarmouth* was ordered to put a salvage crew on board and determine whether *Sheffield* could be taken under tow. As the sea was

Another victim of the small number of Exocets in the Argentinian inventory was the civilian container ship *Atlantic Conveyor*, a Cunard-owned RO/RO ship, which was hit by a single missile on 25 May and burned for five days before finally sinking.

starting to rise, the transfer was made late on the 8th rather than waiting for daylight on the 9th. Examination of *Sheffield* showed her hull to be basically intact and no signs of flooding were found, so she was taken under tow early on the 9th, heading east. As the weather worsened on the 9th, the salvage crew was pulled off *Sheffield* by helicopter, but the tow continued until the next morning. During the night, the sea had risen to the point that waves were washing through the hole on *Sheffield's* starboard side, and, with no power to pump out the accumulating water, the ship began to list to starboard, which only made the problem worse. By first light on the 10th, it was obvious that *Sheffield* was sinking and the tow was cast off. *Yarmouth* had towed *Sheffield* for twenty-nine hours and had reached a position approximately 150 nautical miles east of the point where she had been hit, just outside the TEZ. At that point she foundered at 0400 on 10 May 1982, witnessed by, among others, Captain Salt from the quarterdeck of *Yarmouth*.

Sheffield was not the only loss for the Royal Navy in that war, nor even the only ship lost to damage by an Exocet. The third and fourth of Argentina's five air-launched Exocets were fired at the task group's aircraft carriers on 25 May, but these launches were detected and the carriers were able to fire chaff and avoid the missiles. One of the missiles, however, acquired a new target and hit the civilian container ship *Atlantic Conveyor*, which burned out and finally sank five days later. (The fifth AM 39 was launched at the British fleet but failed to find a target. On 12 June, one MM 38 was launched from a truck on the Argentinian mainland and actually hit HMS *Glamorgan*, but because that ship was manoeuvering to avoid the missile, it struck only a glancing blow. There was considerable fire and some structural damage, but damage control was able to control the fires and the ship was never in danger of sinking.)

Lessons learned

The world watched this little war and learned a great deal. It was obvious that missiles such as the Exocet represented a new kind of threat to all surface

The Royal Navy's experience in the Falklands War showed that the danger posed by Exocets and similar small cruise missiles was not so much in the actual explosive warhead carried by the missile, but primarily in the kinetic damage of the heavy mass of the missile striking lightly constructed modern warships at high speed, which caused massive internal structural damage, and in the burning of residual rocket fuel, which started intense fires in any flammable materials. The Americans learned this lesson on 17 May 1987 when USS *Stark* (FFG 31) was struck by two Exocets fired by an Iraqi Mirage F1 in the Persian Gulf. She survived because the two missiles struck close to each other on her port side in line with her bridge. The damage did not affect her firefighting ability or engineering plant, so she was able to keep power on and pressure in her firemains throughout the successful fight to save the ship. Nevertheless, thirty-seven sailors were killed and a further twenty-one injured. (USN)

combatants, particularly frightening because the missiles were relatively cheap and did not require an extensive infrastructure to be deployed. In the years following the Falklands War, navies around the world tried to apply the lessons of this war, designing new ships or upgrading old ones with better radars, more effective ESM, rapid-reaction close-in defence weapons and improved firefighting capabilities. Much more attention was paid to the flammability of materials inside ships and even to the uniforms sailors wore. (As had many navies, the Royal Navy had by 1980 outfitted their sailors in new uniforms made of synthetic fabrics because they were much easier to care for and tended to wear well, but on *Sheffield* it was found that the synthetic fabrics melted in high heat and actually caused burns that sailors might not otherwise have suffered.)

For all the valuable lessons learned, both sides in this war had paid an exorbitant price in money and human lives over a collection of barely habitable islands of not terribly great value. It is possible to think of multiple scenarios where the issue of who owns the Falklands could have been worked out without paying this price, but given the desperation of the Argentinian junta and the carefully crafted reputation for pugnacity of the British Prime Minister it is hard to imagine how this war over very nearly nothing could have been avoided.

Notes

1 The role of the United States in South American politics at this time, and indeed until quite recently, was ambiguous at best. While loudly and frequently proclaiming support for democracy, business interests – always a major player in American politics – strongly supported the conservative classes. US intervention, whether direct, as in the presence of US Marines fighting the original *Sandinistas* in Nicaragua in the 1920s, or indirect, as in the proxy war fought against latter-day *Sandinistas* by the US-supported *Contras* in the 1980s, was frequent and frequently in support of some rather unsavoury regimes.

2 A contemporary example of this strange mix can be found in Venezuela's Hugo Chávez.

3 The Argentinian plans for occupying the Falklands called for it to take place in the winter, which would in the southern hemisphere mean between July and October, when storms in the South Atlantic would hinder any British response. By the time the weather improved in November, it was hoped the British would have calmed down and been willing to accept the Argentinian occupation.

4 Not only was the Royal Navy ill prepared to take a war to the South Atlantic, but the Royal Air Force similarly lacked the ability to provide air support for the invasion force. The only RAF support came from Vulcan bombers flying from Ascension Island. Since the Vulcans lacked the range to reach the Falklands from Ascension without refuelling, and since the available aerial tankers were themselves short-ranged, it took eleven tankers to enable two Vulcans to bomb the airport outside Stanley.

5 At 6100 tons, the Type 82 destroyer was about as large as the type can get without needing another term to describe the ships. Some sources, in fact, call the Type 82 destroyer a 'light cruiser' (eg, *Janes73,* p. 319) The US Navy was building ships of this size at the time, calling them 'frigates', the same term other navies used to describe small destroyers (or what had been called 'destroyer escorts' by the US Navy in World War II and into the 1960s). To further confuse matters, the US Navy then began, in the 1970s, building both a class of large destroyers (the *Spruance* class) and one of smaller destroyers (the *Oliver Hazard Perry* class) which it now designated 'frigates'. In a final bid to confuse everyone, a variant of the *Spruance*-class destroyers, built on the same hull but equipped with AEGIS electronics, were classified as 'guided-missile cruisers' (hull type CG).

6 For reasons that remain obscure, the Royal Navy's 4.5in (114mm) gun has an actual calibre of 4.45in (113mm). The several iterations of the ADAWS (Action Data Automation Weapons System) have the same intent and many of the same capabilities as the US Navy's AEGIS systems.

7 *Shef,* p. 1. 'Action Stations' means that all crew are at their assigned combat stations; 'State 1, Condition ZULU' means that all watertight doors are closed and that the ship is in the highest state of readiness for damage control.

8 *Green.* As seen from HMS *Yarmouth,* the task group went to state 'Air Yellow' five times on 1 May and to 'Air Red' once. These were states of heightened air defence alert, with 'Red' being higher than 'Yellow'. As is always the case with military units, states of defensive alert often interfere with the performance of a unit's offensive tasks, and must be invoked sparingly.

9 Op cit, p. 1. CTG stands for Commander, Task Group.

10 This count was of air-launched AM 39s. Argentina also had a small number of surface-launched MM 38s carried on naval vessels, some of which were rigged to be launched from improvised launchers mounted on trucks.

11 The Russian P-15 Termit anti-ship cruise missile (NATO codename SS-N-2 'Styx'), was a large subsonic, liquid-fuelled missile with a 513-kilogram warhead and an active radar seeker for terminal guidance. The Chinese made and exported several versions of the P-15, the best known being the CSS-C-2 'Silkworm'. INS *Eilat* was originally HMS *Zealous,* a war-built Z-class destroyer of 1710 tons.

12 Aérospatiale was a French aircraft and missile manufacturer that became part of EADS, whose missile activities were then consolidated with those of BAE Systems and Finmeccanica to form MBDA.

13 Like the Styx, the Exocet relies on the radar of the launch platform to provide an initial course and then uses its own radar for terminal guidance. The warhead is much smaller than Styx's at 165 kilograms.

14 Ibid, p. 2.

15 *DeHoust,* p. 1.

16 The latest generation of attack aircraft are 'network-centric', meaning that target data can be downloaded from one aircraft to another. The source of the target data does not even have to be another aircraft; it can come from a ship or even from a satellite. The missile carrier need not ever acquire the target with its own radar.

17 Op cit, p. 2. By classifying the targets as 'CONDOR', *Glasgow* was identifying them as hostile and dangerous. 'ZIPPO 4' was a state of anti-air defence that called for, among other actions, the launching of a pattern of twelve N4 Chaff D rounds. There was real concern in the task group over the consumption of Chaff rockets. According to Annex C of the Board of Inquiry, *Sheffield* only carried enough Chaff to launch ZIPPO 4 patterns seven times, without any

hope for immediate resupply. This led to reluctance on the part of the AAWC to declare unnecessary ZIPPO alerts. 'Had full Zippo reactions been applied to all such EW/radar detections on 1 May, most of the Task Group's CHAFF DELTA would have been expended on the first day in the Exclusion Zone.'

18 Bedacarratz and his wingman were carrying the first two of Argentina's five Exocets to be committed to combat. Some accounts claim a single Exocet was fired from a range of 100 miles on 1 May, falling harmlessly into the sea at the end of its range, but this was a mistaken identification, one of many that first day of combat. That was an air-to-air missile mistakenly launched by a Mirage III.

19 *Shef*, the most authoritative source for these events, is silent on this time period. Four critical lines have been redacted in the publicly released version of this document.

20 Most of *Sheffield's* survivors believe the warhead exploded, but the opinion of technical experts is that there would have been much more damage and many more injuries had that happened.

21 *Shef*, pp. 2–3. 'Dieso' is diesel fuel. 'Fearnought suit' was the standard RN firefighting garment, made of chemically treated wool. 'BA' is Breathing Apparatus.

22 Ibid, p. 3.

23 More than a few accounts attribute the uncontrollable fire on *Sheffield* to the use of aluminum in her superstructure. There had been cases where ships built with aluminum superstructures had burned down to the steel hull. The best known example was USS *Belknap* (CG-26) which collided with an aircraft carrier during night operations off Sicily on 22 November 1975. *Belknap's* aluminum superstructure caught fire and the metal structure burned. *Sheffield* and her sisters, however, were built entirely of steel.

24 Ibid, p. 3.

25 Accounts differ as to the timing of the arrival of the two Exocets. Some say the one that hit *Sheffield* came first, others that it came later. While there does not appear to be convincing evidence one way or the other, the story makes more sense to this author if the hit on *Sheffield* came first, though the length of time that elapsed between the attacks, at least as reported in *Green,* remains hard to explain. I have tried my best to come up with a reasonable explanation, but it is surmise at best.

26 This account comes from *Green*. The only change I've made is to subtract three hours from his reported times to agree with local time.

27 *Shef*, p. 3.

28 Ibid, p. 3. The time is given in ZULU, which is GMT and was three hours ahead of local time. The order to abandon *Sheffield* came at 1450 local time.

Chapter 12

A Look Back from an Asymmetrical Future – Aden
(12 October 2000)

T HERE WAS MUCH that was seen to be new and foreboding about the
attack on the USS *Cole* (DDG 67) in the Yemeni port of Aden ("Adan) on
12 October 2000, as well as some aspects that were eerily, ironically familiar.
After the fact, there was much talk about this being an early skirmish in an
asymmetrical conflict being waged between the United States, representing the
forces of modern liberalism, and a new and little known entity called Al-Qaeda,
representing an older, darker form of human society.[1] The asymmetry came
from the mismatch between the mechanised, computerised weapons of the
West, as epitomised by the sophisticated and expensive *Cole* – a guided-missile
destroyer of the *Arleigh Burke* class – and the simple device with which she was
attacked. It came also from the horror and indignation with which the
American people and their government reacted to the loss of the seventeen
sailors who died in *Cole* in a sneak attack in an undeclared war, compared to
the willingness with which the two suicide bombers met their death and the
praise their sacrifice received in much of the Arab world.

    Cole was not designed or built to fight this kind of asymmetrical war, a war
for which it was poorly suited. *Cole* had been designed in the 1980s to fight a
conventional war against a conventional enemy. That enemy was the Soviet
Union, and the war was to have been fought with sophisticated aircraft, missiles
and submarines: a clearly identifiable enemy fighting with deadly, but clearly
identifiable weapons. She was the seventeenth unit in the *Arleigh Burke* class.
Ordered in 1991, she was launched at Ingalls Shipbuilding, Pascagoula,
Mississippi on 10 February 1995 and commissioned a little over a year later.

    The *Arleigh Burke* class was designed with the lessons of the Falklands War
very much in mind. All-steel construction was mandated in the hull and
superstructure (despite the fact that the presence of light metals had not
contributed materially to the loss of any Royal Navy warships in that conflict).
The large mast structure, however, is built of aluminum to save topweight. A

pair of 20mm Phalanx CIWS mounts was specifically included in the design to protect against Exocet–like cruise missiles. The entire physical structure was designed with a minimum of curved surfaces and sharp angles to reduce the ships' radar cross-section. This makes them harder for radar-guided missiles, such as the Exocet, to find and lock on to them. Their AEGIS radar was specifically tuned to detect incoming sea-skimming missiles. They additionally have an air-filtration system that is designed to keep out external aerosol agents, such as biological or chemical weapons, but which would have the added benefit of limiting the spread of toxic smoke that was such a major factor in the loss of *Sheffield*.

The *Arleigh Burke*-class destroyers were designed to fulfil all the roles to which destroyers are currently assigned, with a single 5in (127mm)/54 gun capable of firing extended-range guided munitions and various surface-to-air, anti-ship, anti-submarine and land-attack missiles firing from a multitude of launchers. They displace 8315 tons, making them more massive than many World War II-vintage light cruisers, yet their gas-turbine engines can take them from dead stop to full speed in a matter of minutes. That size, speed and the advanced self-protection systems make them quite possibly the most survivable destroyers ever built.

It was this very versatility and self-reliance that brought *Cole* to the port of Aden in October 2000. She was detached, sailing alone, on her way from the Mediterranean, where she was part of the *George Washington* Battle Group, to Bahrain, where she was to make a port call. This should have been an easy transit, the 3300-mile voyage well within the designed range of the class. However, a number of factors led to a decision to refuel *Cole* midway through this transit, rather than wait to arrive at Bahrain and refuel there. One was the relatively short cruising range of the *Arleigh Burke*-class destroyers.[2] Another was the relative lack of oilers in the modern US Navy. With only about a dozen oilers in commission, it was out of the question for one to be made available to refuel *Cole* on a simple transit from the Mediterranean to the Persian Gulf. Finally, there was the prudent '50 per cent fuel' policy of the US Navy that required that all vessels on station never allow their fuel onboard to drop below 50 per cent of capacity under normal operating conditions, in order that they are always ready for emergency deployment.

For a number of years in the mid-to-late 1990s, the refuelling stop of choice between Suez and the Gulf was Djibouti, but the escalating war between Eritrea and Ethiopia threatened to spill over into Djibouti and a decision was made by USCENTCOM in 1998 to look for alternative ports of call.[3] To provide an alternative to Djibouti, a contract was signed with a private fuelling station in

USS *Cole* (DDG 67), seen in March 1998 en route to Southeast Asia, is a member of the largest class of destroyers built by the US Navy since World War II. The sixty-second and last of the *Arleigh Burke* class is to be delivered in 2010. They are true multi-purpose ships, mounting weapons and sensors effective against the aircraft, submarines and surface threats prevalent in the late stages of the Cold War. It remains to be seen whether they will be as effective against the more enigmatic threats of an ongoing asymmetric conflict against resourceful and determined political and religious movements that seems to have replaced the Cold War. (USN)

the port of Aden to provide fuel for US Navy vessels. From January 1999, that fuelling station was used twelve times by navy ships before *Cole* was directed there in October 2000.

A high level of threat

As *Cole* approached Aden on the morning of 12 October, there was much that her captain, Commander Kirk S Lippold, knew, or should have known, about the situation in Yemen. He knew that Aden was not necessarily a safe harbour. Fourteen of the twenty nations in USCENTCOM's AOR (Area of Responsibility) were characterised as posing threats to US forces stationed inside or passing through their borders. This included Yemen. Prior to entering Aden harbour, *Cole* went to ThreatCon Bravo, the second of four possible levels of alert against external threats to the ship.[4] There was no standard definition of any of the threat levels; each ship was expected to develop and file a Force Protection Plan that defined the steps required in each threat condition for that ship. However, there were guidelines and these required certain precautions as part of ThreatCon Bravo. Several of these specifically addressed potential threats from small boats, such as are found in any harbour:

> Harbor craft 'require special concern because they can serve as an ideal platform for terrorists.' Unauthorised craft should be kept away from the ship; authorised craft should be carefully controlled and monitored.
>
> Crews for picket boats should be designated and placed on 15-minute alert. 'If the situation warrants, make random picket boat patrols in the immediate vicinity of the ship.' The picket boat crews should be armed with M16 rifles, one M60 with 200 rounds of ammunition and 10 concussion grenades.
>
> Fire hoses should be prepared for use in repelling small boats or boarders.[5]

There was much that Lippold had no way of knowing, that might have heightened the awareness of the threat facing *Cole* as she entered Aden harbour.[6] In fact, the atmosphere on board *Cole* that morning was rather relaxed and the observance of ThreatCon Bravo was spotty at best. That certainly would have been different had he understood that the United States was at war and that *Cole* was sailing into the middle of a war zone. This was in the last months of the Clinton Presidency and technically the United States was not at war with any state, nor were there even any of those nasty undeclared conflicts going on that had replaced formally declared wars since the mid-twentieth century, at least not any involving the United States. But Lippold should have been aware, even if many in the United States were not, that the nation had been at war since at least 1994.

It had started as Cold War politics as usual. In some ways the roots extend even further back, to the Great Game, the struggle for control of south central Asia between Britain and Russia. In the nineteenth century, Afghanistan had been the prize that both sides sought and it appeared to be in play again in the 1980s, when the Soviets sent troops in to support an unpopular Marxist government. Starting during the Carter administration and vastly expanded under Ronald Reagan, the United States supported various *Mujahideen* guerilla groups fighting the Russians. In the process, the Americans found themselves with some strange bedfellows who would come to haunt them in the future. Not the least of these was a young Saudi, the scion of a family grown wealthy through association with the royal family, Osama bin Laden. The withdrawal of the last Soviet troops in 1989 did not leave behind a peaceful Afghanistan, nor did the many foreign volunteers who had come to fight alongside the native resistance simply return to peaceful occupations.

Al-Qaeda, an organisation set up by bin Laden in 1988 as the conflict in Afghanistan was changing into a civil war between *Mujahideen* factions, enters this story in 1992. Despite American support for the *Mujahideen* in Afghanistan, bin Laden never saw the United States as an ally and the first known terrorist attack by Al-Qaeda was a pair of bombings of hotels in Aden which were believed to be housing American troops en route to Somalia in December 1992.[7] A brief civil war broke out in Yemen in 1994 between the official government in the north of the country and separatists based at Aden in the south. When the southerners declared a Marxist state in May 1994, both the United States and Al-Qaeda announced support for the northern government, probably the last time the two would be on the same side of an issue. The military support provided by bin Laden was a significant factor in the rapid victory of the northern faction and accounted for the willingness of the Yemeni government to allow Al-Qaeda virtually unimpeded use of Yemen as a training and staging ground for the next six years.

It is not clear at what point a decision was made to attack a US warship at Aden, but there is evidence that it was first brought to the attention of the Americans during the investigation following the bombings of two US embassies in Africa in 1998.[8] Unfortunately, as is far too often the case, the information was too unspecific to allow action – nothing more than a warning that an attack was possible at some point in the future. In fact the warning was correct in all details, and an attack on a US warship was in fact carried out at Aden on 3 January 2000, only, at the time, the United States was completely unaware of it. A sister-ship to *Cole*, USS *The Sullivans* (DDG 68), was refuelling in Aden that day.[9] Al-Qaeda had prepared a small boat loaded with explosives and sent it out into the harbour with the intent of coming alongside *The Sullivans* and detonating the charge. Incredibly, they had miscalculated the weight of the explosives and the capacity of the small boat and the boat sank in the harbour before it could draw near *The Sullivans*. Even more incredibly, the event was apparently not noticed by anyone on the destroyer and, if it was observed by anyone else in the harbour, word was never passed to any Western authorities, so the US Navy remained completely unaware that the attempt had been made. Most importantly, Al-Qaeda knew that the United States was not aware of the attempt and that the plan remained valid if the weight of explosives could be correctly calculated.

An innocent-looking killer

Thus it was that just over ten months later, *Cole*, at a somewhat relaxed ThreatCon Bravo, approached the fuelling point in Aden harbour soon after dawn on 12 October. The fuelling point is in the centre of the commercial harbour, at a set of concrete pilings to which ships moor. Fuel is piped under water from tanks on shore. The pipes emerge at the pilings and ships simply connect their supply hoses to outlets at the pilings. Mooring was thus very simple and *Cole* was secured to the fuelling station at about 0930.[10] refuelling started an hour later. At approximately 1118, a small boat, about 10.6 metres in length and manned by two men, approached *Cole's* exposed port side. A large, canvas-covered mass took up most of the available space on the small craft. Assuming that this was a garbage scow making the rounds of the harbour, sailors

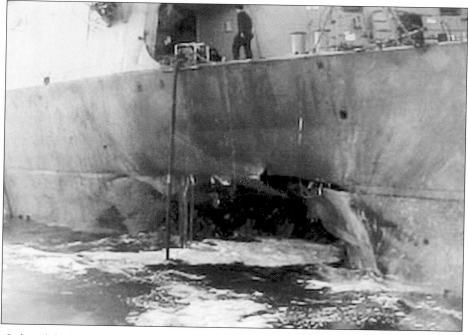

In broad daylight in the busy harbour at Aden, *Cole* was seriously damaged by the detonation of an explosives-filled small boat along her portside, 12 October 2000. The resulting hole in the ship's exterior extended well below the waterline, bringing with it the threat of uncontrollable flooding and loss of stability. It took more than forty-eight hours of active damage control before it was certain that *Cole* would not sink. Compared to *Sheffield*, the immediate damage to *Cole* was far more serious, but *Cole* did not have to deal with the massive fires caused by rocket propellant that ultimately doomed *Sheffield*. (USN)

waved it aft towards the fantail. The two men waved back and saluted as the boat came alongside almost exactly amidships and then exploded.

The Chief Engineer, Lieutenant Commander Deborah Courtney, recalled that she was in her cabin when the explosion occurred. First the ship seemed to move and then, almost immediately, the lights went out. The shaking of the ship was sufficient to knock her off her chair and to the deck.[11] It is not certain how much explosive the small boat contained, but it has been estimated to have been as much as 227 kilograms of C-4 or some other form of RDX explosive. A hole 9.75 x 11 metres was torn in *Cole*'s outer shell plating centred just above the waterline. The refuelling had been proceeding faster than expected, so the day's routine was altered to allow the off-duty crew an early lunch, so they would be available when the ship was ready to get underway. Almost all of the seventeen dead and thirty-nine injured were queuing outside the galley, just inboard of the site of the explosion. No trace of the small boat or its two occupants has ever been found.

On 29 October 2000, *Cole* was sufficiently stable that she could be backed away from the fuelling point in the middle of Aden harbour to which she had been moored when she was attacked. Three local tugs pull her stern and bow away from the fuelling dock, while a fourth stands by ready to start pulling her out of the harbour. (USN)

The crew reacted correctly and in a timely manner. As had happened on *Sheffield* almost two decades earlier, thick, acrid smoke immediately filled the area around the site of the explosion. Unlike on *Sheffield*, however, the hole in the shell plating extended below the waterline, adding the danger of uncontrollable flooding. The electrical distribution net was severed by the blast and the entire ship forward of the damage was without power. To add to the danger, several fuel tanks were ruptured by the blast and a volatile and highly flammable fuel-air mixture rapidly filled the damaged area.[12] The sparking of severed electrical cables led to a very real risk of explosion and fire.

However lax the force protection measures may have been before the attack, the reaction of *Cole*'s crew was exemplary. Immediate damage-control measures spread AFFF foam over the leaking fuel and rerouted electrical service around the damaged area.[13] Sufficient redundancy had been designed into the fire-mains, so that water pressure was never lost. The single greatest priority was cutting into the damaged mess spaces and getting the wounded out. However, the greatest danger was flooding in the adjacent forward engineering spaces. That space filled quickly, and the flooding was threatening the after engine room. If that space flooded as well, it would be difficult to keep the ship afloat.

It was far from certain that *Cole* could be saved. The second day after the attack was the crisis point. The emergency generator failed and the crew started losing the battle against the flooding. Late in the day, the bulkhead between the engine rooms began to give way and it looked as if the after engineering spaces would indeed flood. For most of that night, there was little the crew could do but watch as the water levels rose and the ship's list increased. Between lack of sleep, the constant stench of gas fumes and rotting food, morale on board reached a nadir. But dawn on the third day brought hope and progress. Yemeni port authorities brought over a portable generator and the pumps were restarted. Later that day, the crew got the emergency generator going again and from then on the progress against the water was steady.

By this time, help had arrived, first in the form of HMS *Marlborough*, a Type 23 frigate, soon followed by detachments of US Marines who took over responsibility for the physical security of the ship and several US Navy units, which provided the crew with berthing and hot food away from the all-pervasive stench. A diver went over the side and ascertained that *Cole*'s basic structure was intact. After a week had passed, the last of the dead had been recovered and *Cole* was clearly no longer in danger of sinking.

USNS *Catawba* (T-ATF 168), a large ocean-going tug, took over towing responsibilities outside the harbour. The size of the gash in *Cole's* side plating can be seen. Fortunately, the weather was calm and she did not have far to go. (USMC)

Waiting not far off shore was the semi-submersible heavy lift ship MV *Blue Marlin*, normally used to transport deep ocean drilling platforms, which was just large enough to carry *Cole* back to an American shipyard for repairs. The full extent of the damage can be seen in this view. (USN)

Coming full circle

The next question was how to get the damaged ship to a repair facility. In 1942, an American warship, the light cruiser USS *Marblehead* (CL 12), had been seriously damaged in fighting in the Java Sea. She made an incredible 9000-mile journey under her own power, with stops at shipyards at Trincomalee, Simonstown and Recife where sufficient repairs were made to allow her to reach New York. But in the year 2000 that kind of odyssey was impossible. Even had *Cole* been in condition to undertake a voyage in the open ocean, there simply are no longer so many ports willing to take in a damaged American warship and even fewer capable of repairing a warship of any nationality. The US Navy quickly contracted with the Norwegian owners of the semi-submersible heavy lift ship MV *Blue Marlin*. Designed to transport large submersible oil rigs of up to 30,000 tons, *Blue Marlin* arrived at Aden on 29 October and loaded *Cole* on board the next day. The voyage to the Ingalls yard in Mississippi was slow but uneventful; she arrived there on 13 December and began repairs that took $250 million and eighteen months to complete. *Cole* returned to service on 19 April 2002.

Commander Lippold remained in command of *Cole* until she was taken out of commission at the dockyard at the beginning of 2001. He was given a succession of desk assignments until he was informed on 21 August 2006 that he would not be promoted to Captain. He retired from the US Navy in May 2007.

In a very real sense, with the bombing of *Cole*, the story of destroyers has

A glimpse at one of the possible futures for the destroyer type is provided by the helicopter destroyer (DDH) JMSDF *Hyuga*, seen here at her launch at Yokahama, 23 August 2007. There has been considerable debate whether she is indeed a destroyer, but her lack of capability to operate fixed-wing aircraft or assault craft, and her specialisation to perform anti-submarine warfare (ASW) argue in favour of that designation. (JMSDF)

Another possible future for the type is embodied in the *DDG 1000* design now under development by the US Navy. With a hull form designed for low observability and a weapons suite designed for command of the sea and air space around her, she would be the ultimate 'one-size-fits-all' surface warship. However, at more than 14,000 tons and a cost estimated in 2005 to exceed $3 billion each (nearly three times the cost of a current-generation *Burke*-class destroyer), the planned procurement of thirty-two ships of this class has been reduced by stages to seven, with only two authorised to date. Smaller, cheaper, more expendable ships will still be needed to take on many of the more dangerous tasks that have traditionally fallen to destroyers. (USN).

come full circle. In 1904, destroyers attacked the stationary giants of the Russian fleet at Port Arthur and ushered in a new age of naval warfare. Now, ninety-six years later, it was a destroyer – the new capital ship for the navies of a new century – that sat immobile while a tiny craft made a surprise attack. It is impossible to predict the future of the destroyer as a type. It is not impossible that they will pass into history, as did the battleships and cruisers they were originally designed to attack and protect. But the very adaptability of the type argues against that. At the time of writing, in late 2007, two destroyer projects in two navies, both very familiar with destroyer combat, continue to stretch the definitions of the type. On 23 August 2007, the Japanese Maritime Self-Defence Force launched a helicopter destroyer, JMSDF *Hyuga*. Something of a hybrid between a destroyer and helicopter carrier, she will be almost twice the size of

Cole, in terms of displacement.[14] In the United States, the construction of two *DDG-1000*-class destroyers has been authorised by Congress. These will also be almost double the size of *Cole* and will cost so much that current plans call for a maximum of only seven to be built. As such, they will be too valuable to risk close in to shore and in other high-risk situations. The job of going into harm's way will necessarily fall to new types, such as the 'Littoral Combat Ship' and 'Fast Sea Frame' being built and tested today. Perhaps one of these, or some similar type, will emerge as the destroyer in the navy of the future.

Notes

1 The irony that the United States, particularly under President George W Bush, should be the standard bearer for the Western Democracies in the fight against religious fundamentalism is not lost on many.

2 There are many arguments for and against gas-turbine propulsion for warships. The strongest argument in its favour is the extremely rapid acceleration possible with gas turbines; the strongest counter-argument is that gas turbines are not very fuel efficient. It is for this reason that many gas-powered ships combine high-speed gas turbines with some other form of propulsion designed to allow high-endurance cruising. The most popular of these are CODAG (COmbined Diesel And Gas) and COGOG (COmbined Gas Or Gas). The disadvantage of combined propulsion systems is that they take up a lot of space and can, as in the case of CODAG systems, require complex logistics to keep a ship supplied with different fuels for its different engines. By using a single model of gas turbine optimised for high speed, the *Arleigh Burke* class pays the penalty of having relative short range (less than 5000 nautical miles).

3 *CRS*, pp. 4–5. USCENTCOM, based at McDill AFB, Florida, is responsible for US military activity in the Middle East, northeastern Africa and southwestern Asia as far east as the borders of India and China. *Cole* entered CENTCOM's AOR (Area of Responsibility) as soon as she transited the Suez Canal.

4 The lowest level of alert was ThreatCon Alpha, the first step up from not being on alert; the highest was ThreatCon Delta.

5 *Bud*. The M16 was the standard infantry rifle of the US military. The M60 was the standard light machine gun.

6 There have been many claims of foreknowledge of the level of threat at Aden, but none stood out sufficiently from the 'noise' to cause action to be taken in the form of issuing a specific alert. After the fact, there have been claims that a little-known military intelligence unit codenamed 'Able Danger', which specialised in the then new art of data mining in open source information, reported a specific warning of danger at Aden two days before the attack on *Cole,* but were unable to persuade their superiors to issue the appropriate warnings.

7 There is disagreement as to whether bin Laden ever actually received money from the CIA. Even if American money never actually reached bin Laden, there is no question that the United States supported other groups that fought alongside bin Laden's Arab fighters in Afghanistan.

8 *Com*.

9 This was the second US Navy warship to bear this interesting name. Five Sullivan brothers from Waterloo, IA enlisted in the navy together right after the attack on Pearl Harbor and, at

their request, went through training together and were assigned duty on the same ship, USS *Juneau* (CL 52). All five died when that ship was sunk by the Japanese submarine *I-26* in the aftermath of the First Naval Battle of Guadalcanal, 13 November 1942.

10   Initial press releases by the US DOD stated that *Cole* was bombed while mooring and that the suicide bombers had slipped in among the tugs and other small craft that normally attended the entry of a new ship into harbour. It is not clear whether this was a genuine mistake based on incomplete information or a feeble attempt to cover up security lapses on *Cole*. The mistake was not corrected until independent press reports made it clear that *Cole* had been berthed at the fuelling point for more than an hour when she was attacked.

11   *Med*, p. 1.

12   Marine turbines can use a variety of fuels, but function best on fuels similar to aviation jet fuel. The current generation of jet fuels, such as JP-5 and JP-8, are less volatile and have higher flash points than earlier jet fuels, but are far more explosive than the bunker oil used to fuel World War II–vintage destroyers.

13   AFFF – Aqueous Film Forming Foam – a water-based foam that rapidly spreads over the surface of a fuel spill, forming a barrier to evaporation of the fuel. Compared to the protein-based foams originally used in World War II, AFFF spreads faster, but breaks down more quickly and needs to be renewed more frequently.

14   It has been stated by numerous sources that *Hyuga* is only called a destroyer for political reasons, that she is in fact a helicopter carrier in all but name, but compared to helicopter carriers in the US Navy, such as the *Wasp*-class LHDs, *Hyuga* is a quite different ship. She is not an amphibious assault ship, like the LHDs, nor will she carry V/STOL fixed-wing attack aircraft like small aircraft carriers in the Italian and Spanish navies. Rather, her primary mission is to provide anti-submarine protection for the Japanese fleet, an entirely appropriate role for a destroyer.

Appendix – Gun Calibres

THERE WERE THREE basic systems in use simultaneously to describe gun sizes, at least through the end of World War II: the British, American and Metric (used by almost everyone else). For clarity and consistency, throughout this book they are given in inches first, with metric conversion in millimetres in brackets.

The Royal Navy used the 'pdr' (pounder) designation of gun sizes for much of the time period covered by this book. It is a system dating back to the beginning of artillery design and designates a gun by the weight of the projectile it fired. In the earliest days, every gun was different and the balls that fit one cannon might not fit any other in the world. The onset of the Industrial Revolution and the mass-production of guns led to standardisation on a few basic gun calibres. This led to certain pdr designations being associated with specific gun calibres, even though shell weight might vary considerably for any given calibre depending on the type of shell. This, however, did not cause the pdr designations to be dropped until after World War II.

To make matters worse, for guns larger than 25pdr, and even a few smaller ones, the British used inch or metric designations, sometimes interchangeably. In recent years, the Royal Navy has adopted solely metric gun designations.

Most European nations referred to guns solely by calibre (shell diameter) using the metric system throughout this period.

The US Navy also referred to guns by calibre, but used (and still uses) inch measurements (with some notable exceptions, such as anti-aircraft guns, which were sometimes given metric designations, depending mainly on where the design originated). Very small guns of less than an inch bore diameter were given 'calibre' designations, such as the Browning 50-calibre machine gun. A calibre, in this system, was ¹⁄₁₀₀ of an inch, so that 50-calibre was a half-inch (or 12.7mm).

The following table covers most of the gun sizes mentioned in this book and, for the sake of completeness, some that are not. Please note that the listed equivalences are approximate and that these are gun designations and not necessarily actual shell diameters. Also note that these equivalences between nomenclatures changed over time, so that a 12 pdr of the Napoleonic era was quite different from a 12 pdr of World War II.

1 pdr	37mm	1.46in
2 pdr	40mm	1.57in
4 pdr	50mm	1.97in
6 pdr	57mm	2.24in
9 pdr	65–70mm	2.55–2.75in
12 pdr	75mm	2.95in
17 pdr	76.2mm	3.00in
18 pdr	83.8mm	3.30in
25 pdr	87.6mm	3.45in

Sources

IT SHOULD BE noted that, given the research resources available at the beginning of the twenty-first century, some sources I have used exist only in cyberspace. In these cases, I have given the hyperlink to the source rather than the more traditional publisher information. It is a characteristic of such sources that they are more ephemeral than paper-and-ink sources. When the site that serves the pages is changed or ceases to exist, the effect can be as if every copy of a book was instantly vaporised. All links listed here were active and available at the time this manuscript was written.

Not all of these sources are directly referenced in my notes, but those that are may be identified by the short name given in the first column below.

Primary Sources

Cole   Cole, Commander William M, USN, *Action Report*, 3 December 1942, http://www.destroyerhistory.org/actions/421130_445fletcher.pdf. (Commander Cole was captain of USS *Fletcher* (DD 445) at the Battle of Tassafaronga. One of many useful source documents relating to this battle to be found at this valuable web site.)

Comp   *Compilation of despatches and TBS transmissions sent and received, from November 28 to December 1, 1942 relating to the Fifth action off Savo Island*, http://www.destroyerhistory.org/actions/tf67_421130_dispatches.pdf.

Crest   Crenshaw, Captain Russell S, Jr, USN (Ret), *Crest of the Wave: Memoirs of a Naval Officer – 1937–67*, self-published, 1993. (A well-written, perceptive account of much of the crucial struggle in the Solomons.)

Chums   Evans, Vice Admiral E R G R, RN, *The Broke's Glorious Fight*, in *Chums*, No. 1820, vol 36, 31 July 1927, pp. 47–8. (*Chums* was a British weekly boy's adventure magazine that started in 1892 and continued publishing, becoming a monthly in 1933, until 1934.)

Green   Green, Peter J, *Falklands War Diary: My View from HMS Yarmouth – 2nd April to 28th July 1982*, http://twogreens.co.uk/navy/FALKLANDS/falklands.html. (A straight-forward day-by-day account of the events of this conflict as seen from the midst of the fight. Very useful.)

Hansen   Hansen, Lieutenant J R, USN, USS Chevalier *DD 451, Action report of enemy engagement night of 6 October 1943*, 14 October 1943. (This is the report of *Chevalier*'s XO. Available at http://www.destroyerhistory.org/fletcherclass/usschevalier/xoactionreport.html.)

OpPlan   Kinkaid, T C, Rear Admiral, USN, *Operation Plan No. 1–42*, 27 November 1942. (Available at http://www.destroyerhistory.org/actions/tf67_421127_operationplan.pdf.)

Shef   *Loss of* HMS Sheffield – *Board of Inquiry*, Office of Commander-in-Chief, Fleet, 28 May 1982. (This report was released in response to freedom-of-information requests and is available on the internet, though some sections have been excised. The actual report is dated 22 July 1982.)

Khar   *Loss of* Khartoum, ADM 1/11210, 21 August 1940. (This is a cover letter for a report, attached in this reference, describing the loss of HMS *Khartoum* by her CO, Commander D T Dowler. Neither this report nor the two cover letters make any mention of the engagement with *Torricelli* earlier on the day *Khartoum* sank.)

Mustin   Mustin, Vice Admiral Lloyd M, USN (Ret), *Reminiscences*, interviewed by John T Mason, Jr, US Naval Institute Oral History Program, Annapolis, Md, 2003.

Ali   Onen, Yekta Ragip, *Memories of Torpedo Officer Navy Lt Ali Haydar, Yillarboyu Tarih* (History over the Years), Vol. 8, No. 4, April 1982. (This was kindly translated from the Turkish by Tosun Saral. I have taken the liberty of converting his literal translation into more colloquial English.)

Poor   Poor, Henry V, Henry A Mustin and Colin G Jameson, *The Battles of Cape Esperance, 11 October 1942 and Santa Cruz Islands, 26 October 1942*, Office of Naval Intelligence, Washington, DC, 1943. (This combat narrative was found at http://www.ibiblio.org/hyperwar/USN/USN-CN-SantaCruz/index.html#page1.)

Reed   Reed, Robert B, *Recollection*, from E Andrew Wilde, Jr, *The* USS Preston *(DD-379) in World War II: Documents, Recollections and Photographs*, Needham, MA, 2001. (This is a privately published document available in pdf form at the web site http://www.destroyerhistory.org. Reed served on *Preston*, which was in *Enterprise*'s screen at the Battle of the Santa Cruz Islands, which gave him a front-row seat to the events related in Chapter 7.)

Court   *Report of the Court of Enquiry into the circumstances attending the action between* HMS SWIFT, HMS BROKE *with enemy destroyers on the night of 20th/21st April, 1917*, ADM 137/3659, 22 April 1917. (Obtained from the British National Archives, Kew Richmond, Surrey, TW9 4DU. This appears to be a subsection of a longer report, being the minutes of interviews between the court of enquiry and some of the officers and crew of HMSs *Swift* and *Broke*, made the day after the action.)

Memo   Smith, William Y, *Memorandum for the Record of White House Staff Meeting, August 5, 1964, 8 a.m.*, National Defense University, Taylor Papers, T-202-69, http://www.gwu.edu/~nsarchiv/NSAEBB/NSAEBB132/tonkin.pdf

Bush   Westholm, Commander R E, USN, *Action Report, USS* Bush *(DD 529), 6–7 April 1945*, http://www.ussbush.com/far.htm. (This is an excellent and informative site dedicated to this destroyer lost to *kamikaze* attack off Okinawa.)

Chevalier   Wilson, Lieutenant Commander George R, USN, USS Chevalier DD 451, *Report of Enemy Action Resulting in Loss of Vessel*, 15 October 1943. (Available at http://www.destroyerhistory.org/fletcherclass/usschevalier/coactionreport.html.)

Colhoun   Wilson, Commander George R, USN, *Action Report, USS* Colhoun *(DD 801), 6–7 April 1945*, 27 April 1945, http://www.ussbush.com/resculgs.htm. (The extracts used in this book were taken from the excellent USS *Bush* web site.)

Wright   Wright, Rear Admiral Carleton H, USN, *Report on Action off Cape Esperance, Night of November 30, 1942*, 9 December 1942, http://www.destroyerhistory.org/actions/tf67_421130_actionreport01.pdf.

Secondary Sources (author known)

Andrade, Dale and Kenneth Conboy, 'The Secret Side of the Tonkin Gulf Incident', in *Naval History*, Vol. 13, No. 4, August 1999.

Brown, Louis, *Technical and Military Imperatives: A Radar History of World War II*, Taylor & Francis Group, New York, 1999.

Campbell, John, *Jutland: An Analysis of the Fighting*, Conway Maritime Press Ltd., London, England, 1986.

Crenshaw   Crenshaw, Captain Russell S, Jr. USN (Ret), *The Battle of Tassafaronga*, The Nautical & Aviation Publishing Company of America, Baltimore, MD, 1995.

DeHoust   DeHoust, Major Walter F, USMC, *War Since 1945 Seminar: Offensive Operations of the Falklands War*, USMC Staff College, Quantico, VA, 2 April 1984.

del Campo, Juan, *Britons and Peruvians Fight at Sea*, http://members.lycos.co.uk/Juan39/BATTLE_OF_PACOCHA.html.

Narvik   Dickens, Captain Peter, RN, *Narvik: Battles in the Fjords*, Naval Institute Press, Annapolis, MD, 1997. (Originally published by Ian Allen Ltd. in 1974.)

Bud   Doehring, Thoralf, *Unofficial US Navy Site*, http://www.navybuddies.com/index.htm. (An excellent source of information on the current state of the US Navy.)

Dull, Paul S, *A Battle History of the Imperial Japanese Navy (1941–45)*, Naval Institute Press, Annapolis, MD, 1978.

Jut   Fawcett, H W and G W W Hooper, (eds), *The Fighting at Jutland*, Hutchinson & Co., London, England. (The edition of this book in my possession, while intact and in good condition, carries no copyright or publication date. Based on references in the Introduction, it is likely the book dates from the mid-1920s.)

Frank   Frank, Richard B, *Guadalcanal: The Definitive Account of the Landmark Battle*, Penguin Books, New York, 1992. (An excellent general history of the Guadalcanal campaign. Easily the best such available.)

Radar   Friedman, Norman, *Naval Radar*, Naval Institute Press, Annapolis, MD, 1981. (Originally published in that same year by Conway Maritime Press Ltd. Still the most useful book on the subject.)

Rules   Gordon, Andrew, *The Rules of the Game: Jutland and the British Naval Command*, John Murray (Publishers), London, England, 1996. (An interesting examination of the psychology of the Royal Navy officer corps in the years between Trafalgar and Jutland.)

Skunks   Hanyok, Robert J, 'Skunks, Bogies, Silent Hounds, and the Flying Fish: The Gulf of Tonkin Mystery, 2–4 August 1964', in *Cryptologic Quarterly*, Winter 2000/Spring 2001 Edition, Vol. 19, No. 4/Vol. 20, No. 1. (*Cryptologic Quarterly* is a classified publication of the US National Security Agency (NSA). This article, with minor redactions, was made public on 3 November 2005 due to persistent FOIA (Freedom of Information Act) requests. This is the most complete analysis of the SIGINT failures that were important in the US escalation in Vietnam. Available at http://www.nsa.gov/vietnam/releases/relea00012.pdf.)

Hara   Hara Tameichi, Captain, with Fred Saito and Roger Pineau, *Japanese Destroyer Captain: Pearl Harbor, Guadalcanal, Midway – The Great Naval Battles as Seen through Japanese Eyes*, Naval Institute Press, Annapolis, MD, 1967.

Hocking, Charles, *Dictionary of Disasters at Sea during the Age of Steam*, Naval and

Military Press Ltd, 1994. (This is available, without index, online starting at http://perso.orange.fr/cdasm.56/dictionnaire/001.pdf.)

McCul McCully, Lieutenant Commander Newton A, USN, *The McCully Report: The Russo-Japanese War 1904–05*, Naval Institute Press, Annapolis, MD, 1977.

McSh McSherry, Patrick, *Whitehead Torpedo*, http://www.spanamwar.com/torpedo.htm.

Med Medwick, Cathleen, 'An Officer and a Gentle Woman – Lieutenant Commander Deborah Courtney experiences of the USS *Cole* bombing', in *O: The Oprah Magazine*, December 2001. (This article was found on the internet at the BNET Research Center site: http://findarticles.com/p/articles/mi_m0KNJ/is_12_2/ai_80206417/pg_1. The article contains some details of the *Cole* bombing not reported elsewhere.)

Janes73 Moore, Captain John E, RN, (ed), *Jane's Fighting Ships 1973–74*, Jane's Yearbooks, London, England, 1973.

Buzz Moore, Stephen L, William J Shinneman and Robert Gruebel, *The Buzzard Brigade: Torpedo Squadron Ten at War*, Pictorial Histories Publishing Co., Missoula, MT, 1996.

Struggle Morison, Samuel Eliot, *The Struggle for Guadalcanal, August 1942–February 1943, History of United States Naval Operations in World War II, Vol. V*, Little, Brown & Co., Boston, 1948.

Break Morison, Samuel Eliot, *Breaking the Bismarcks Barrier, 22 July 1942–1 May 1944, History of United States Naval Operations in World War II, Vol. VI*, Little, Brown & Co, Boston, 1950.

Victory Morison, Samuel Eliot, *Victory in the Pacific, 1945, History of United States Naval Operations in World War II, Vol. XIV*, Little, Brown & Co., Boston, 1960.

O'Hara O'Hara, Vincent P, *The US Navy Against The Axis: Surface Combat 1941–1945*, Naval Institute Press, Annapolis, MD, 2007.

Blood Parkin, Robert S, *Blood on the Sea: American Destroyers Lost in World War II*, Da Capo Press, Cambridge, MA, 2001.

CRS Perl, Raphael and Ronald O'Rourke, *Terrorist Attack on USS Cole: Background and Issues for Congress*, Congressional Research Service, US Library of Congress, Washington, DC, 30 January 2001.

Ops Roscoe, Theodore, *United States Destroyer Operations in World War II*, US Naval Institute Press, Annapolis, MD, 1953. (The standard reference for US destroyer activities in WWII.

Ross Rosselli, Alberto, *The Military Operations of the Italian Fleet on Red Sea June 1940–April 1941*, http://www.regiamarina.it/redsea.htm.

Hist Stevens, William O and Allan Westcott, *A History of Sea Power*, Doubleday, Doran & Co., Inc., Garden City, NY, 1942.

Tarrant, V E, *Jutland: The German Perspective*, Arms & Armour Press, London, England, 1995.

Tarrant, V E, *The U-Boat Offensive 1914–45*, Arms & Armour Press, London, England, 1989.

Warner, Denis and Peggy Warner, *The Tide at Sunrise: A History of the Russo-Japanese War 1904–05*, Routledge, Taylor and Francis Group, London, 2004.

Secondary Sources (author unknown/uncredited)

Box   *Boxing the Compass,* http://www.gwpda.org/naval/boxco000.htm.
(An extremely useful site about compass and steering terminology.)

Com   *Cooperative Research History Commons,*
http://www.historycommons.org/index.jsp.
(A supremely useful sight for well-annotated timelines of many recent events. I used this site for its excellent coverage of the intelligence context of the *Cole* bombing.)

Gol1   *Goliath Sunk,* http://diggerhistory2.info/graveyards/pages/history/goliath.htm.
(An evenhanded account of *Goliath*'s loss.)

Gol2   HMS *Goliath,*
http://www.isle-of-man.com/manxnotebook/fulltext/gw1922/goliath.htm.
(This page contains a number of excerpts from *The Naval Review, Vol IV* giving various eye-witness accounts of *Goliath*'s sinking.)

Makarov, Stepan Osipovich, http://www.russojapanesewar.com/makaroff.html.
(This website, maintained by The Russo-Japanese War Research Society, is an invaluable resource for anyone, particularly those like this author not fluent in Russian or Japanese, interested in this war and these navies. I have made use of several other pages at this site as well.)

Nav   *Naval History Of The War,*
http://www.1911encyclopedia.org/Naval_History_Of_The_War.
(A useful summary of naval activity in World War I.)

The Falklands War, http://guest.xinet.com/ignacio/polsi342/falklands.html. (An excellent, concise account of the conflict.)

The Russo-Japanese War, http://www.navy.ru/history/hrn10-e.htm.
(This site is another valuable resource, giving the Russian perspective on many incidents of this war.)

Indispensable Sites

These are sites I referenced constantly during the writing of this and many other books.

NavWeaps: Naval Weapons, Naval Technology and Naval Reunions, http://www.navweaps.com/.
(This site covers, in magnificent detail, very nearly all the weapons used by the world's navies in the twentieth century, excepting aviation ordnance. Additionally provides some useful coverage of naval electronics.)

Destroyer History, http://www.destroyerhistory.org/.
(This site, maintained by Dave McComb, is a tremendously useful resource for anyone interested in US Navy destroyers from World War II to the present.)

DANFS   *Dictionary of American Naval Fighting Ships,*
http://www.history.navy.mil/danfs/index.html.
(An invaluable first stop for anyone looking for information on any US Navy vessel. This compilation has been going on for years and the quality of the entries is uneven, but it is an invaluable resource.)

Long   *Long Lancers,* http://www.combinedfleet.com/lancers.htm. (The entire site is an indispensable reference on the Imperial Japanese Navy, and this page is the portal to individual records for each IJN destroyer.)

PTF – Patrol Torpedo Fast – The 'Nasty Class' Fighting Boat, http://ptfnasty.com/.
(This site, maintained by Dan Withers, is the best source of information on these craft that saw duty in the Vietnam War.)

Index

The presence of the indexed term or name in the text on a page are in standard face (e.g., 45); the presence of a person or ship in a photograph is shown in boldface (e.g., **45**); a mention in a note on a page is shown by the page followed by 'n' and the note number (e.g., 45n3). The nationality of ships is given in parentheses after the name using standard two-letter codes, where such codes exist. When two or more ships or classes of the same name and nationality are indexed, they are further distinguished by type or date, as needed.